George W Waite

A Straight Road to Caesar

For Beginners in Latin

George W Waite

A Straight Road to Caesar
For Beginners in Latin

ISBN/EAN: 9783743407374

Manufactured in Europe, USA, Canada, Australia, Japa

Cover: Foto ©ninafisch / pixelio.de

Manufactured and distributed by brebook publishing software (www.brebook.com)

George W Waite

A Straight Road to Caesar

A

STRAIGHT ROAD TO CAESAR

FOR BEGINNERS IN LATIN

BY

GEORGE W. WAITE, A.M.
SUPERINTENDENT OBERLIN PUBLIC SCHOOLS

AND

GEORGE H. WHITE, A.M.
PRINCIPAL OBERLIN COLLEGE PREPARATORY SCHOOL

BOSTON, U.S.A.

GINN & COMPANY

1892

GIFT

Typography by J. S. Cushing & Co., Boston, U.S.A.

Presswork by Ginn & Co., Boston, U.S.A.

To

Our Brethren

of the

NORTH-EASTERN OHIO TEACHERS ASSOCIATION

This Book is

with their consent

RESPECTFULLY INSCRIBED

PREFACE.

THE aim of this book is indicated by the title. Caesar is properly the first Latin author read by American students, for no writer illustrates more clearly the spirit and principles of the language. A mastery of Caesar is the best possible foundation for Latin scholarship.

But Caesar is too difficult to be read freely and enthusiastically without definite preparation. The road to Caesar should be as direct and easy as a Roman road; it must, however, be long enough to carry the traveller not merely within sight of the city, but to the golden milestone in its very centre.

Our plan includes : —

1. *An abundance of easy sentences*, both English and Latin, for translation. The Latin is to be learned by constant and rapid translation, both Latin-English and English-Latin. The grammar-work is essential; but the grammar is quoted to explain the sentences, not the sentences to illustrate the grammar. The work begins with the sentence and is developed by sentences, so easy at first, and increasing in difficulty so gradually, that the hour of recitation is filled with the rapid practical use of the language.

2. *The inductive method*, used with moderation. The pupil first sees the Latin word in sentences, and, — in the earlier part of the book, — in all its case-forms ; then, and not till then, he is called upon to learn the paradigm. The rules of syntax are developed in a similar way. There is thus, in every moment of study, the "joy of discovery," the "scientific method," laboratory practice. Words, as truly as rocks and flowers, are products of nature ; and their right study should cultivate the observing faculties of the young as successfully, and in a very important direction.

3. *The use of Caesar's vocabulary and of sentences taken from Caesar.* In the choice of words for the earlier pages, we were obliged to take into account not only the frequency of their occurrence in Caesar, but as well, their availability for both paradigms and sentences. We can hardly expect that the amount of labor expended upon this portion of our book will be appreciated by any who have not attempted the

v

same thing. Our words are, with but two or three exceptions, Caesarian, and the sentences, as soon as the extent of the pupil's vocabulary allows, are largely taken from Caesar without essential change of form. We find, on concluding the work with classes, that the outline of thought in the First Book of Caesar, and a considerable portion of the difficult expressions, have become familiar to our pupils, so that their first days in Caesar are not, as has too often been the case, the most discouraging of their whole Latin course. And we regard it as of some importance that pupils should receive their first impressions of Latin not from such sentences as, *The rose is red*, but from Roman expressions like those of Caesar.

4. *Systematic arrangement, and such constant repetition* of all the previous work to the very end of the book, not through repeated references to the grammar, but through the construction of sentences, that term-reviews are not necessary, but that the pupil may constantly and safely move forward. Words are given so many times in the exercise where they first occur, and called up so regularly afterwards, that the pupil need never go to the lexicon for them a second time, and is able, thus, to give his full thought to the inflectional endings. And yet, toward the end, new words are freely introduced, that the pupil may have practice in the rapid acquisition of words. Equal care has been expended in arranging the principles of syntax; new rules are called up so regularly that they cannot pass out of mind.

5. *Provision for the most thorough drill upon paradigms.* No new method can secure substantial progress without such drill. All our paradigms are divided into syllables and accented, that there may be no possibility of mistake. It is hoped that the arrangements made for carrying the whole sentence through a paradigm may have some value.

6. *Adequate means for teaching pronunciation correctly from the beginning.* The first few days are all-important for this. We have not only given a key to the sounds and carried this as a foot-note for several pages, but have divided words into syllables and marked the accents for fifteen pages, and have throughout marked vowels known to be long.

7. *The least possible use of the verb before the verb paradigms are given.* Not many verbs are given at first, and these are used only in the third person of the present, imperfect, and future indicative. This is no burden to the pupil, yet it gives a good insight into the verb as Caesar employs it, and makes the study of the verb comparatively easy when it is reached.

8. *Prominence to rules, not to exceptions.* If rules are acquired, exceptions are noticed as exceptions when they occur, and this is sufficient in the early stages of language study.

9. *Adequate emphasis* upon the third declension of nouns, the pronouns, and the third conjugation of verbs.

10. *No division into Lessons;* the teacher being left free to divide the work according to his judgment.

Our reason for attempting to add another to the list of First Latin Books now before a long-suffering public, is that, after trying many books, we have not found among those in use one which exactly meets our needs. All with which we are acquainted demand a solid year of work, and do not enable the pupil even then to enter Caesar with comfort. We have found, by repeated trials, that good classes will accomplish this book and a large portion of the First Book of Caesar, in thirty-six weeks, each of five one-hour recitations. Many teachers — if many teachers do us the honor to use this book — will prefer to devote the whole thirty-six weeks to the mastery of the book alone. Others may think it wise to introduce the pupils to Caesar when they have reached RESULT CLAUSES, p. 144, and to take the remainder of this book in connection with the study of Cæsar. This we have sometimes done.

We desire to express our thanks to Miss Mary L. Atwood and Miss Frances J. Hosford, of the Oberlin College Preparatory School, and to Miss Grace Safford of the Oberlin Public High School, for their patient and appreciative use of our exercises, while we were experimenting with trial-editions.

OBERLIN, July, 1891.

TO THE PUPIL.

The Latin language is very different from the English. Observe attentively the following points : —

1. It is not enough in Latin to know words; it is equally important to know the endings of words. In the sentence, **Puer** (*the boy*) **capit** (*captures*) **latrōnem** (*the robber*), *puer* is the subject of the verb ; but in **Latrō capit puerum**, the word *puerum* is marked as the object by its suffix. To say *Latrō capit puer* is no more correct than to say in English, *Her don't want we ; us don't belong to she.*

2. (See *Gradātim*, p. 19, published by Ginn & Co., Boston, 1889.) In English, the meaning depends upon the order of the words.

means one thing;
> *The boy captures the robber*

> *The robber captures the boy*

means quite another thing.
But in Latin,
> *Puer latrōnem capit,*
> *Puer capit latrōnem,*
> *Latrōnem puer capit,*
> *Latrōnem capit puer,*
> *Capit latrōnem puer,*

all mean
> *The boy captures the robber.*

On the other hand,
> *The robber captures the boy*

may be expressed in Latin,
> *Latrō puerum capit,*
> *Latrō capit puerum,* etc.

We have an illustration of this in the use of the English personal pronouns, e.g.
> *All men praise* HIM,

and
> HIM *all men praise,*

have the same meaning.

3. Many relations which in English are expressed by a preposition, are in Latin denoted by a change of ending in a noun, e.g. *The boat (scapha) of Sulla*, is, in Latin, *Scapha Sullae*. The correct use or omission of prepositions in Latin is highly important.

4. The verb in a Latin sentence usually stands last.

PROGRAM OF A RECITATION.

[Observe that the major part of the hour is assigned to *translation*, from Latin to English and from English to Latin.]

I. Assignment of advance lesson, with advice as to method of learning . . . . 5 minutes.

II. Rapid oral review of previous lesson . . . . 10 minutes.

III. Part of the class recite new paradigms, rules, etc.; part write paradigms on the board . . . . 10 minutes.

IV. Oral or blackboard translation of the advance from Latin to English . . . . 10 minutes.

V. Part of the class write on the board the advance translation from English to Latin. The rest take drill work, — pronunciation, paradigms, translation from dictation. All unite in correcting blackboard work. 20 minutes.

55 minutes.

The above plan provides for reciting each lesson twice: once in advance, once in review. This is sufficient. Another plan, which secures at least two recitations of each lesson, would devote the first half-hour to reciting the assigned lesson for the day and the review, and the second half-hour to going over the morrow's lesson; the teacher supplying the meanings of new words and making suggestions as to the best methods of study. This gives fine scope for the teacher's power, is in accordance with the modern methods of teaching, and will create enthusiasm; and, if the assigned lesson of each day is recited with thoroughness, the results will be satisfactory.

The only term-reviews necessary with this book are a few recitations upon the paradigms and rules of syntax. Words and constructions are so graded and repeated that there is no occasion for reviewing the sentences at the end of the term.

SUGGESTIONS.

1. That the pupil be required to pronounce each Latin and English sentence before translating.

2. That for the first ten recitations the teacher pronounce each Latin sentence before requiring the pupil to do so.

3. That the class frequently read Latin in concert.

4. That halting recitations be not allowed.

5. That the pupil be required often to translate both English and Latin sentences from the teacher's dictation.

6. That the endings and paradigms be learned at the places, and in the order, indicated.

7. That the teacher encourage the pupil to gather the thought in the Latin order of the words.

8. That the pupil be required to combine rapidity of recitation with thoroughness of work, and that the length of lessons bend to this.

9. That translation, both Latin-English and English-Latin, be made the chief work of the class-room.

10. That much written work, outside the class-room, be required; but that the pupil be not allowed, in the class-room, to lean upon his written work.

11. That the SUGGESTIONS which precede the Exercises be not committed to memory in place, but carefully read and applied in connection with the study of the Exercises.

TABLE OF CONTENTS.

——◦◦——

xi

A STRAIGHT ROAD TO CAESAR.

NOUNS. FIRST OR *A*-DECLENSION.

NOMINATIVE AND ACCUSATIVE CASES. SINGULAR NUMBER.

ILLUSTRATION. — Sul'la fē'mi nam lau'dat,
Sulla praises the woman.

In the above sentence, Sul'la is in the nominative case, fē'mi nam in the accusative (English objective). The sign of the nominative is the case-ending -a ; of the accusative, the case-ending -am.

SUGGESTIONS. — 1. The Latin has no article. Supply *a, an,* or *the* in English when necessary, as in the above illustration.

2. The words *long* and *short* when used of English vowels refer to *quality;* e.g. *nōte, nŏt.* When used of Latin vowels they refer to *quantity* only, a long syllable occupying more time in pronunciation than a short syllable, as indicated in the schedule below.

3. In this book, vowels long by nature are marked with the macron (‑). Diphthongs are long.

1.

1. Sul'la Gal'bam vo'cat.　2. Gal'ba Sul'lam vo'cat.　3. Fē'mi na fī'li am iu'vat.　4. Fī'li a fē'mi nam iu'vat.　5. Cot'ta sca'pham lau'dat.　6. Fē'mi na Mi ner'vam lau'dat.　7. Mi ner'va fī'li am· lau'dat.　8. Gal'ba Sul'lam iu'vat.　9. Sul'la fē'mi nam iu'vat.　10. Cot'ta Mi ner'vam vo'cat.　11. Mi ner'va Cot'tam vo'cat.　12. Fī'li a Gal'bam lau'dat.

NOTE. — Pronounce the Latin according to the following schedule : —
ă, ā, păpā ; ŏ, ō, ŏhō ; ŭ, ū, fŭll mōōn ; ĕ, ē, văcātion (ĕ nearly the sound of *e* in met); ī, machīne ; ĭ, holĭness ; œ, ay ; œ, boy ; au, now ; eu, feud ; ei, veil ; ui, we ; c, come ; g, go ; i consonant, yes ; s, yes ; t, time ; v (u consonant), we ; qu, quart ; ch, king ; th, thick ; ph, fun ; bs, like ps ; other consonants as in English.

1

DIRECTION. — Apply the following statements to the words in the above Exercise : —

a. The subject of a finite verb is in the nominative case.

b. A finite verb agrees with its subject in number and person.

c. The direct object of a transitive verb is in the accusative case.

Commit these statements carefully to memory.

2.

1. Minerva summons the woman. 2. Sulla summons the daughter. 3. The daughter assists Sulla. 4. Cotta assists Minerva. 5. Minerva praises the boat. 6. Galba praises the daughter. 7. Cotta summons Galba. 8. Sulla assists the daughter. 9. Minerva summons Sulla. 10. The woman assists Cotta. 11. The daughter praises the woman. 12. Galba praises Sulla.

GENITIVE, DATIVE, VOCATIVE, AND ABLATIVE CASES.
SINGULAR NUMBER.

ILLUSTRATIONS. — Sul'la sca'pham Gal'bae (genitive case) lau'dat, *Sulla praises the boat* of *Galba*, or, *Sulla praises Galba's boat.*

Sul'la Gal'bae (dative case) sca'pham dat, *Sulla gives the boat* to *Galba*, or, *Sulla gives Galba the boat.*

Sul'la, Gal'ba (vocative case), sca'pham lau'dat, (O) *Galba*, *Sulla praises the boat.*

Sul'la Gal'bam sca'phā (ablative case) iu'vat, *Sulla assists Galba* with *a boat.*

Fē'mi na, fī'li a (apposition) Gal'bae, Cot'tam iu'vat, *A woman, the daughter of Galba, assists Cotta.*

The Latin case-endings given above, and their equivalents, are —

ă, ā, păpā ; ŏ, ō, ŏhō ; ŭ, ū, fŭll mo͞on ; ĕ, ē, văcātion ; ī, machīne ; ĭ, holĭness ; œ, ay ; œ, boy ; au, now ; eu, feud ; ei, veil ; ui, we.

LATIN.	ENGLISH.
Genitive, -ae,	Objective with of, or the possessive case,
Dative, -ae,	Objective with to (or for),
Vocative, -a,	Nominative of address,
Ablative, -ā,	Objective with by, from, with, in, etc.

SUGGESTIONS.—1. Cum (in 8 below) is a preposition governing the ablative.

2. The vocative generally stands after one or more words in its sentence (as in 5 below).

3.

1. Mi ner'va sca'pham Cot'tae lau'dat. 2. Cot'ta Mi ner'vae sca'pham dat. 3. Gal'ba ga'le am Sul'lae lau'dat. 4. Sul'la Gal'bae ga'le am dat. 5. Sul'la, Cot'ta (vocative), fī'li am Gal'-bae vo'cat. 6. Fī'li a Gal'bae Mi ner'vam vo'cat. 7. Sul'la cum fē'mi nā Mi ner'vam iu'vat. 8. Fī'li a Gal'bae cum Mi ner'vā Sul'lam iu'vat. 9. Sul'la fī'li am Gal'bae sca'phā iu'vat. 10. Fē'-mi na, fī'li a Sul'lae, Gal'bam pe cū'ni ā iu'vat. 11. Gal'ba cum fī'li ā Sul'lae Mi ner'vam lau'dat. 12. Mi ner'va fē'mi nae pecū'-ni am et sca'pham dat.

Learn and repeat the following paradigms, and all given hereafter, till they are as familiar as the alphabet:—

		BOAT (F.)	MINERVA (F.)	WOMAN (F.)	HELMET (F.)
Sing.	Nom.	sca'pha	Mi ner'va	fē'mi na	ga'le a
	Gen.	sca'phae	Mi ner'vae	fē'mi nae	ga'le ae
	Dat.	sca'phae	Mi ner'vae	fē'mi nae	ga'le ae
	Acc.	sca'pham	Mi ner'vam	fē'mi nam	ga'le am
	Voc.	sca'pha	Mi ner'va	fē'mi na	ga'le a
	Abl.	sca'phā	Mi ner'vā	fē'mi nā	ga'le ā

Like sca'pha, decline Cot'ta, Gal'ba, and Sul'la; like ga'le a, fī'li a and pe cū'ni a.

DIRECTIONS.—1. Use, occasionally, the progressive form of the verb, e.g. is praising for praises.

c, come; g, go; i consonant, yes; s, yes; t, time; v (u consonant), we; qu, quart; ch, king; th, thick; ph, fun; bs, like ps.

2. Apply and learn the following statements : —

a. Any noun which modifies another noun and does not denote the same person or thing, is in the genitive.

b. The indirect object of an action is in the dative.

c. The vocative is used for direct address.

d. The means or instrument of an action is expressed by the ablative.

e. A noun which modifies another noun and denotes the same person or thing, agrees with it in case. This agreement is called *apposition.*

4.

1. Sulla summons Galba's daughter.   2. Galba, with [his] daughter, is assisting Sulla.   3. Sulla praises Minerva's daughter.   4. Minerva gives Galba the boat.   5. Galba is giving a boat to Sulla's daughter.   6. Galba summons the woman's daughter.   7. The woman, with [her] daughter, is assisting Galba.   8. The daughter of Galba gives money to Minerva.   9. Galba is giving Sulla a helmet.   10. Sulla assists Galba with money and a boat.   11. Minerva, with the daughter of Galba, assists Sulla.   12. The woman, daughter of Galba, gives a boat to Sulla.

NOMINATIVE AND ACCUSATIVE CASES. PLURAL NUMBER.

Suggestions. — 1. Nominative case-ending, -ae ; accusative, -ās.

2. The personal ending -t of the verb in the singular number becomes -nt in the plural.

5.

1. Sul'la fī'li ās Gal'bae vo'cat.   2. Fī'li ae Sul'lae (dative) pe cū'ni am dant.   3. Gal'ba cum Mi ner'vā fē'mi nās iu'vat. 4. Fē'mi na, cum fī'li ā Cot'tae, Mi ner'vae ga'le ās dē mōn'strat. 5. Fī'li ae Gal'bae fē'mi nās vo'cant.   6. Fē'mi nae fī'li ās Gal'bae

---

ă, ā, păpā ; ŏ, ō, ŏhō ; ŭ, ū, fŭll mōōn ; ĕ, ē, văcātion ; ī, machīne ; ĭ, holi-ness ; œ, ay ; œ, boy ; au, now ; eu, feud ; ei, veil ; ui, we.

iu'vant. 7. Mi ner'va et Cot'ta ga'le ās Sul'lae lau'dant. 8. Fē'-mi nae Sul'lae (dative) sca'phās Gal'bae dē mōn'strant. 9. Fī'li ae Sul'lae Mi ner'vae (dative) ga'le ās dant. 10. Sul'la et Mi ner'va fī'li ās Cot'tae pe cū'ni ā iu'vant.

6.

1. The woman praises Sulla's helmets. 2. The women, daughters of Sulla, praise Galba's boats. 3. Sulla is showing [his] helmets and boats to Minerva. 4. Minerva assists the women, daughters of Galba, with money. 5. The women summon the daughters of Cotta. 6. Galba's daughters are assisting Sulla with a boat. 7. The women give the daughter of Galba money and boats. 8. Galba gives helmets and boats to Sulla. 9. The woman, daughter of Galba, assists Sulla. 10. The daughters of Galba and of Sulla are showing Minerva the boats.

OTHER CASES, PLURAL NUMBER.

SUGGESTION. — Genitive case-ending, -ārum; dative, -īs; vocative, -ae; ablative, -īs. The dative and ablative plural of fī'li a is fī li ā'bus.

7.

1. Per'fu ga cum nau'tīs est in Ger mā'ni ā. 2. Gal'ba per'fu-gīs pe cū'ni am dat. 3. Nau'ta per'fu gam sca'phīs iu'vat. 4. Fē'-mi nae cum fī li ā'bus Sul'lam iu'vant. 5. Mi ner'va fī li ā'bus Gal'bae ga'le ās dat. 6. Gal'ba fē'mi nīs sca'phās per fu gā'rum dē mōn'strat. 7. Nau'tae cum per'fu gīs sunt in Ger mā'ni ā. 8. Fī'li ae per'fu gae sunt in Ī ta'li ā, et nau'tīs pe cū'ni am dant. 9. Pe cū'ni a fī li ā'rum est in sca'phā. 10. Fē'mi nae sunt in sca'phīs et fī'li ās iu'vant. 11. Ga'le ae per fu gā'rum et sca'-phae nau tā'rum in Gal'li ā sunt. 12. Fē'mi nae et nau'tae et per'fu gae sunt in sca'phīs.

---

c, come ; g, go ; i consonant, yes ; s, yes ; t, time ; v (u consonant) we ; qu, quart ; ch, king ; th, thick ; ph, fun ; bs, like ps.

DIRECTION. — Apply and learn the following statement: —
Most nouns of the first declension are feminine; but, in all
declensions, names of male beings, and of rivers, winds, months,
and mountains, are masculine; and names of female beings, and
of countries, cities, plants, and trees, are feminine.

		BOATS (F.)	WOMEN (F.)	HELMETS (F.)
Plur.	Nom.	sca'phae	fē'mi nae	ga'le ae
	Gen.	sca phā'rum	fē mi nā'rum	ga le ā'rum
	Dat.	sca'phīs	fē'mi nīs	ga'le īs
	Acc.	sca'phās	fē'mi nās	ga'le ās
	Voc.	sca'phae	fē'mi nae	ga'le ae
	Abl.	sca'phīs	fē'mi nīs	ga'le īs

Combine these paradigms with the corresponding singulars
(Exercise 3) and commit all thoroughly to memory.   Like
sca'pha decline nau'ta; like fē'mi na, per'fu ga; like ga'le a,
pe cū'ni a and (in the singular) Gal'li a, Ger mā'ni a and
Ī ta'li a.   Fī'li a is declined like ga'le a, but has fī li ā'bus
(not fī'li īs) in the dative and ablative plural.

8.

1. Galba's daughter is in the boat with the women.   2. Galba
is in Italy and is assisting the deserters with boats.   3. Sulla
gives the deserters money.   4. The woman is in Germany with
the daughters of Sulla.   5. Minerva summons the sailor's daughters.   6. The sailors' daughters assist Galba with money.   7. Galba gives Sulla's daughters a boat.   8. The deserters are showing
helmets to the women.   9. Minerva assists the women with
boats.   10. The money of the daughters is in the boats.   11. Galba
gives helmets to the deserters.   12. The sailors' money is in the
helmet, the helmet in the boat.

ă, ā, păpā; ŏ, ō, ŭhō; ŭ, ū, fŭll mo͞on; ĕ, ē, văcātion; ĭ, machīne; ĭ, holĭness; œ, ay; œ, boy; au, now; eu, feud; ei, veil; ui, we.

RECAPITULATION, IMPERFECT AND FUTURE TENSES.

SUGGESTIONS.—1. The imperfect tense has -ba before the personal endings -t and -nt; e.g. *lau dā'bat, he was praising; lau dā'bant, they were praising.*

2. The future tense has -bi (singular), -bu (plural) before the endings -t and -nt; e.g. *lau dā'bit, he will praise; lau dā'bunt, they will praise.* When the letter before -ba or -bi is *ā* (or *a* before the personal endings, e.g. *lau'dat, lau'dant*), the verb is said to be of the first conjugation. A is generally long before -ba, -bi, -bu; but is short in *da'bat, da'bit*, etc.

3. The imperfects e'rat, *he was,* e'rant, *they were;* and the futures e'rit, *he will be,* e'runt, *they will be;* are irregularly formed.

9.

1. Fē'mi *na* e'rat fī'li *a* Cot'tae.   2. Sul'*la* nau'ta (appositive) e'rit in sca'phā.   3. Fī'li *a* Cot'tae (dative) sca'pham Gal'*bae* per'fu *gae* dē mōn strā'bit.   4. Per'fu *ga* Sul'*lam* nau'tam vo cā'-bat.   5. Cot'ta Gal'bam iu vā'bit et per'fu *gae* (dative) pe cū'-ni *am* Sul'*lae* da'bit.   6. Gal'ba per'fu *ga* sca'pham Sul'*lae* et ga'le *am* Cot'tae lau dā'bat.   7. Fē'mi *nae* e'rant fī'li *ae* nau tā'-*rum.*   8. Nau'tae fī li *ā'bus* pe cū'ni *am* et sca'phās da'bant.   9. Fī'-li *ae* cum nau'tīs e'runt in sca'phīs.   10. Per'fu *gae*, Cot'ta et Gal'ba (appositives), sca'phās fī li *ā'rum* lau dā'bant.   11. Nau'tae cum fī li *ā'bus* Cot'tam et Gal'bam per'fu *gās* iu vā'bant.   12. Fī'li *ae* per'fu *gīs* pe cū'ni *am* et ga'le *ās* da'bunt.   13. Pe cū'ni *a* fī li *ā'rum* e'rat in ga'le *īs*, ga'le *ae* in sca'phīs.   14. Fī'li *ae* per fu gā'*rum* fī'li *ās* nau tā'*rum* iu vā'bunt.

10.

1. The deserter was in Gaul with Sulla.   2. The sailor will give money to the daughter of Sulla.   3. The women will assist the deserters with Sulla's boat.   4. Cotta's daughter will show Sulla's boat to a deserter.   5. Galba, the deserter, is giving money to the sailor's daughters.   6. The sailors were in the boat with the deserters.   7. The sailors were assisting the deserters.

---

c, come; *g, go; i consonant, yes; s,* yes; *t, time; v (u consonant) we; qu, quart; ch, king; th, thick; ph, fun; bs,* like *ps.*

8. The deserters were praising the sailors.   9. The money of Galba, the deserter, was in a sailor's helmet.   10. The boats of the sailors and the money of the deserters were in Italy.

NOUNS.   SECOND OR *O*-DECLENSION.

NOUNS IN -*US*. ALL CASES, SINGULAR NUMBER.

SUGGESTIONS. — 1. Nominative case-ending, -**us**; genitive, -ī; dative, -ō; accusative, -**um**; vocative, -**e**; ablative, -ō.

2. Notice that here alone the vocative of Latin nouns differs from the nominative.

3. Nouns of the second declension in -**us** are, as a rule, masculine. But, in all declensions, apply first the Direction in Exercise 7.

11.

1. Brū'tus do'mi nī et ser'vī a mī'cus e'rat.   2. Do'mi nus e'rat cap tī'vī a mī'cus.   3. Do'mi nus ser'vum a mī'cī lau dā'bit.   4. Cap-tī'vus, a mī'ce, do'mi nō e'quum da'bat.   5. Do'mi nus ser'vō e'quum da'bit.   6. Do'mi nus e'quī e'rat cap tī'vus.   7. Cap tī'vus et e'quus e'rant in Gal'li ā.   8. Do'mi nus cum cap tī'vō et ser'vō e'rit in Ger mā'ni ā.   9. Ser'vus cum do'mi nō et a mī'cō, Brū'tō, cap tī'vum iu vā'bat.   10. Ser'vus do'mi num vo cā'bit.   11. Ser'vus, Brū'te, e'rit a mī'cus.

	SLAVE (M.)	CAPTIVE (M.)	MASTER (M.)
Sing. Nom.	ser'vus	cap tī'vus	do'mi nus
Gen.	ser'vī	cap tī'vī	do'mi nī
Dat.	ser'vō	cap tī'vō	do'mi nō
Acc.	ser'vum	cap tī'vum	do'mi num
Voc.	ser've	cap tī've	do'mi ne
Abl.	ser'vō	cap tī'vō	do'mi nō

Like *ser'vus* decline *Brū'tus* and *e'quus;* like *cap tī'vus*, *a mī'cus.*

ă, ā, păpā; ŏ, ō, ŏhō; ŭ, ū, fŭll moōn; ĕ, ē, văcātion; ī, machīne; ĭ, holĭ-ness; œ, ay; œ, boy; au, now; eu, feud; ei, veil; ui, we.

12.

1. Slave, [your] master is in Germany with Brutus. 2. The owner of the horse was a friend of Brutus. 3. Brutus gives the captive money and a horse. 4. The captive, in company with [his] friend, was assisting Brutus. 5. The slave is assisting [his] master with a horse and a boat. 6. Brutus, [your] friend is a captive. 7. The slave was praising Brutus, [his] master. 8. The captive is giving a slave to [his] friend Brutus. 9. Brutus was summoning the captive. 10. The friend of Brutus was a captive. 11. Brutus will summon the slave and give money to the captive. 12. The master is praising the captive.

NOUNS IN -*US*, PLURAL NUMBER.

SUGGESTION. — Nominative and vocative case-ending, -**ī**; genitive, -**ōrum**; dative, -**īs**; accusative, -**ōs**; ablative, -**īs**.

13.

1. Ser'vī e'rant do mi nō'*rum* a mī'cī. 2. Do'mi nī sunt ser vō'-*rum* a mī'cī. 3. Prae fec'tī a mī'cōs vo cā'bant. 4. Tri bū'nī sunt prae fec tō'*rum* a mī'cī. 5. Tri bū'nī prae fec'tīs e'quōs da'bunt, ser'vīs nōn. 6. Prae fec'tī do'mi nīs e'quōs dē mōn strā'bant. 7. Prae fec'tī e'rant cap tī'vī. 8. Tri bū'nī prae fec'tōs et do'mi-nōs vo cā'bunt, ser'vōs nōn. 9. Ser'vī tri bū'nōs nōn lau dā'bunt. 10. Do'mi nī et ser'vī cum tri bū'nīs et prae fec'tīs e'rant in Ī ta'li ā. 11. A mī'cī tri bū nō'*rum* cap tī vō'*rum* a mī'cī sunt. 12. Do'mi nī cap tī'vīs et a mī'cīs cap tī vō'*rum* pe cū'ni am dē mōn-strā'bunt. 13. Tri bū'nī cap tī'vōs e'quīs iu'vant. 14. Tri bū'nī cum do'mi nīs et ser'vīs et cap tī'vīs e'rant in Ger mā'ni ā.

	SLAVES (M.)	CAPTIVES (M.)	MASTERS (M.)
Plur. Nom.	ser'vī	cap tī'vī	do'mi nī
Gen.	ser vō'rum	cap tī vō'rum	do mi nō'rum
Dat.	ser'vīs	cap tī'vīs	do'mi nīs

---

c, come ; *g*, *g*o ; *i* consonant, *y*es ; *s*, *y*es ; *t*, *t*ime ; *v* (*u* consonant), *w*e ; *qu*, *qu*art ; *ch*, *k*ing ; *th*, *th*ick ; *ph*, *f*un ; *bs*, like *ps*.

	SLAVES (M.)	CAPTIVES (M.)	MASTERS (M.)
Plur. Acc.	ser'vŏs	cap tĭ'vŏs	do'mi nŏs
Voc.	ser'vī	cap tĭ'vī	do'mi nī
Abl.	ser'vīs	cap tĭ'vīs	do'mi nīs

Combine these paradigms with those of Exercise 11; complete the paradigms of *e'quus* and *a mī'cus;* decline also like *cap tĭ'vus*, *tri bū'nus* and *prae fec'tus.*

14.

1. The friends of the captives were not slaves. 2. The friends of the slaves were not captives. 3. The captives are friends of the commanders. 4. The tribunes were summoning the slaves and [their] friends. 5. The tribunes will give horses to the slaves and [their] friends. 6. The slaves summon [their] masters, and with [their] friends assist the tribunes. 7. The commanders are friends of the masters and the tribunes. 8. The masters were giving money to the captives. 9. The masters with their slaves will assist the commanders. 10. The masters with the commanders and tribunes were assisting the captives. 11. The captives were giving [their] horses to the masters, not to the commanders. 12. The commanders are with the masters and captives.

NOUNS IN -*ER*, -*IR*, AND -*IUS*. ALL CASES, SINGULAR AND PLURAL NUMBERS.

SUGGESTIONS. — 1. Nouns in -er and -ir have no case-ending in the nom. and voc. sing. In the other cases, the endings are like those of nouns in -us.

2. In some of these nouns, e.g. *a'ger*, e of the nom. and voc. sing. is not found in the other cases; thus, the gen. sing. is *a'grī*, not *a'ge rī*.

3. Nouns in -*ius* usually have -*ī* instead of -*iī* in the genitive singular, e.g. *Clau'dī* and *so'cī* (3 and 18 below), and in the vocative singular of proper names (also *fi'li us*), -*ī* instead of -*ie*, e.g. *Clau'dī* and *fi'lī* (17 and 18).

ă, ā, păpā; ŏ, ō, ŏhō; ŭ, ū, fŭll mōͅon; ĕ, ē, văcātion; ĭ, machīne; ī, holiness; œ, ay; œ, boy; au, now; eu, feud; ei, veil; ui, we.

15.

1. Fa'ber pu'e *rum* cōn fir'mat. 2. Pu'er cum fa'brō est in a'grō. 3. Vir fī'li ōs Clau'dī (-iī) ser'vat. 4. Tri bū'nus pu'e rō pe- cū'ni am da'bat. 5. Ser'vī in a'grīs e'rant cum pu'e rīs. 6. Pu'e rī, fī'li ī fa brō'*rum*, fī'li ās tri bū'nī iu vā'bunt. 7. Fa'brī sunt a mī'cī pu e rō'*rum*. 8. Do'mi nus vi'rīs et fē'mi nīs et lī'be rīs pe cū'ni am dat. 9. Vi'rī pu'e rōs cōn fir'mant. 10. Sul'la fa'brīs et so'ci īs a'grōs dat. 11. So'ci ī fī'li *um* Clau'dī (-iī) cōn fir mā'bant. 12. Fī'- li *us* fa'brī a mī'cus pu'e rī est. 13. Ser'vī fa'brōs et so'ci ōs ser'- vant. 14. Sul'la fa'brō a'gr*um*, pu'e rīs e'quum dē mōn strā'bit. 15. Lī'be rī cum vi'rīs sunt in sca'phā. 16. Fa'ber fē'mi nās iu vā'bit, vi'rōs et lī'be rōs, nōn. 17. Fa'ber, Clau'dī, vi'rō ser'vum dē mōn strā'bat. 18. Brū'tus, fī'lī, est so'ci *us*, Clau'di *us* a mī'cus so'cī (-iī).

		FIELD (M.)	BOY (M.)	ALLY (M.)	CLAUDIUS (M.)
Sing.	Nom.	a'ger	pu'er	so'ci us	Clau'di us
	Gen.	a'grī	pu'e rī	so'cī (-iī)	Clau'dī (-iī)
	Dat.	a'grō	pu'e rō	so'ci ō	Clau'di ō
	Acc.	a'grum	pu'e rum	so'ci um	Clau'di um
	Voc.	a'ger	pu'er	so'ci e	Clau'dī
	Abl.	a'grō	pu'e rō	so'ci ō	Clau'di ō

Sing. MAN (M.)

		FIELD (M.)	BOY (M.)	ALLY (M.)	MAN (M.)
Plur.	Nom.	a'grī	pu'e rī	so'ci ī	vir
	Gen.	a'grō'rum	pu e rō'rum	so ci ō'rum	vi'rī
	Dat.	a'grīs	pu'e rīs	so'ci īs	vi'rō
	Acc.	a'grōs	pu'e rōs	so'ci ōs	vi'rum
	Voc.	a'grī	pu'e rī	so'ci ī	vir
	Abl.	a'grīs	pu'e rīs	so'ci īs	vi'rō

Like *a'ger* decline *fa'ber;* like *pu'er, lī'be rī* (used only in the plural) ; like *Clau'di us* and the plural of *so'ci us* decline *fī'li us.* Complete *vir* as follows : Plur. nom. *vi'rī*, gen. *vi rō'- rum*, dat. *vi'rīs*, etc.

16.

1. The boys are in the field with the engineers. 2. The engineers are encouraging the boys. 3. The men are protecting the commanders. 4. The engineer was a friend of the boys. 5. The boys were sons of engineers. 6. The commanders will give the boys boats, the men horses. 7. A man will be with the boys in the boat. 8. The boys will be with the men in the boats. 9. The slave of the man Claudius (appositive) was not the boy's friend. 10. Claudius, Sulla is giving fields to slaves and deserters. 11. Boys, the engineers were allies, not slaves. 12. To the man, Claudius (appositive), the engineer gives money. 13. To the boy, the son of Brutus, Claudius was showing [his] helmet. 14. The men are protecting the allies.

NOUNS IN -*UM*. ALL CASES, SINGULAR AND PLURAL NUMBERS.

SUGGESTIONS. — 1. The case-ending of the nominative, accusative, and vocative singular is -um ; that of the nom., acc., and voc. plural, -a. Other case-endings are as in nouns in -us ; but nouns in -*i* um usually have -ī instead of -*i* ī in the gen. sing.

2. Nouns of the second declension in -um are neuter. But apply directions (Exercise 7). The neuter *vul'gus* has no plural, and its case-ending in nom., acc., and voc. is -us.

3. **Est** at the beginning of a sentence is to be translated *there is;* sunt, *there are;* e'rat, *there was*, etc.

4. *Au xi'li* um (singular) means *assistance;* *au xi'li* a (plural), *auxiliary forces, auxiliaries.*

17.

1. Con ci'li *um* dē crē'tum pa'rat. 2. Vul'gus prae fec'tō dē crē'- tum dē mōn strā'bit. 3. Con ci'li *a* dē crē'ta, prae fec'tī op'pi da, pa'rant. 4. Au xi'li *a* dē crē'ta con ci li ō'rum lau dā'bant. 5. Au-

---

ă, ā, păpā ; ŏ, ō, ōhō ; ŭ, ū, fŭll mōon ; ĕ, ē, văcātion ; ī, machīne ; ĭ, holĭness ; œ, ay ; œ, boy ; au, now ; eu, feud ; ei, veil ; ui, we.

xi'li *um* con ci'lĭ prae si'di *a* cŏn fir'mat.   6. Con ci'li *um* op'pi dō et prae si'di ŏ au xi'li *um* da'bit.   7. E'quī au xi li ŏ'*rum* e'rant in ca'str*ĭs*.   8. Ca'stra et op'pi d*a* et prae si'di *a* sunt in pe rī'cu lō. 9. Op'pi d*um* est in pe rī'cu lō et prae fec'tus bel'*lum* pa rā'bit. 10. A mī'cī ser vŏ'rum con ci'li ŏ pe rī'cu l*um* dē mŏn strā'bant. 11. Tri bū'nus au xi'li *a* ar'mat.   12. Est bel'l*um* et prae fec'tī ca strŏ'*rum* so'ci ōs ar'mant.   13. Prae si'di *um* cum au xi'li *ĭs* est in op'pi dō.   14. Bel'la et pe rī'cu la bel lō'*rum* vul'g*us* nōn cōn-fir mā'bunt.

	WAR (N.)	DECREE (N.)	TOWN (N.)	COUNCIL (N.)
Sing. Nom.	bel'**lum**	dē crē'**tum**	op'pi d**um**	con ci'li u**m**
Gen.	bel'**lĭ**	dē crē'**tĭ**	op'pi d**ĭ**	con ci'l**ĭ** (-i**ī**)
Dat.	bel'**lō**	dē crē'**tō**	op'pi d**ō**	con ci'li **ō**
Acc.	bel'**lum**	dē crē'**tum**	op'pi d**um**	con ci'li u**m**
Voc.	bel'**lum**	dē crē'**tum**	op'pi d**um**	con ci'li u**m**
Abl.	bel'**lō**	dē crē'**tō**	op'pi d**ō**	con ci'li **ō**
Plur. Nom.	bel'**la**	dē crē'**ta**	op'pi d**a**	con ci'li **a**
Gen.	bel lō'**rum**	dē crē tō'**rum**	op'pi dō'**rum**	con ci li ō '**rum**
Dat.	bel'**lĭs**	dē crē'**tĭs**	op'pi d**ĭs**	con ci'li **ĭs**
Acc.	bel'**la**	dē crē'**ta**	op'pi d**a**	con ci'li **a**
Voc.	bel'**la**	dē crē'**ta**	op'pi d**a**	con ci'li **a**
Abl.	bel'**lĭs**	dē crē'**tĭs**	op'pi d**ĭs**	con ci'li **ĭs**

Like the sing. of *bel'lum* decline *vul'gus*, but see Suggestion 2, above; like the plur. of *bel'lum*, *ca'stra;* like *op'-pi dum*, *pe rī'cu lum;* like *con ci'li um*, *au xi'li um* and *prae-si'di um*.

18.

1. The council is arming the auxiliary [forces].   2. The aux-iliary [forces] will be in camp.   3. Claudius with the auxiliaries protects the camp.   4. Italy is in danger, the slaves are pre-paring war.   5. There is war, the women and children are in the town.   6. The tribunes will protect the council of the common people.   7. The common people with the tribune protect the

---

c, come; *g*, *go*; *i consonant*, yes; *s*, yes; *t*, *time*; *v* (*u consonant*) *we*; *qu*, quart; *ch*, *king*; *th*, *thick*; *ph*, *fun*; *bs*, like *ps*.

town. 8. The garrison of the town will assist the common people. 9. The commanders arm the auxiliaries and the allies. 10. Garrisons of auxiliary [forces] protect the towns. 11. The commander of the camp gives the town assistance. 12. The commanders of the garrison are in the camp.

LETTERS.

A, e, i, o, u, y, are vowels; all other letters are consonants. The combinations *ae, au, ei, eu, oe, oi, ui,* are diphthongs. *P, b, c (k), q, g, t, d, ch, th,* are mutes ; *l, m, n, r,* liquids ; *x* and *z* double consonants. *I* is *a consonant* before another vowel in the same syllable.

SYLLABICATION.

1. Make the syllables of a Latin word the same in number as its vowels and diphthongs; e.g. *nau'ta, a mī'cus.*

2. Write a single consonant, or *x*, or two or more consonants which can be used to begin a word, with the latter of two vowels; e.g. *do'mi nus, au xi'li um, sca'pha, ca'stra.*

3. Of other two consonants, write one with each vowel; of more than two, join with the latter vowel those which can be used to begin a word ; e.g. *Sul'la, dē mōn'strat.*

QUANTITY OF VOWELS AND SYLLABLES.

1. For quantity of *vowels,* see Exercise 1, Suggestions 2 and 3.

2. A *syllable* containing a long vowel or a diphthong is a *long syllable;* e.g. *nōn, nau'ta* (first syllable).

3. A *syllable* containing a short vowel is a *long syllable* when its vowel is followed by two or more consonants or a double consonant, but when the first of two consonants is a mute and the second a liquid, the *syllable* is common, that is, short in prose, but sometimes long in poetry ; e.g. *Cot'ta, a'grī* (first syllables).

ă, ā, păpā ; ŏ, ō, ŏhō ; ŭ, ū, fŭll mo͞on ; ĕ, ē, văcātion ; ĭ, machĭne ; ī, holĭness ; œ, ay ; œ, boy ; au, now ; eu, feud ; ei, veil ; ui, we.

4. Name syllables as indicated by the following word: —

5 4 3 2 1
Pe cŭ ni ā' rum.

1. *Ultima.*   2. *Penult.*   3. *Antepenult.*
4. *First syllable preceding the antepenult, etc.*

ACCENT.

1. Accent the *penult* of a word of *two syllables;* e.g. *Gal'ba.*
2. Accent the *penult* of a word of *three or more syllables, if the penult be a long syllable; otherwise, accent the antepenult;* e.g. *a mī'cus, prae fec'tus; fē'mi na, do'mi nus.*
Verify these rules by the preceding Exercises, and apply them hereafter till mastered.

THE CHANGE FROM THE ACTIVE TO THE PASSIVE VOICE.

SUGGESTIONS. — 1. The *subject* (nominative) of the Active Voice, if a voluntary agent, is put in the *ablative with ā* or *ab* in the Passive; e.g. **Brūtus** in 1 becomes **ā Brūtō** in 2.

2. The *object* (accusative) of the Active Voice becomes the *subject* (nominative) of the Passive ; e.g. **auxilia** and **sociōs** (accs.) in 9 become **auxilia** and **sociī** in 10.

3. The personal endings -t and -nt of the Active Voice become respectively -**tur** and -**ntur** in the Passive ; e.g. **vo'cat,** *he summons;* **vo cā'tur,** *he is summoned;* **vo'cant,** *they summon ;* **vo can'tur,** *they are summoned.*

4. In translation, such forms as *they are summoned* (Passive Voice) should be carefully distinguished from *they are summoning* (Progressive Form, Active Voice).

19.

1. *Brūtus* līberōs sociōrum vocat et cōnfirmat. 2. Līberī sociōrum *ā Brūtō* vocantur et cōnfirmantur. 3. *Tribūnī* servum iuvant. 4. Servus *ā tribūnīs* iuvātur. 5. *Fīliae* fabrī līberōs captīvōrum laudant et iuvant. 6. Līberī captīvōrum *ā fīliābus* fabrī laudantur et iuvantur. 7. *Auxilia* castra et oppida servant. 8. Castra et oppida *ab auxiliīs* servantur. 9. Praefectī *auxilia*

et *sociōs* armant. 10. *Auxilia* et *sociī* ā praefectīs armantur. 11. Nautae *amīcum* captīvōrum cōnfirmant. 12. *Amīcus* captīvōrum ā nautīs cōnfirmātur. 13. Perfuga *equōs* et *scaphās* parat. 14. *Equī* et *scaphae* ā perfugā parantur. 15. Faber puerīs *pecūniam* dat. 16. *Pecūnia* puerīs ā fabrō datur. 17. Claudius servō *scapham* dēmōnstrat. 18. *Scapha* servō ā Claudiō dēmōnstrātur.

20.

1. The commander summons the auxiliaries. 2. Auxiliaries are summoned by the commander. 3. The engineers are preparing a camp. 4. A camp is prepared by the engineers. 5. The council praises the sailors. 6. The sailors are praised by the council. 7. Brutus, the friend of the slave, assists the allies. 8. The allies are assisted by Brutus, the friend of the slave. 9. The captive is showing [his] helmet to the tribune. 10. The helmet is shown to the tribune by the captive. 11. Sulla gives the deserters money. 12. Money is given to the deserters by Sulla. 13. The master is encouraging [his] slaves. 14. The slaves are encouraged by the master. 15. The garrisons protect the women and children. 16. The women and children are protected by the garrisons.

ADJECTIVES IN -US, -A, -UM, SINGULAR NUMBER. PASSIVE VOICE, OTHER TENSES.

SUGGESTIONS. — 1. Observe that the masculine, feminine, and neuter forms of these adjectives are declined like *servus*, *scapha*, and *bellum* respectively.

2. Genitives in -ī for -iī accent the penult; e.g. con *ci'lī.*

3. The letters -bā (imperfect), -bi, -bu (future), are used before the personal ending of the passive, as in the active ; e.g. *lau dā* bā'*tur, he was* (being) praised, *lau dā'*bi *tur, he will be praised; lau dā* bun' *tur, they will be praised.*

21.

1. Dominus bonus ā servō vocātur. 2. Fēmina bona ā fīliā vocābātur. 3. Concilium bonum ā praefectō vocābitur. 4. Sulla

equum dominī bonī laudat. 5. Puer fīliam fēminae bonae laudābat. 6. Praefectus dēcrētum concilī bonī laudābit. 7. Servus
dominō bonō auxilium dat. 8. Nauta fēminae bonae scapham
dabat. 9. Tribūnus conciliō bonō pecūniam dabit. 10. Praesidium dominum bonum cōnfirmat. 11. Minerva fēminam bonam
cōnfirmābat. 12. Galba concilium bonum cōnfirmābit. 13. Galba,
domine bone, captīvum servat. 14. Sulla, fēmina bona, līberōs
servābat. 15. Brūtus, concilium bonum, praesidium servābit.
16. Galba ā sociō bonō servātur. 17. Minerva ā fēminā bonā
servābātur. 18. Praefectus ā conciliō bonō servābitur.

22.

1. The good master encourages [his] slave. 2. The good
daughter was encouraging the children. 3. The good garrison
will encourage the common people. 4. The master of the good
slave was in camp. 5. The money of the good daughter is in
the town. 6. The commander of the good garrison will be in
Germany. 7. Brutus gives the good slave a horse. 8. The sailor
will give [his] good daughter a boat. 9. Galba was giving the
good garrison assistance. 10. The master assists [his] good
slave. 11. The woman will assist [her] good daughter. 12. The
auxiliaries were assisting the good garrison. 13. Good slave, the
master will be in camp. 14. Good daughter, Claudius was an
ally, not a deserter. 15. Good garrison, the camp is not in
danger. 16. The sailor is summoned by the good slave. 17. The
boy was summoned by the good daughter. 18. The commanders
will be summoned by the good garrison.

ADJECTIVES IN -US, -A, -UM, PLURAL NUMBER.

23.

1. Dominī bonī servōs cōnfirmant. 2. Fēminae bonae fīliās cōn-
firmābant. 3. Concilia bona captīvōs cōnfirmābunt. 4. Equī
dominōrum bonōrum ā servīs laudantur. 5. Fīliae fēminārum

bon*arum* ā puerīs laudābantur.   6. Dēcrēta conciliō*rum* bonō*rum* ā praefectō laudābuntur.   7. Equī domin*īs* bon*īs* ā servīs dantur. 8. Scaphae fēmin*īs* bon*īs* ā nautīs dabantur.   9. Dēcrēta conciliī*s* bon*īs* ā praefectīs dabuntur.   10. Servī dominō*s* bonō*s* iuvant.   11. Amīcī fēmin*ās* bon*ās* iuvābant.   12. Tribūnī concilia bon*a* iuvābunt.   13. Est bellum, domin*ī* bon*ī*, in Galliā. 14. Līberī, fēmin*ae* bon*ae*, erant in scaphā.   15. In castrīs, concilia bon*a*, auxilia erunt et sociī.   16. Galba cum domin*īs* bon*īs* erit in Galliā.   17. Minerva cum fēmin*īs* bon*īs* erat in Germāniā. 18. Dēcrēta ā conciliī*s* bon*īs* servābuntur.

	M.	F.	N.		M.	F.	N.
Sing. Nom.	bo'nus	bo'na	bo'num	Plur.	bo'nī	bo'nae	bo'na
Gen.	bo'nī	bo'nae	bo'nī		bo nō'rum	bo nā'rum	bo nō'rum
Dat.	bo'nō	bo'nae	bo'nō		bo'nīs	bo'nīs	bo'nīs
Acc.	bo'num	bo'nam	bo'num		bo'nōs	bo'nās	bo'na
Voc.	bo'ne	bo'na	bo'num		bo'nī	bo'nae	bo'na
Abl.	bo'nō	bo'nā	bo'nō		bo'nīs	bo'nīs	bo'nīs

24.

1. The good slaves were assisting [their] masters.   2. The good daughters are assisting Minerva.   3. The good garrisons will assist the common people.   4. The master of the good slaves is in camp.   5. The friends of the good daughters were in the town.   6. The commanders of the good garrisons will be in Gaul.   7. The tribune gives the good slaves money.   8. The sailor was giving [his] good daughters assistance.   9. The commander will give the good garrisons auxiliary [forces].   10. The masters will praise [their] good slaves.   11. The woman was praising [her] good daughters.   12. The auxiliary [forces] are praising the good garrisons.   13. Good slaves, your master was not in danger.   14. Good daughters, the children are not captives.   15. Good garrisons, the allies will be in camp.   16. The boy is protected by the good slaves.   17. The woman was protected by [her] good daughters.   18. The town will be protected by [means of] good garrisons.

ATTRIBUTIVE AND PREDICATE ADJECTIVES.

SUGGESTIONS. — 1. When a Latin noun is limited by two adjectives, as in 11, below, do not omit the conjunction.
2. An attributive adjective is applied directly to its noun; *e.g.* **vir bonus**, *a good man*. Adjectives otherwise applied are predicate adjectives; *e.g.* **vir est bonus,** *the man is good.*

25.

1. Nauta erat saucius. Scapha erit nova. Concilium est clārum. 2. Fīlia nautae sauciī saepe invābātur. 3. Auxilium multum nautae sauciō ā tribūnō clārō dabātur. 4. Minerva fēminae clārae pecūniam dabit. 5. Sociī dominum saucium et fīliam clāram iuvābant. 6. Praefectus, cum fabrō clārō, māgnō in perīculō erat. 7. Dēcrētum conciliī clārī erit bonum. 8. Virī multī sunt et clārī. Galeae erunt novae. Perīcula erant māgna. 9. Fīliae fēminārum sauciārum erant clārae. 10. Līberī fabrōrum sauciōrum sunt multī. 11. Sulla captīvīs clārīs agrōs multōs et māgnōs dabat. 12. Dēcrēta nova praefectīs dēmōnstrantur. 13. Fabrī cum virīs multīs oppidum servābant. 14. Erant in castrīs captīvī multī et sauciī.

		M.	F.	N.
Sing.	Nom.	sau'ci us	sau'ci a	sau'ci um
	Gen.	sau'ci ī	sau'ci ae	sau'ci ī
	Dat.	sau'ci ō	sau'ci ae	sau'ci ō
	Acc.	sau'ci um	sau'ci am	sau'ci um
	Voc.	sau'ci e	sau'ci a	sau'ci um
	Abl.	sau'ci ō	sau'ci ā	sau'ci ō
Plur.	Nom.	sau'ci ī	sau'ci ae	sau'ci a
	Gen.	sau ci ō'rum	sau ci ā'rum	sau ci ō'rum
	Dat.	sau'ci īs	sau'ci īs	sau'ci īs
	Acc.	sau'ci ōs	sau'ci ās	sau'ci a
	Voc.	sau'ci ī	sau'ci ae	sau'ci a
	Abl.	sau'ci īs	sau'ci īs	sau'ci īs

The masculine of *sau'ci us* is declined like the noun *so'ci us* with -*iī* instead of -*ī* in the gen. sing.; the feminine like *ga'-le a;* the neuter like *con ci'li um.* Like *bo'nus* decline *clā'rus, mā'gnus, mul'tus,* and *no'vus.*

26.

1. The man will be illustrious. The daughter is good. The town was large. 2. The children of the wounded slave are many. 3. The decree of the illustrious council will encourage the garrison. 4. The allies are armed and will give assistance to many wounded slaves. 5. The tribune was giving the illustrious captive money. 6. The commander shows the auxiliary [forces] the new danger. 7. The engineer and the illustrious captive are armed. 8. The auxiliaries with many allies will be in the town. 9. The tribunes are illustrious. The boats were large. The garrisons will be many. 10. The horses of the allies were praised by the auxiliaries. 11. The children of the wounded allies were in great danger. 12. The common people will assist the wounded allies. 13. The engineers are preparing a large camp. 14. The illustrious commander was the son of a great man.

GENITIVE WITH ADJECTIVES.

SUGGESTIONS. — 1. As a general rule, a noun limiting an adjective is put in the *dative*. Some adjectives, however, like **cupidus** and **plēnus**, are followed by the *genitive*. For the *ablative* with adjectives, see Exercise 31.

2. Figures and letters joined to words refer to the Directions at the end of the Exercise. *Grammatical sections designated by figures are to be learned; those designated by letters are to be read and applied.*

27.

1. Perfuga est auxilī[1] cupidus. 2. Bellum erit perīculī[1] plēnum. 3. Captīvus saucius bellī nōn erat cupidus. 4. Oppida virōrum sauciōrum plēna erunt. 5. Praefectī cum sociīs[2] multīs erunt in oppidīs. 6. Minerva cum fīliā[2] clārā māgnō in perīculō erat. 7. Dēcrētum parābitur et conciliō clārō dēmōnstrābitur. 8. Concilium erit virōrum clārōrum plēnum. 9. Dēcrētum concilī bonī tribūnum saepe iuvābit. 10. Nautae scaphārum novārum cupidī erant. 11. Fabrī scaphās multās parābunt. 12. Scapha erat nautārum et līberōrum plēna. 13. Praesidium equōrum multōrum est cupidum.

DIRECTION. — Learn A. & G. : ¹218, *a* ; Rule 18 (p. 381).   ²248, *a* ;
Rule 47.
II. : ¹399 and I., 1, 2, 3 ; Rule XVII. (p. 326) ;
²419, 1 ; Rule XXIV. I.

	M.	F.	N.
Sing. Nom.	cu'pi dus	cu'pi da	cu'pi dum
Gen.	cu'pi dī	cu'pi dae	cu'pi dī
Dat.	cu'pi dō	cu'pi dae	cu'pi dō
Acc.	cu'pi dum	cu'pi dam	cu'pi dum
Voc.	cu'pi de	cu'pi da	cu'pi dum
Abl.	cu'pi dō	cu'pi dā	cu'pi dō
Plur. Nom.	cu'pi dī	cu'pi dae	cu'pi da
Gen.	cu pi dō'rum	cu pi dā'rum	cu pi dō'rum
Dat.	cu'pi dīs	cu'pi dīs	cu'pi dīs
Acc.	cu'pi dōs	cu'pi dās	cu'pi da
Voc.	cu'pi dī	cu'pi dae	cu'pi da
Abl.	cu'pi dīs	cu'pi dīs	cu'pi dīs

Decline *plē'nus* like *bo' nus*.

28.

1. There is a large garrison in the town.   2. The town will be protected by auxiliary [forces].   3. The garrison was desirous of new auxiliaries.   4. New auxiliaries are often desirous of war. 5. There were many auxiliary [forces] in the camp.   6. The town was full of women and children.   7. The women and children praise the illustrious garrison.   8. The great council will be full of illustrious men.   9. The council is desirous of new allies and much money.   10. The commander was encouraged by a decree of the council.   11. The allies were desirous of new horses.   12. There were many horses in the fields.

DATIVE WITH ADJECTIVES.

SUGGESTIONS. — 1. **Amīcus** has thus far been used as a noun with the genitive.   It is properly an adjective, declined like **bonus** and limited by a noun in the dative.   Carefully distinguish these uses.

2. **Inimīcus**, 7, is the preposition **in**, compounded with **amīcus**.   In the syllabication of compounds the parts should be separated ; hence, **in i mī'cus**, not **i ni mī'cus**.

3. **Et** . . . **et**, as in 4, below, is to be translated *both* . . . *and*.

29.

1. Servī dominīs¹ saepe sunt amīcī.   2. Dominī saepe sunt ser-
vōrum amīcī.   3. Tribūnus conciliō erat acceptus.   4. Dēcrētum
et praesidiō et auxiliīs erit acceptum.   5. Praesidium auxiliīs
erit amīcum.   6. Perīculum auxiliōrum praesidiō erat nōtum.
7. Vulgus bellō est inimīcum.   8. Praesidium nōn erat bellī cupidum.   9. Castra erunt nautārum sauciōrum plēna.   10. Servus
erat et captīvōrum et perfugārum amīcus.   11. Sociī captīvīs sunt
amīcī, perfugīs inimīcī.   12. Perfugae sociīs erant nōtī.·

DIRECTIONS. — Learn A. & G.: ¹**234** and *a* ; Rule 28.

H.: ¹**391** and I.; Rule XIV.

		M.	F.	N.
Sing.	Nom.	a mī'cus	a mī'ca	a mī'cum
	Gen.	a mī'cī	a mī'cae	a mī'cī
	Dat.	a mī'cō	a mī'cae	a mī'cō
	Acc.	a mī'cum	a mī'cam	a mī'cum
	Voc.	a mī'ce	a mī'ca	a mī'cum
	Abl.	a mī'cō	a mī'cā	a mī'cō
Plur.	Nom.	a mī'cī	a mī'cae	a mī'ca
	Gen.	a mī cō'rum	a mī cā'rum	a mī cō'rum
	Dat.	a mī'cīs	a mī'cīs	a mī'cīs
	Acc.	a mī'cōs	a mī'cās	a mī'ca
	Voc.	a mī'cī	a mī'cae	a mī'ca
	Abl.	a mī'cīs	a mī'cīs	a mī'cīs

Like *a mī'cus* decline *ac cep'tus*, also *in i mī'cus ;* decline
nō'tus like *bo'nus.*

30.

1. The sailor was well known to the commander.   2. The commander is friendly to the children of the sailor.   3. There is
danger in camp; the allies are unfriendly to the tribune.   4. The
tribune was not a friend of the allies.   5. Assistance will be
acceptable to the tribune.   6. Both the commanders and the ·
tribunes were well known to the allies.   7. The camp was full of
deserters.   8. The deserters were not unfriendly to the commander of the camp.   9. The commander of the camp was well
known to the garrison.   10. Money will be acceptable to the

engineers. 11. The engineers are friendly to the sons of Claudius. 12. The dangers of war are not acceptable to many men.

ABLATIVE WITH ADJECTIVES.

SUGGESTIONS. — 1. A few adjectives like **dīgnus** and **indīgnus** are followed by the *ablative*.

2. Possessive pronouns are adjectives agreeing with their nouns in gender, number, and case. They also refer to a *possessor*, expressed or implied; **meus**, *my;* **tuus**, *thy, your,* to *one possessor;* **suus**, *his, her, its, their,* to *one* or *more.*

3. **Suus** refers to the *subject* of a proposition, as *a possessor; e.g.* in 2, below, **suō** refers to **vir**, the subject (*the possessor*), but agrees with **tribūnō**.

31.

1. Praefectus est saucius et auxiliō[1] tuō dīgnus. 2. Vir dīgnus ā tribūnō suō laudābātur. 3. Castra tua erant fabrō tuō indīgna. 4. Castra mea ā fabrō tuō nōn parābantur. 5. Dēcrēta concilī tuī et multa et accepta erant. 6. Sociī tuī dēcrētīs tuīs dīgnī erant. 7. Dominus servō suō pecūniam multam dabat. 8. Servus bonus dominō suō erat dīgnus. 9. Amīcī tuī auxilī meī nōn erunt cupidī. 10. Amīcī meī ā servīs suīs servābuntur. 11. Faber, fīlī mī, est amīcus et tuus et meus. 12. Fēminae fīliābus suīs pecūniam multam dabant. 13. Fīliae tuae pecūniā tuā sunt dīgnae. 14. Meī līberī fīliārum tuārum amīcī sunt.

DIRECTIONS. — Learn A. & G.: [1]245 and *a*, 1; Rule 42.
H.: [1]421, III.; Rule XXVI., III.

	M.	F.	N.		M.	F.	N.
Sing. Nom.	me'us	me'a	me'um	Plur.	me'ī	me'ae	me'a
Gen.	me'ī	me'ae	me'ī		me ō'rum	me ā'rum	me ō'rum
Dat.	me'ō	me'ae	me'ō		me'īs	me'īs	me'īs
Acc.	me'um	me'am	me'um		me'ōs	me'ās	me'a
Voc.	mī	me'a	me'um		me'ī	me'ae	me'a
Abl.	me'ō	me'ā	me'ō		me'īs	me'īs	me'īs

Like *me'us* decline *tu'us* and *su'us*, omitting the vocative; like *bo'nus*, *dī'gnus;* like *a mī'cus*, *in dī'gnus.*

32.

1. The good master was praised by his slave. 2. The slave was not unworthy of his master. 3. My commander is praising his auxiliary [forces]. 4. The auxiliary [forces] are worthy of my commanders. 5. The town was friendly both to your allies and to your auxiliaries. 6. Your allies were not unfriendly to their commanders. 7. My well-known friends are desirous of your boat. 8. Your son will be in the boat with your daughter. 9. The daughters of your commanders were in my camp. 10. My commander with his daughters was in your camp. 11. Your commanders are worthy of their friends. 12. Your daughter is not unworthy of her friends.

ADJECTIVES IN -ER.

SUGGESTIONS. — 1. The possessive pronouns, **noster**, *our*, and **vester**, *your*, are adjectives agreeing with their nouns, but they refer to *more than one possessor*, expressed or implied.

2. When a noun is limited by an adjective and a noun in the genitive, a common order is, *adj., gen., noun.* See 7.

33.

1. Auxilia nostra[1] vulgus miserum dēlectant. 2. Vulgus miserum ab auxiliīs nostrīs dēlectātur. 3. Dēcrētum vestrum sociīs nostrīs nōn erit acceptum. 4. Amīcī nostrī scaphīs suīs dēlectantur. 5. Noster captīvus miser nōn erat cupidus bellī. 6. Bellum nostrum captīvum miserum nōn dēlectat. 7. Misera Claudī fīlia māgnō in perīculō est. 8. Vestrī sociī nōtī agrōs nostrōs vastant. 9. Agrī nostrī ā sociīs vestrīs vastantur. 10. Oppidum nostrōrum sociōrum miserōrum praesidiō vastātur. 11. Praesidium vestrum oppida nostra vastat. 12. Praefectus nostrō captīvō miserō equum suum dabit. 13. Amīcī fīliārum vestrārum perfugīs auxilium dabunt. 14. Fīliae captīvōrum nostrōrum nōn sunt in Galliā.

DIRECTION. — Learn A. & G.: [1]**197**; Rule 2.
II.: [1]**438** and 1; Rule XXXIV.

		M.	F.	N.
Sing.	Nom.	no'ster	no'stra	no'strum
	Gen.	no'strī	no'strae	no'strī
	Dat.	no'strō	no'strae	no'strō
	Acc.	no'strum	no'stram	no'strum
	Voc.	no'ster	no'stra	no'strum
	Abl.	no'strō	no'strā	no'strō
Plur.	Nom.	no'strī	no'strae	no'stra
	Gen.	no strō'rum	no strā'rum	no strō'rum
	Dat.	no'strīs	no'strīs	no'strīs
	Acc.	no'strōs	no'strās	no'stra
	Voc.	no'strī	no'strae	no'stra
	Abl.	no'strīs	no'strīs	no'strīs

		M.	F.	N.
Sing.	Nom.	mi'ser	mi'se ra	mi'se rum
	Gen.	mi'se rī	mi'se rae	mi'se rī
	Dat.	mi'se rō	mi'se rae	mi'se rō
	Acc.	mi'se rum	mi'se ram	mi'se rum
	Voc.	mi'ser	mi'se ra	mi'se rum
	Abl.	mi'se rō	mi'se rā	mi'se rō
Plur.	Nom.	mi'se rī	mi'se rae	mi'se ra
	Gen.	mi se rō'rum	mi se rā'rum	mi se rō'rum
	Dat.	mi'se rīs	mi'se rīs	mi'se rīs
	Acc.	mi'se rōs	mi'se rās	mi'se ra
	Voc.	mi'se rī	mi'se rae	mi'se ra
	Abl.	mi'se rīs	mi'se rīs	mi'se rīs

Like *no'ster* decline *ve'ster*.

34.

1. Our new boat delights the children.   2. Both sons and daughters are delighted with our boat.   3. Our auxiliary [forces] delight their commander.   4. Our commander is delighted with his auxiliary forces.   5. The fields of our allies are laid waste by the unworthy garrison.   6. The wounded commander was assisted by our friends.   7. The field will be protected by our auxiliaries.   8. The garrisons of your towns were desirous of assistance.   9. Your towns are worthy of good garrisons.   10. The friends of our slaves lay waste many unfortunate towns.   11. In our council there were many illustrious men.   12. The council

will be friendly to your allies. 13. The unworthy garrison lays waste our unfortunate town. 14. Our unfortunate town is laid waste by the unworthy garrison.

ADJECTIVES USED AS NOUNS.

SUGGESTION. — Adjectives and possessive pronouns are often used as nouns ; e.g. amīcus, a friend. Especially are many masc. and neut. pl. forms thus used ; e.g. multī, the many, — many, — many men ; multa, many things ; bonī, the good, — good men ; bona, goods ; nostrī, our forces, our men ; suī, his (their) forces, his (their) men; sua, his (their) property.

35.

1. Multī* bonōs laudant. 2. Auxilia nostrōs[1] servābunt. 3. Nostrī[2] agrōs vulgī vastābant. 4. Bonī nōn erunt bellōrum cupidī. 5. Brūtus amīcō meō sua dabit. 6. Praefectī tribūnō suōs dēmōnstrābant. 7. Tribūnus ā suīs servābitur. 8. Multa fīliās nostrās dēlectābunt. 9. Fēminae bonae fīliābus meīs multa dabunt. 10. Bona captīvōrum sociīs nostrīs dabantur. 11. Sociī nostrī amīcīs suīs bona dēmōnstrant. 12. Amīcī sociōrum ā nostrīs cōnfirmābuntur.

DIRECTIONS. — 1. Read A. & G. : *188 and Remark ; 190, a ; 197, d.
II. : *441 and 1 ; 449 and 4.
2. Learn A. & G. : [1] Rule 30. [2] Rule 13.
II. : [1] Rule V. [2] Rule III.

36.

1. Ours (our forces) were assisting the garrison. 2. Worthy friends will assist ours (our forces). 3. There will be many good [men] in the council. 4. The council will give many [things] to our slaves. 5. Many [things] will be acceptable to our slaves. 6. The good are worthy of their friends. 7. The commander will protect the goods of his friends. 8. Our friends will give their [property] to the commander. 9. Worthy men were encouraging the good. 10. The tribune was encouraged by

his [forces]. 11. Ours (our men) often praise the well-known tribune. 12. The well-known tribune is praised by ours (our men).

RECAPITULATION, WITH NEW NOUNS OF THE FIRST DECLENSION.

SUGGESTION.— Glōriae causā in 15, below, is to be translated *for the sake of glory*.

37.

1. Fuga fēminārum[1] et līberōrum causam tuam nōn iuvābit. 2. Causa fugae erat perīculum prōvinciae nostrae. 3. Nostra prōvincia ā sociīs tuīs vastābātur. 4. Praefectus glōriā māgnā erat dīgnus. 5. Māgna est glōria causae tuae. 6. Sociī nostrī causae tuae erant amīcī. 7. Praesidium nostrum prōvinciam tuam nōn vastābit. 8. Est silva māgna in prōvinciā nostrā. 9. Erant in silvā perfugae multī. 10. Silvae multae et māgnae prōvinciās servābunt. 11. Sunt oppida multa in prōvinciīs nostrīs. 12. Misera oppidōrum praesidia auxilī erant cupida. 13. Nostrī oppidīs[2] auxilium dabunt. 14. Bellum prōvinciīs nōn est acceptum. 15. Sociī nostrī glōriae causā armābantur. 16. Glōria bellī nostrōs sociōs dēlectābit.

DIRECTIONS. — 1. Learn A. & G.: [1] 213; Rule 14. [2] 224; 225; Rule 21.
H.: [1] 395; Rule XVI. [2] 384 and II.; Rule XII., II.
2. Decline *cau'sa, fu'ga, sil'va* like *nau'ta; prō vin'ci a* like *pe cū'ni a*.

38.

1. Ours (our forces) were protected by a forest. 2. The forest is in our province. 3. A slave shows the forest to the commanders. 4. There were many wounded men in the forest. 5. The illustrious commander of the province is a worthy man. 6. The worthy commander will give the province assistance. 7. The province will be protected by new auxiliary [forces]. 8. The well-known allies will be friendly to our cause. 9. Our cause is

the cause of our provinces. 10. The good will encourage our cause and protect our glory. 11. Our garrisons and auxiliary forces are the glory of our commanders. 12. Our provinces were full of large forests. 13. Many [men] were praising the forests and the friendly provinces.

RECAPITULATION, WITH NEW NOUNS OF THE SECOND DECLENSION.

SUGGESTION.—**Hīberna** was originally the neuter plural of an adjective declined like **bonus**, the expression **hīberna castra** meaning *winter camp, winter quarters.* Later, **castra** was omitted, leaving **hīberna** with the combined signification of both words. Many adjectives are thus used in all numbers and genders. Compare Suggestion, Exercise 35.

39.

1. Nūntius lēgātum et praefectum cōnfirmābat. 2. Lēgātus nūntium et praesidium cōnfirmābit. 3. Prōvincia et lēgātō et nūntiō erit amīca. 4. Nūntiī amīcī et lēgātī populō Rōmānō erant dīgnī. 5. Lēgātus erat prōvinciae acceptus. 6. Māgnum est imperium populī Rōmānī. 7. Imperium māgnum populō[1] Rōmānō dabātur. 8. Populus Rōmānus lēgātō dīgnō imperium dabit. 9. Domicilium lēgātō clārō dīgnum est. 10. Lēgātī nostrī domicilia in Galliā parābant. 11. Nōta nūntiōrum domicilia sunt in prōvinciā. 12. Nūntiī ā lēgātīs servābantur. 13. Lēgātī nūntiīs pecūniam multam dabant. 14. Pecūnia lēgātōrum nūntiōs dēlectābat. 15. Nostrī hīberna parābunt. 16. Hīberna ā nostrīs parābuntur.

DIRECTIONS. — 1. Learn A. & G. : [1]**225,** *e.*
II. : [1]**384** and I.
2. Decline *nūn'ti us* like *so'ci us; lē gā'tus* and *prae fec'tus* like *capti'vus; po'pu lus* like *do'mi nus; Rō mā'nus* like *a mī'cus; im pe'ri um* and *do mici'- li um* like *con ci'li um; hī ber'na* like the plural of *dē crē'tum.*

40.

1. Many [men] were protecting the worthy messenger. 2. The Roman people will give the messenger a new abode. 3. The

abode of the messenger is in our province. 4. The well-known messenger is worthy of the Roman people. 5. New power was given to a friend of the illustrious lieutenant. 6. The lieutenant will protect the power of the Roman people. 7. The good are not unfriendly to the ambassador and the Roman people. 8. The flight of the messengers will not delight the Roman people. 9. The messengers are unworthy of power. 10. Friends will assist the unfortunate messengers. 11. The abodes of the deserters are well-known to the messengers. 12. The danger to (genitive) the winter [quarters] was not great. 13. The winter [quarters] were protected by our lieutenants. 14. Our lieutenants with many messengers are in the winter [quarters].

———••o‡o‡oo••———

NOUNS. THIRD DECLENSION.

NOUNS IN -OR, MASCULINE GENDER, SINGULAR NUMBER.

SUGGESTION. — Nom. and voc. sign—; gen., -is; dat., -ī; acc., -em; abl., -e.

41.

1. Ōrātor est amīcus meus. 2. Victor erat ōrātōris amīcus. 3. Ōrātor honōre[1] māgnō dīgnus est. 4. Victor clārus nostrōs cōnfirmābit. 5. Honor victōris ōrātōrem dēlectābit. 6. Honor novus victōrī ab ōrātōre dabātur. 7. Concilium novum honōre victōris dēlectātur. 8. Ōrātor et victōrem et bellum laudābat. 9. Populus Rōmānus nostrō ōrātōrī clārō honōrem māgnum dat. 10. Populus Rōmānus honōris est cupidus. 11. Glōria populī Rōmānī ā victōre servābātur. 12. Honor populī Rōmānī ab ōrātōre servābitur.

DIRECTIONS. — 1. Learn A. & G.: [1] 65, a.
II. : [1] 99.
2. Nouns in -or are masculine ; but apply Direction, Exercise 7. Exceptions to the special rules for endings of the third declension will be elsewhere noted.

42.

1. The orator was a friend of the victor. 2. The victor will assist the children of the orator. 3. The orator was protecting the honor of the victor. 4. Honor was given to the illustrious victor. 5. The victor was worthy of honor. 6. The well-known orator delights the Roman people. 7. The Roman people praise the orator and the victor. 8. The victor was showing our camp to the orator. 9. The tribune was summoned by the orator and the victor. 10. The tribune is a friend of the orator. 11. Our commanders are friendly to the honor of worthy men. 12. The orator and the victor were not unworthy of honor.

NOUNS IN -OR, PLURAL NUMBER.

SUGGESTIONS. — 1. Nom., acc., and voc. case-ending, -ēs; gen., -um; dat. and abl., -ĭbus.

2. A collective noun usually takes a singular verb, but if the thought of *the individual* prevails, the plural is often used.

43.

1. Populus Rōmānus victōrēs armābat et ōrātōrēs cōnfirmā-bat. 2. Ōrātōrēs victōribus honōrēs dabunt. 3. Victōrēs saepe honōrum cupidī sunt. 4. Honōrēs et victōribus et ōrātōribus dabuntur. 5. Līberī ōrātōrum et victōrum honōribus nōn sunt indīgnī. 6. Bonī ab ōrātōribus et victōribus cōnfirmābuntur. 7. Uxor senātōris erat soror uxōris meae. 8. Vulgus uxōrem senātōris, sorōrem fēminae bonae, laudat. 9. Senātor uxōre suā est dīgnus. 10. Senātōrēs uxōrēs suās et sorōrēs vocābant. 11. Uxōrēs senātōrum sorōribus ōrātōrum pecūniam dabunt. 12. Sorōrēs uxōrī victōris pecūniam dēmōnstrant. 13. Amīcī sorōrum ā senātōribus cōnfirmābantur.

Sing. Nom.	ho′nor	ō rā′ tor	Sing. Acc.	ho nō′rem	ō rā tō′rem
Gen.	ho nō′ris	ō rā tō′ris	Voc.	ho′nor	ō rā′tor
Dat.	ho nō′rī	ō rā tō′rī	Abl.	ho nō′re	ō rā tō′re

Plur. Nom. ho nō'rēs   ō rā tō'rēs | Plur. Acc. ho nō'rēs   ō rā tō'rēs
Gen. ho nō'rum   ō rū tō'rum | Voc. ho nō'rēs   ō rā tō'rēs
Dat. ho nō'rĭ bus ō rā tō'rĭ bus | Abl. ho nō'rĭ bus   ō rā tō'rĭ bus

Like *ho'nor* decline *so'ror, u'xor* and *vic'tor ;* like *ōrā'tor, se nā'tor.*

44.

1. The senators were protecting their wives and sisters. 2. The sisters were protected by the senators. 3. The sisters of the senators were the wives of orators. 4. The orators were worthy of their good wives. 5. The friends of our wives and sisters are sons of senators. 6. Our good wives are with the victors and their sisters. 7. The victors will be in Gaul with our orators. 8. The honors of the victors will delight our orators. 9. Orators will praise the victors and the worthy senators. 10. The senators will be encouraged by honors. 11. The Roman people give honors to their senators. 12. Honors are given both to the victors and the orators. 13. Our [property] will be given to our wives and sisters.

NOUNS IN -*IŌ*, FEMININE GENDER.

SUGGESTIONS. — 1. Case-endings will be as in Exercises 41 and 43 until further mention.

2. Nouns in -*iō* have lost a final n from the nom. and voc. sing., which must be replaced to form *the stem* to which the case signs are affixed ; *e.g.* **legiō,** the nom., becomes **legiōn,** *the stem ;* gen., **legiōnis,** etc.

3. *To Vesontio, to Rome,* etc., meaning *in the direction of,* is expressed by the accusative case: e.g. *Vesontiōnem, Rōmam,* etc.

4. Verbs like **monet;** *i.e.* Pres. *monet, monent;* Imp. *monēbat, monēbant ;* Fut. *monēbit, monēbunt,* are of the *Second Conjugation.*

5. Verbs like **dūcit;** *i.e.* Pres. *dūcit, dūcunt;* Imp. *dūcēbat, dūcēbant ;* Fut. *dūcet, dūcent,* are of the *Third Conjugation.*

45.

1. Vesontiō[1] et Avaricum in Galliā sunt. 2. Praefectus Vesontiōnis nātiōnem[2] monet. 3. Nātiō ā praefectō Vesontiōnis monētur. 4. Tribūnus legiōnem Rōmam[3] dūcit. 5. Legiō Rōmam

ā tribūnō dūcitur. 6. Honor nātiōnis glōria legiōnis est. 7. Populus Rōmānus Vesontiōnem auxilium mīttit. 8. Auxilium Vesontiōnem ā populō Rōmānō mīttitur. 9. Senātor nātiōnī amīcus erat, legiōnī inimīcus. 10. Ōrātor legiōne et nātiōne est dīgnus. 11. Nātiōnēs Galliae Genāvam legiōnēs multās mīttunt et auxilia sua monent. 12. Legiōnēs multae Genāvam ā nātiōnibus Galliae mīttuntur et auxilia monentur. 13. Victōrēs legiōnibus nostrīs et nātiōnibus Galliae erant nōtī. 14. Amīcī nātiōnum erant legiōnum nostrārum amīcī. 15. Victōrēs legiōnēs suās Avaricum dūcunt. 16. Multae legiōnēs Avaricum dūcuntur.

DIRECTION. — Learn A. & G.: ¹29, 1, 2, and Note. ²65, b. ³258, b.
H.: ¹42, I., 1, 2 ; II., 1, 2. ²105 and 100, 3.
³380 and II.; Rule X., II.

Sing. Nom.	nā'ti ō	Plur. nā ti ō'nēs	Sing. Ve son'ti ō
Gen.	nā ti ō'nis	nā ti ō'num	Ve son ti ō'nis
Dat.	nā ti ō'nī	nā ti ō'ni bus	Ve son ti ō'nī
Acc.	nā ti ō'nem	nā ti ō'nēs	Ve son ti ō'nem
Voc.	nā'ti ō	nā ti ō'nēs	Ve son'ti ō
Abl.	nā ti ō'ne	nā ti ō'ni bus	Ve son ti ō'ne

Like *nā'ti ō* decline *le'gi ō*. Decline new nouns of the first and second declension wherever introduced.

46.

1. There is in Gaul an unfriendly nation. 2. Allies give assistance to the unworthy nation. 3. The allies of the nation lay waste our provinces. 4. The Roman people send many legions to Geneva. 5. A tribune with his legion is sent to Vesontio. 6. The garrison of Vesontio is well-known to the legion. 7. The commander of a legion leads auxiliary [forces] to Avaricum. 8. The auxiliary [forces] with our legions will protect the province. 9. The nations of Germany will be unfriendly to our legions. 10. The commanders of our legions warn the nations of Germany. 11. Illustrious men of many nations are sent to Rome. 12. Our ambassadors will not be acceptable to the nations of Germany.

NOUNS IN -ĀS, FEMININE GENDER.

SUGGESTIONS. — 1. The case-ending of the nom. and voc. sing. is -s.
2. In these nouns a final t of the stem has been suppressed before the case
ending -s: e.g. *cīvitās* is for *cīvitā(t)s*. Decline, therefore, nom. *cīvitās*;
gen. *cīvitātis*, etc.
3. **Studet**, *he is devoted to*, i.e. *he desires;* **persuādet**, *he makes it pleasant to*, i.e. *he persuades;* and **favet**, *he is favorable to*, i.e. *he favors;* are
followed by the dative.

47.

1. Cīvitās lībertātī favet et potestātī* studet. 2. Populus
Rōmānus lībertāte est dīgnus. 3. Rōma est potestātis et lībertātis domicilium. 4. Māgna est potestās et lībertās cīvitātis.
5. Senātōrēs nōbilitātī[1] favent et cīvitātī[1] persuādent. 6. Cīvitās potestātem māgnam nōbilitātī dabit. 7. Nōbilitās legiōnibus
multīs lībertātem populī Rōmānī servābit. 8. Māgna est glōria
et honor nōbilitātis. 9. Praefectus clārus nōbilitātem dūcēbat. 10. Imperium cīvitātum inimīcārum nōbilitātem monēbat.
11. Ōrātor nōtus et nōbilitātī et cīvitātibus persuādet. 12. Nōbilitās cīvitātēs Galliae monēbant. 13. Amīcī nōbilitātis ā cīvitātibus monēbantur. 14. Virī clārī Rōmam ā nōbilitātę mīttēbantur.
15. Praefectī auxilia Vesontiōnem mīttēbant.

DIRECTION. — Read A. & G.: *227, *e* and 3.
H.: *385 ; 371, III., Note 3.
Learn A. & G.: [1]227 ; Rule 22.
H.: [1]385, I., II.

Sing. Nom.	cī'vi tās	Plur.	cī vi tā'tēs
Gen.	cī vi tā'tis		cī vi tā'tum (ium)
Dat.	cī vi tā'tī		cī vi tā'ti bus
Acc.	cī vi tā'tem		cī vi tā'tēs (īs)
Voc.	cī'vi tās		cī vi tā'tēs
Abl.	cī vi tā'te		cī vi tā'ti bus

Sing. Nom.	lī ber'tās	Plur.	lī ber tā'tēs
Gen.	lī ber tā'tis		lī ber tā'tum (ium)
Dat.	lī ber tā'tī		lī ber tā'ti bus
Acc.	lī ber tā'tem		lī ber tā'tēs (īs)
Voc.	lī ber'tās		lī ber tā'tēs
Abl.	lī ber tā'te		lī ber tā'ti bus

Like *cī'vi tạs* decline *nō bi'li tās ;* like *lī ber'tās, po te'stās.*

48.

1. The nobility desires power. 2. The Roman people will give power to the nobility. 3. The power of the nobility is great. 4. The state is desirous of liberty and power. 5. Liberty will give power to a state. 6. The state is not unworthy of power and liberty. 7. The good were praising the state and the nobility. 8. The nobility was worthy of the state. 9. The states of Germany favor liberty. 10. Our senators were admonishing (warning) the states. 11. Unfriendly orators favor the states. 12. The nobility of the states was sending many legions to Geneva. 13. The commander was sending the auxiliaries to Avaricum.

NOUNS IN -DŌ (gen. -ĭnĭs), FEMININE GENDER. ALSO HOMŌ AND CAESAR.

SUGGESTIONS. — 1. **Homō** and nouns in -dō have lost a final n of the stem in the nom. and voc. sing. In the other cases ō preceding n has become i. Hence, nom. *homō*, gen. *homĭnĭs*, etc. ; nom. *fortĭtūdō*, gen. *fortĭtūdĭnĭs*, etc.

2. **Ex-pellit** means *he drives out;* it is followed by the ablative, often with a preposition, to denote the place from which.

49.

1. Vir clārus est Caesar, servus Caesaris bonus homō. 2. Caesar hominī bonō, servō suō, lībertātem dabit. 3. Amīcī Caesaris hominem dīgnum cōnfirmābunt. 4. Est multitūdō hominum inimīcōrum in Galliā. 5. Sociī īgnōtī multitūdinī inimīcæ favēbant. 6. Nostrī cīvitāte[1] hominēs indīguōs expellunt. 7. Fuga multitūdinis Caesarem monēbit. 8. Caesar nostrōs, nōn multitūdinem, armābit. 9. Caesar fortitūdinem cōnfirmābit et victōrēs multīs cum honōribus Rōmam mittet. 10. Vesontiō fortitūdine tribūnī, hominis clārī, servābitur. 11. Tribūnus cum Caesare et multitūdine nōbilitātis Vesontiōnem mittētur. 12. Māgna est potestās fortitūdinis. 13. Praefectī indīgnī multīs cum hominibus, perfugīs et servīs, prōvinciā expelluntur. 14. Praefectus prōvinciae

Caesarī et hominibus multīs est nōtus. 15. Multī hominēs glōriae causā fortitūdinī student. 16. Tribūnī legiōnēs multās Genāvam dūcent.

DIRECTION. — Learn A. & G.: [1]243 and *a*; Rule 38.
H.: [1]413; 414, I.; Rule XXII.

Sing. Nom.	ho'mō	Plur.	ho'mi nēs
Gen.	ho'mi nis		ho'mi num
Dat.	ho'mi nī		ho mi'ni bus
Acc.	ho'mi nem		ho'mi nēs
Voc.	ho'mō		ho'mi nēs
Abl.	ho'mi ne		ho mi'ni bus

Sing. Nom.	for ti tū'dō	Plur.	for ti tū'di nēs
Gen.	for ti tū'di nis		for ti tū'di num
Dat.	for ti tū'di nī		for ti tū di'ni bus
Acc.	for ti tū'di nem		for ti tū'di nēs
Voc.	for ti tū'dō		for ti tū'di nēs
Abl.	for ti tū'di ne		for ti tū di'ni bus

Like *for ti tū'dō* decline *mul ti tū'dō*. Write the declension of *Cae'sar* from the Latin sentences.

50.

1. The illustrious commander is the son of an unworthy man. 2. Caesar will send the illustrious man to Rome. 3. Rome is the abode of bravery. 4. The bravery of the multitude will delight Caesar. 5. Caesar will encourage bravery. 6. The nobility desire war and persuade the multitude. 7. The multitude is encouraged by Caesar's bravery. 8. Caesar is not unworthy of the multitude. 9. The multitude desire a worthy man. 10. A good cause is not assisted by an unworthy man. 11. Men unfriendly to Caesar were laying waste our fields. 12. Deserters are friendly to the unworthy men. 13. There were many sailors with the unfriendly men. 14. Slaves are friends of the unworthy men. 15. The states prepare war and drive the unworthy multitude from the province.

NOUNS IN -Ō (gen. -ōnis), MASCULINE GENDER.

SUGGESTIONS. — 1. These nouns, like those in -iŏ, and -dŏ, have lost the final n of the stem in the nom. and voc. sing., but unlike those nouns retain ŏ before n in the other cases.

2. **Ad** means *to*, i.e. *up to;* **in** means *to*, i.e. *to a position within, into, into the midst of;* **in**, with the ablative, means *in (situation in a place).*

3. *Do, does* and *did*, when used as auxiliary verbs, are not to be translated; e.g. *he does praise*, **laudat**; *they do favor*, **favent.**

•

51.

1. Homō saucius est cālō, et perfuga miser latrō est.   2. Auxilium et latrōnī et cālōnī est acceptum.   3. Erant cum latrōne et cālōne hominēs multī et inimīcī.   4. Hominēs indīgnī ad Caesarem [1] dūcēbantur.   5. Caesar cālōnem ad castra, [1] latrōnem ad oppidum, Genāvam, mīttēbat.   6. Fīlius cālōnis et fīlia latrōnis ad prōvinciam mīttentur.   7. Cicerō clārus erat ōrātor nōtus.   8. Ōrātor māgnus nōn est latrōnum et cālōnum amīcus.   9. Cālōnēs et latrōnēs Cicerōnī sunt nōtī.   10. Cicerō cālōnibus et latrōnibus nōn favēbit.   11. Potestās Cicerōnis cālōnēs et latrōnēs cīvitāte expellit.   12. Cīvitās ā Cicerōne monēbātur.   13. Populus Rōmānus Cicerōnem laudat.   14. Praefectus inimīcus cum cālōnibus multīs et latrōnibus suōs in prōvinciam dūcet.

DIRECTION. — Learn A. & G. : [1] **258**, last clause.
H. : [1] **380** and I. ; Rule X., I.

Sing. Nom.	cā'lō	Plur. cā lō'nēs	Sing. Ci'ce rō
Gen.	cā lō'nis	cā lō'num	Ci ce rō'nis
Dat.	cā lō'nī	cā lō'ni bus	Ci ce rō'nī
Acc.	cā lō'nem	cā lō'nēs	Ci ce rō'nem
Voc.	cā'lō	cā lō'nēs	Ci'ce rō
Abl.	cā lō'ne	cā lō'ni bus	Ci ce rō'ne

Like *cā'lō* decline *la'trō.*

52.

1. A robber was led into camp by a servant.   2. The robber shows the servant his goods and money.   3. The servant is desirous of the robber's money.   4. Our commander [does] not

favor the robber. 5. The commander of the camp will send the servant to Italy, the robber to the town, Geneva. 6. Friends of the servant drive the robber from the town. 7. The forests of Italy are full of servants and robbers. 8. Sulla leads many servants and robbers to Rome. 9. Sulla's commanders are not friends of Cicero and the nobility. 10. Sulla with many servants and robbers will lay waste our fields. 11. The well-known victor will give the servants and robbers the fields of Italy. 12. Sulla is not encouraged by Cicero. 13. Robbers [do] not praise Cicero. 14. The Roman people will give Cicero much honor.

NOUNS IN -L. ALSO FRATER.

SUGGESTIONS.— 1. Nouns in -l are usually masculine by signification.

2. The nom. and voc. form *frāter* is replaced by a shorter stem *frātr* in the other cases. Decline nom. *frāter*, gen. *frātris*, etc.

3. *From Avaricum, from Geneva*, etc., is expressed by the ablative case ; e.g. *Avaricō, Genāvā*, etc.

53.

1. Frāter meus cōnsulem socium[1] appellat, exsulem amīcum. 2. Cōnsul ā frātre meō socius[2] appellātur, exsul amīcus. 3. Meus frāter clārus et cōnsulī et exsulī persuādēbat. 4. Cīvitās frātrī meō favēbat. 5. Populus Rōmānus frātrem meum Avaricō,[3] cōnsulem Genāvā vocābat. 6. Nūntius cum exsule Rōmā ā cōnsule in prōvinciam mīttēbātur. 7. Māgna est potestās cōnsulis, honor exsulis, fortitūdō frātris meī. 8. Frātrēs senātōris cōnsulēs et exsulēs monēbunt. 9. Nōbilitās cum cōnsulibus et exsulibus ā frātribus monēbitur. 10. Et cōnsulēs et exsulēs frātrēs senātōris armābunt. 11. Perīculum exsulum et cōnsulum nōn est frātribus īgnōtum. 12. Auxilium frātrum cōnsulibus erit acceptum. 13. Nostrī frātrem meum tribūnum creant. 14. Frāter meus ā nostrīs tribūnus creātur.

DIRECTIONS.— Learn A. & G.: [1]239, 1 and *a* ; Rule 32. [2]239, 1, Note 2. [3]258. *a*.

H.: [1]373 ; Rule VI. [2]373, 2. [3]412 and II.

Sing. Nom.	frā'ter	Plur.	frā'trēs		Sing. cōn'sul	Plur. cōn'su lēs
Gen.	frā'tris		frā'trum		cōn'su lis	cōn'su lum
Dat.	frā'trī		frā'tri bus		cōn'su lī	cōn su'lī bus
Acc.	frā'trem		frā'trēs		cōn'su lem	cōn'su lēs
Voc.	frā'ter		frā'trēs		cōn'sul	cōn'su lēs
Abl.	frā'tre		frā'tri bus		cōn'su le	cōn su'lī bus

Like *cōn'sul* decline *ex'sul*.

· 54.

1. The brother of the consul was a prisoner and an exile. 2. The prisoner was sent to the consul from Geneva. 3. The consul will favor his brother, the exile. 4. The servant of the exile was a slave of the consul. 5. The slave was given to the exile by his brother, the consul. 6. Money will be sent from Vesontio to the consul by the exile. 7. The consul calls the exile his illustrious brother. 8. The states elect brothers consuls. 9. A senator calls the exiles friends and brothers. 10. The exiles with their brothers, the consuls, desire power. 11. The state protects the friends of the consuls and the exiles. 12. The nation was giving to the brothers and the exiles great honor. 13. Great honor was given to the consuls by the worthy exiles.

NOUNS IN -ES, MASCULINE GENDER. ALSO *PRĪNCEPS.*

SUGGESTIONS.— 1. These nouns change i of the stem to e before s, the case-sign of the nom. and voc. sing. Before s, p is retained, while t and d are dropped.

2. *Princeps* is the masculine form of an adjective.

3. Ā, ab means *from, away from* (the outside) ; ex, *from, out of* (the interior).

55.

1. Nōbilitās prīncipem cīvitātis obsidem[a] Rōmam mīttēbat. 2. Obses ex[b] Galliā[1] in[b] Ītaliam[1] ab mīlite dūcēbātur. 3. Mīles prīncipī, obsidī[2] dīgnō, agrōs Galliae dēmōnstrābat. 4. Erat cum prīncipe amīcus mīlitis. 5. Amīcus erat cālō obsidis, prīncipis[2]

clārī. 6. Cālō erat mīlitī amīcus et obside nōn indīgnus. 7. Prīnceps mīlitem bonum mīttet. 8. Cōnsulēs sunt obsidum cupidī et mīlitēs in Galliam mīttent. 9. Mīlitēs nostrī prīncipēs Galliae monēbant. 10. Prīncipēs cīvitātum obsidēs armābant. 11. Obsidēs dīgnī ā principibus dabantur. 12. Sunt cum obsidibus līberī prīncipum. 13. Obsidēs ā[b] mīlitibus ab Galliā ad[b] Italiam dūcentur. 14. Praefectī mīlitum et obsidibus et prīncipibus favēbunt.

DIRECTION. — Read A. & G.: [a]184 and 2 ; 185. [b]258, 2. Note 2.
H.: [a]373, 1. [b]412 and I. ; 380 and I.
Learn A. & G.: [1]258 ; Rule 56. [2]183 ; Rule 1.
H.: [1]Rules XXI. and X. [2]363 ; Rule II.

Sing. Nom.	ob'ses	Plur. ob'si dēs	Sing. prīn'ceps	Plur. prīn'ci pēs
Gen.	ob'si dis	ob'si dum	prīn'ci pis	prīn'ci pum
Dat.	ob'si dī	ob si'di bus	prīn'ci pī	prīn ci'pi bus
Acc.	ob'si dem	ob'si dēs	prīn'ci pem	prīn'ci pēs
Voc.	ob'ses	ob'si dēs	prīn'ceps	prīn'ci pēs
Abl.	ob'si de	ob si'di bus	prīn'ci pe	prīn ci'pi bus

Like *ob'ses* decline *mī'les*, gen. *mī'li tis*.

56.

1. A hostage was given to the state by a chief of Gaul. 2. A messenger with a soldier was sent to the chief. 3. The chief gives the hostage to the soldier. 4. The hostage warns the soldier. 5. The power of the soldier and of the chief is well-known to the hostage. 6. The soldier with the hostage is summoned from (out of) Gaul to (into) Italy. 7. Our leading men (chiefs) are desirous of hostages. 8. The province is arming its soldiers and desires assistance. 9. The nations of Gaul will send leading men with many hostages to the province. 10. The allies of the leading men are well-known to the soldiers. 11. Many soldiers were sent by our leading men into Gaul. 12. Honors worthy of illustrious soldiers were given to our leading men.

NOUNS IN -US. FEMININE GENDER.

ALSO LAUS AND CUSTŌS.

SUGGESTIONS. — 1. These nouns are alike in that they drop the consonant (*t*, *d*) before -**s**, the case-ending of the nom. and voc. sing., and retain the preceding vowel quantity.
2. Translate the ablative in 6, below, *because of*.
3. Most verbs, like **venit**; i.e. Pres. *venit*, *veniunt*; Imp. *veniēbat*, *veniē-bant*; Fut. *veniet*, *venient*; are of the *fourth conjugation*.

57.

1. Custōs est vir māgnae virtūtis.[1] 2. Virtūs custōdis mīlitēs nostrōs dēlectābit. 3. Caesar virtūtem laudat et custōdem cōn-firmat. 4. Vir bonus saepe est laudis cupidus. 5. Laus māgna custōdī dīgnō dabitur. 6. Tribūnus virtūte[2] suā māgnum in perī-culum venit. 7. Tribūnus auxiliō studet et ā cōnsule custōdēs postulat. 8. Praefectī multī cum custōdibus ad tribūnum veni-unt et auxilium postulant. 9. Virtūs custōdum laude māgnā est dīgna. 10. Custōdēs nostrī laudī et virtūtī nōn erunt inimīcī. 11. Populus Rōmānus māgnam[3] laudem et honōrem custōdibus dabat. 12. Custōdēs nostrī mīlitēs honōris māgnī erunt.

DIRECTION. — Learn A. & G.: [1] **215**; Rule 15. [2] **245**; Rule 41. [3] **187** and *a*, 1.
H.: [1] **396**, V.; .Rule XVI. [2] **416**; Rule XXII. [3] **439** and 1.

Sing. Nom.	cu'stōs	Sing. laus	lau'dis	Sing. vir'tūs	vir tū'tis
Gen.	cu stō'dis		lau'dis		vir tū'tis
Dat.	cu stō'dī		lau'dī		vir tū'tī
Acc.	cu stō'dem		lau'dem		vir tū'tem
Voc.	cu'stōs		laus		vir'tūs
Abl.	cu stō'de		lau'de		vir tū'te

Plur. Nom.	cu stō'dēs	Plur. lau'dēs		Plur. vir tū'tēs	
Gen.	cu stō'dum		lau'dum		vir tū'tum
Dat.	cu stō'di bus		lau'di bus		vir tū'ti bus
Acc.	cu stō'dēs		lau'dēs		vir tū'tēs
Voc.	cu stō'dēs		lau'dēs		vir tū'tēs
Abl.	cu stō'di bus		lau'di bus		vir tū'ti bus

58.

1. A good soldier desires praise. 2. The commander will give praise to the good soldiers. 3. The guard is a soldier of well-known valor. 4. The state demands from a guard great valor. 5. The state will praise the valor of the guard. 6. Praise will be given to the guard because of valor. 7. The state by its praise encourages the guard. 8. Guards were sent from the province to Geneva. 9. Assistance will be sent to the guards from Rome. 10. The valor of our guards will protect the honor of the Roman people. 11. The honor of the Roman people will be protected by our guards. 12. The guards [do] not protect the state for the sake of praise.

NOUNS IN -X. FEMININE GENDER.

SUGGESTIONS.—1. These nouns have the case-ending -s in the nom. and voc. sing.; c and g of the stem unite with -s to form x; e.g. stem duc, nom. *duc-s* = dux, gen. *ducis*, etc.

2. Many nouns in -x are masc. by signification.

3. **Facit**, though of the *third conjugation*, is in the present, imperfect, and future, inflected like the *fourth conjugation*.

59.

1. Phalanx erat ducis bonī cupida. 2. Phalanx rēgis duce bonō est dīgna. 3. Rēx frātrem suum ducem phalangis facit. 4. Rēx phalangem suam Rōmā ad prōvinciam dūcet. 5. Dux cum phalange in prōvinciam veniēbat. 6. Nūntius ā rēge in Galliam mīttētur. 7. Nātiōnēs Galliae lēgātōs ad rēgem mīttēbant et pācem postulābant. 8. Pāx rēgī et ducī et phalangī est accepta. 9. Vulgus erit pācis cupidum. 10. Ducēs pācem postulābunt et rēgibus persuādēbunt. 11. Amīcī rēgum pācī favēbunt. 12. Amīcī pācis ducibus nostrīs persuādēbant. 13. Cīvitātēs ducibus et rēgibus suīs sunt dīgnae.

Sing. Nom.	dux (x = c-s)	Plur.	du'cēs
Gen.	du'cis		du'cum
Dat.	du'cī		du'ci bus

Sing.	Acc.	du'cem	Plur.	du'cēs
	Voc.	dux		du'cēs
	Abl.	du'ce		du'ci bus

Sing.	Nom.	pha'lanx ($x = g$-s)	Plur.	pha lan'gēs
	Gen.	pha lan'gis		pha lan'gum
	Dat.	pha lan'gī		pha lan'gi bus
	Acc.	pha lan'gem		pha lan'gēs
	Voc.	pha'lanx		pha lan'gēs
	Abl.	pha lan'ge		pha lan'gi bus

Like *dux* decline *rēx*, gen. *rē'gis*, *pāx*, gen. *pā'cis*.

60.

1. The leader, a man worthy of the king, was arming his phalanx.   2. The king summons the leader with his phalanx to
Rome.   3. The phalanx was friendly to the king and worthy
of its leader.   4. The king was giving the leader and the phalanx much praise.   5. The friends of the king will be delighted
by the valor of the phalanx.   6. The friends of the leader
will assist the king.   7. Unfortunate kings were desiring peace.
8. Messengers of the kings were sent to Rome for the sake of
peace.   9. A decree of the state gives peace to the kings.   10. Ambassadors will be sent to the kings.   11. Peace will be granted
(given) by the kings.   12. Great nations are delighted with peace.

NOUNS IN -ĒS, ALSO URBS AND PLĒBS (I-STEMS).
FEMININE GENDER.

SUGGESTIONS. — 1. Case-endings in this Exercise are the same as in Exercise 59. The i of the stem appears only *before* the case-ending of the gen.
plur. (-ium) and *within* the case-ending of the acc. plur. (regularly -īs
instead of -ēs).

2. For the meaning and use of the word *stem*, read A. & G. 21 and foot-
note 2; H. 46 and 1.

3. Fert is irregular: Pres. fert, ferunt; Imp. ferēbat, ferēbant; Fut.
feret, ferent.

61.

1. Perīculum urbis rēgem monēbit.   2. Rēx urbī mīlitēs auxili causā[1] dat.   3. Mīlitēs cum plēbe auxilium ferunt.   4. Plēbs cum mīlitibus urbem fortitūdine servābat.   5. Urbs virtūte plēbis et mīlitum servābātur.   6. Rēx plēbem iuvābat et hominēs inimīcōs ex urbe expellēbat.   7. Caedēs exsulum urbibus Ītaliae persuādē-bit.   8. Causa caedis miserum concilī dēcrētum est.   9. Plēbs caedī et famī nōn studēbat.   10. Caedēs et famēs plēbī nōn persuādēbunt.   11. Urbēs inimīcae caede et fame vastābantur.   12. Bellum urbīs (-ēs) nostrās vastābat et famis causa erat.   13. Prīncipēs urbium Rōmam pācis causā veniēbant.   14. Pāx famem et caedem urbibus nostrīs expellet.   15. Caedēs saepe famem fert.

DIRECTION. — Learn A. & G. : [1] 245, c.
II. : [1] Rule XXII.

Sing.	Nom.	cae'dēs	Plur.	cae'dēs	Sing.	urbs	Plur.	ur'bēs
	Gen.	cae'dis		cae'dĭ um		ur'bis		ur'bĭ um
	Dat.	cae'dī		cae'di bus		ur'bī		ur'bi bus
	Acc.	cae'dem		cae'dīs (ēs)		ur'bem		ur'bīs (ēs)
	Voc.	cae'dēs		cae'dēs		urbs		ur'bēs
	Abl.	cae'de		cae'di bus		ur'be		ur'bi bus

Notice in these nouns, -i before -um in the gen. plur. (cae'dēs sometimes omits it), and the endings -īs or -ēs in the acc. plur. Like urbs decline plēbs ; like the sing. of cae'dēs, fa'mēs.

62.

1. The slaughter of the common people will warn the cities of the province.   2. The cities will be warned by the slaughter of the common people.   3. The danger of famine will persuade the unfortunate cities.   4. The guards of the cities will be warned by famine.   5. Famine will drive the populace away from the cities.   6. War is the cause of famine and slaughter.   7. The unfortunate populace desire the assistance of the city.   8. The city is friendly to the populace and [does] not favor famine and slaughter.   9. Assistance drives away from the city famine and slaughter.

10. The city is praised by the populace.   11. The populace was giving the city much praise.   12. The nations will praise the city [of] Rome.

NOUNS IN -*IS* (*I-STEMS* CONTINUED), ALSO COHORS.
FEMININE GENDER.

SUGGESTION. — In 8, **prō hoste habet** (*he holds for an enemy*) is to be translated, *he treats as an enemy.*

63.

1. Erat in cohorte[1] hostis.   2. Caedēs partis mīlitum hostī erat nōta, partis īgnōta.   3. Homō indīgnus partī praefectōrum nōtus erat, partī īgnōtus.   4. Māgna cohortis pars hostī nōn favēbat. 5. Praefectus cum parte cohortis hostem monēbat.   6. Laus hostis cohortī nōn erat accepta.   7. Praefectus cohortem in ini- mīcam Galliae partem dūcēbat.   8: Cohors praefectum indī- gnum prō hoste habet.   9. Cohortēs hostium multīs prōvinciae partibus nōn favēbunt.   10. Hostēs partīs (-ēs) cīvitātis vastā- bunt.   11. Partēs cīvitātis ā hostibus vastābuntur, partēs co- hortibus nostrīs servābuntur.   12. Custōdēs urbium cohortibus auxilium ferent.   13. Virtūs cohortium nostrārum hostibus per- suādēbat.   14. Sociī cohortīs (-ēs) nostrās multīs in prōvinciae partibus iuvābunt.

DIRECTION. — Learn A. & G. : [1]**258**, *c*, 1.
H. : [1]**425**, 1.

Sing. Nom.	ho'stis	Plur.	ho'stēs
Gen.	ho'stis		ho'sti um
Dat.	ho'stī		ho'sti bus
Acc.	ho'stem		ho'stīs (ēs)
Voc.	ho'stis		ho'stēs
Abl.	ho'ste		ho'sti bus

Sing. Nom.	co'hors	Plur.	co hor'tēs
Gen.	co hor'tis		co hor'ti um (um)
Dat.	co hor'tī		co hor'ti bus

Sing. Acc.	co hor'tem	Plur. co hor'tīs (ēs)
Voc.	co'hors	co hor' tēs
Abl.	co hor'te	co hor'ti bus.

Like co'hors decline pars, gen. par'tis. It has also an adv. acc. par'tim, meaning partly, and an abl. par'tī.

64.

1. An enemy was leading the cohort. 2. The leader is unfriendly to a large part of the cohort. 3. The leader is treated by the cohort as an enemy. 4. The cohort calls the leader an enemy of the Roman people. 5. The cohort will not favor an enemy. 6. The bravery of the leader [does] not persuade the cohort. 7. Claudius is desirous of a part of a cohort, Brutus demands a part. 8. A part was sent to Claudius, a part to Brutus. 9. The danger of parts of the province is well-known to our cohorts. 10. The state will arm its cohorts and warn its enemies. 11. Many cohorts of our enemies were coming into parts of the province. 12. Parts of the province were laid waste by our enemies. 13. Our enemies are driven from a large part of the province by our cohorts. 14. The valor of the cohorts is not unknown to our enemies.

NOUNS IN -IS (I-STEMS CONTINUED). FEMININE GENDER.

SUGGESTIONS.—1. Cīvis, clāssis and nāvis (genitives the same) show the i-stem in the abl. sing., cīvis and clāssis occasionally, nāvis oftener. Nāvis has also sometimes the acc. sing. nāvim.

2. The dative sometimes means for (see 3, 4, 6, 8, 12 and 13).

65.

1. Nāvis māgna cīvem Rōmānum ad Ītaliam ferēbat. 2. Erat in nāve (-ī) praefectus clāssis et amīcus cīvis. 3. Clāssis māgna praefectō[1] ā cīve (-ī) nōtō parābātur. 4. Cīvis praefectō nāvem (-im) novam et clāssem māgnam parābit. 5. Praefectus clāsse (-ī)

dēlectābitur ,et ,cīvī laudem māgnam dabit.   6. Praefectus clāssī[1]
suae nautās dēligit.   7. Fīlius praefectī dēligitur praefectus nāvis.
8. Multitūdō cīvium et fabrōrum nāvīs (-ēs) et clāssīs (-ēs) cōnsulī
parābit.   9. Clāssēs māgnae, multitūdō nāvium, ā cīvibus armā-
buntur.   10. Nostrae nāvēs et cōnsulem et cīvīs (-ēs) dēlectābunt.
11. Cīvēs clāssibus et nāvibus dēlectābantur.   12. Cōnsulēs clāssibus praefectōs, nāvibus nautās multōs dēligunt.   13. Multitūdō
clāssium cīvibus dēliguntur.

DIRECTION. — Learn A. & G.: [1]**233**, *a*; Rule 27.
H.: [1]**384**, 1, 2).

Like *ho'stis* decline *cī'vis*, *clās'sis*, and *nā'vis*. They also have the abl.
sing. *cī'vī*, *clās'sī*, and *nā'vī*. *Nā'vis* has, besides, the acc. sing. *nā'vim*.

66.

1. Our admiral (commander of the fleet) is worthy of a new
ship.   2. An illustrious citizen, an engineer, will prepare a ship
for our fleet.   3. The ship will be equipped (armed) by a Roman
citizen.   4. The assistance of the citizen will be acceptable to the
state.   5. Sailors are selected for the ship from our fleet.   6. Our
fleet will drive the enemy away.   7. The nation will praise the
admiral and the worthy citizen.   8. There is a war; a multitude of
citizens are demanding the assistance of our ships and fleets.   9. The
admiral selects for his fleets and ships many sailors.   10. Many
ships and large fleets will assist our citizens.   11. Leading men
with many citizens were coming to our fleets and ships.   12. Many
illustrious citizens will be protected by our fleets and ships.

NOUNS IN *-IS* (*I- STEMS* CONTINUED).   FEMININE
GENDER.   ALSO *LIGER* AND *ARAR*.

SUGGESTIONS. — 1. **Liger** and **Arar** have the i-stem in both acc. and abl.
Orbis shows the i-stem rarely in the abl. sing., **finis** oftener.   They are of
the *masculine gender*.

. 2. **Orbis terrae (terrārum)** means *the circle of the land (lands)*, i.e. *the world*.

3. Translate **trānsdūcit,** *he leads across.* It takes *two accusatives.* See 3 and 13.

67.

1. Liger et Arar sunt in Galliā. 2. Erant in Ararī scaphae multae, in Ligerī māgnae nāvēs. 3. Caesar legiōnēs[1] multās Ararim[1] trānsdūcit. 4. Fīnis imperī nostrī est māgnus terrae orbis. 5. Imperium nostrum orbem terrae servat et fīnem nōn habet. 6. Māgnum in orbe (-ī) terrārum est imperium populī Rōmānī. 7. Populus Rōmānus imperium sine fīne (-ī) habēbit. 8. Fīnēs hostium nostrōrum sine fīne (-ī) nōn sunt. 9. Hostēs fīnibus novīs studēbant. 10. Hōstēs mīlitēs multōs ē fīnibus suīs in fīnīs (-ēs) nostrōs dūcēbant. 11. Mīlitēs multī, custōdēs fīnium nostrōrum, hostēs prōvinciā expellēbant. 12. Mīlitēs multī Ligerim trānsdūcuntur. 13. Praefectī Ligerim legiōnem trānsdūcunt. 14. Legiō Ararim trānsdūcitur.

DIRECTION. — Learn A. & G.: [1]**239,** 2 and *b*; Rule 33.
H.: [1]**376.**

Sing. Nom.	A'rar
Gen.	A'ra ris
Dat.	A'ra rī
Acc.	A'ra rim
Voc.	A'rar
Abl.	A'ra rī

Like *A'rar* decline *Li'ger*, gen. *Li'ge ris;* like *ho'stis, or'bis,* and *fī'nis.* These have also the abl. sing. *or'bī* and *fī'nī.*

68.

1. The Saône and the Loire were well known to our sailors. 2. Messengers were sent from Geneva to the Saône and the Loire. 3. Our sailors were summoned from the Saône to Vesontio, from the Loire to Avaricum. 4. There is in the great world much territory. 5. The world has a known limit. 6. The valor of our legions will protect the world. 7. The nations of the world are not without limit. 8. The enemy were desiring our territory. 9. The enemy were led across the territory of our allies. 10. The allies were driving the enemy from our cities and territory. 11. The enemy will lead their allies across the Saône.

NOUNS IN -*E* AND -*AL* (*I-STEMS* CONTINUED).
NEUTER GENDER.

SUGGESTIONS. — 1. The case-endings of all neuter nouns of the third declension are as follows: Nom., acc., and voc. —; gen. -is; dat. -ī; and abl. -e; pl., nom., acc., and voc. -a; gen. -um; dat. and abl. -ibus.

2. In the abl. sing. of neuter i-stems, -ī takes the place of -e, and in the nom., acc., and voc. pl., -i appears before -a.

3. In the nom., acc., and voc. sing., i of the stem becomes e unless it is preceded by al or ar, when it is usually dropped; e.g. nom. vectīgāli becomes vectīgal, but nom. mari- becomes mare. Verify Suggestions 1, 2, and 3 by the declensions below.

4. Translate mare nostrum, *Mediterranean sea.*

5. Translate trānsit, *he goes over,* i.e. *he crosses;* trānseunt, *they cross.*

69.

1. Māgnum est mare[1] nostrum. 2. Pars maris nostrī prōvinciae fīnitima est, pars prōvinciae marī nostrō. 3. Caesar māgnō cum vectīgālī mare[2] nostrum trānsit. 4. Vectīgal ad Ītaliam marī[3] saepe mīttitur. 5. Pars vectīgālis ex prōvinciā, pars ex Galliā mīttēbātur. 6. Nātiōnēs fīnitimae maribus multīs vectīgal māgnum Rōmam mīttunt. 7. Sunt in orbe (-ī) terrārum maria multa et māgna. 8. Clāssēs nostrae sunt marium nostrōrum et vectīgālium custōdēs. 9. Nautae nostrī cum vectīgālibus māgnīs maria īgnōta saepe trānseunt. 10. Nostrī nautae clārī maribus clāssīs (-ēs) hostium expellent. 11. Vectīgālia māgna cōnsulem cōnfirmābunt. 12. Cīvēs vectīgālibus māgnīs nōn erant inimīcī. 13. Lēgātī vectīgālia accepta Rōmam ferēbant.

DIRECTION. — Learn A. & G.: [1]65, *c.* [2]237, *d.* [3]258, *g,* and Note; Rule 48.
H.: [1]111. [2]372. [3]Rule XXV.

Sing.		Plur.		Sing.	Plur.
Nom.	ma're	ma'ria		vec tī'gal	vec tī gā'li a
Gen.	ma'ris	ma'ri um		vec tī gā'lis	vec tī gā'li um
Dat.	ma'rī	ma'ri bus		vec tī gā'lī	vec tī gā'li bus
Acc.	ma're	ma'ri a		vec tī'gal	vec tī gā'li a
Voc.	ma're	ma'ri a		vec tī'gal	vec tī gā'li a
Abl.	ma'rī	ma'ri bus		vec tī gā'lī	vec tī gā'li bus

70.

1. Germany is adjacent to an unknown sea. 2. The Mediterranean sea is adjacent to Italy. 3. A fleet crosses the Mediterranean sea with tribute. 4. The tribute of the world is given to the Roman state. 5. The world sends tribute to the city [of] Rome. 6. The state desires large tribute. 7. A large part of the Mediterranean sea will be protected by our fleet. 8. Parts of the great seas are unknown to our sailors. 9. Fleets often cross the seas with our revenues. 10. The seas are often unfriendly to our fleets. 11. Our fleets will drive the enemy from the seas and protect our revenues. 12. A part of our revenues is sent by sea from Gaul. 13. The nobility desire large revenues.

ADJECTIVES IN *-IS* (*I-STEMS*), THIRD DECLENSION, TWO TERMINATIONS.

SUGGESTIONS. — 1. *Omnis* has but two forms for gender, one for masculine and feminine nouns ; e.g. (see 1) *omnis honor; omnis glōria*; the other for neuters ; e.g. *omne imperium*. These *two* forms become *one* in the gen., dat., and abl. sing. and pl. ; e.g. (see 2) *omnis honōris, omnis glōriae, omnis imperī.*

2. The masculine and feminine form of *omnis* is declined like *hostis*, but with the ending *-I* only, in the dat. and abl. sing. ; the neuter form is declined like *mare*.

71.

1. *Omnis* honor et *omnis* glōria et *omne* imperium populō Rōmānō dabantur. 2. *Omnis* honōris et *omnis* glōriae et *omnis* imperī cīvitās est cupida. 3. *Omnī* honōrī et *omnī* glōriae et *omnī* imperiō studēbat cōnsul. 4. *Omnem* honōrem et *omnem* glōriam et *omne* imperium Rōma habēbat. 5. *Omnī* honōre et *omnī* glōriā et *omnī* imperiō dīgna est Rōma. 6. *Omnēs* lēgātī et *omnēs* cōpiae et *omnia* auxilia in Galliam mīttentur. 7. *Omnium* lēgātōrum et *omnium* cōpiārum et *omnium* auxiliōrum māgnum erit perīculum. 8. *Omnibus* lēgātīs et *omnibus* cōpiīs et *omnibus* auxiliīs sociī sunt amīcī. 9. *Omnīs* (*-ēs*) lēgātōs et *omnīs* (*-ēs*)

cōpiās et *omnia* auxilia hostēs urbe expellent.   10. *Omnibus* lēgātīs et *omnibus* cōpiīs et *omnibus* auxiliīs suīs dīgna est Italia.
11. Hostēs nōbilitātem omnem et omne vulgus armābunt.
12. Omnēs hostēs Ararim trānseunt.   13. Omnis nōbilitās cum
hostibus proelium commīttit.

omnis, *all;* stem omni-

		M. F.	N.	M. F.	N.
Sing.	Nom.	om'nis	om'ne	Plur. om'nēs	om'ni a
	Gen.	om'nis	om'nis	om'ni um	om'ni um
	Dat.	om'nī	om'nī	om'ni bus	om'ni bus
	Acc.	om'nem	om'ne	om'nīs (ēs)	om'ni a
	Voc.	om'nis	om'ne	om'nēs	om'ni a
	Abl.	om'nī	om'nī	om'ni bus	om'ni bus

72.

1. All the multitude of the enemy cross the Rhine.   2. The
slaughter of all the nobility brings great misfortune to every part
of the state.   3. Caesar persuades every enemy.   4. Rome will
send fleets to every known sea.   5. Our fleets are upon every sea.
6. Hostages will be sent to Rome from all nations.   7. A conspiracy of all unfriendly nations brings danger to our allies.
8. Friendly allies will lay waste all the territory of the enemy.
9. All [of] the towns are in the territory of the enemy.   10. Caesar
was giving acceptable assistance to all our allies.   11. Our legions
were protecting all parts of Gaul.

**ADJECTIVES IN -*IS* (*I-STEMS* CONTINUED), TWO TER-
MINATIONS.   ALSO THE NOUNS *GENUS* AND
ITER, NEUTER GENDER.**

SUGGESTIONS. — 1. **Genus** is for **gener**. Since the nom., acc., and voc. sing.
of neuter nouns have no case-ending, the use of **us** instead of **er** represents a
change in the stem-ending. This change occurs in many neuter stems.   **Iter**

does not change its stem-ending, but the letters in in the middle of the stem (*itiner-*) do not appear in the forms having no case-ending.
2. Translate **māgna itinera**, *forced marches.* See 7, 8, 9, and 10.

73.

1. Nōbilitās, genus virōrum fortium, iter facit. 2. Iter erat plērum perīculī. 3. Fortēs generis omnis virī in itinere erant. 4. Dux,[1] omnī hominum generī acceptus, itineris causā dēligēbātur. 5. Dux fidēlis itinerī bonum custōdum genus dēligēbat. 6. Nostrī custōdēs fortēs ab omnī populī Rōmānī genere laudantur. 7. Māgna itinera saepe sunt ūtilia. 8. Nostrī mīlitēs fortēs māgna itinera saepe faciunt. 9. Omnia hominum genera in prōvinciam māgnīs itineribus venient. 10. Perīcula māgnōrum itinerum ducibus fortibus sunt nōta. 11. Bonī generum omnium ducēs itineribus dēligēbantur. 12. Nostrī ducēs fidēlēs omnibus generibus sunt ūtilēs. 13. Laus māgna nostrīs ducibus ūtilibus dabātur.

DIRECTION. — Learn A. & G.: [1]30.
II.: [1]43, 2.

ūtilis, *useful;* stem **ūtili-**		**genus**, *a class,* stem **gener-**	**iter**, *a march;* stem **it(in)er-**
M. F.	N.		
Sing. Nom. ū ti lis	ū'ti le	Sing. ge'nus	Sing. i'ter
Gen. ū'ti lis	ū'ti lis	ge'ne ris	i ti'ne ris
Dat. ū'ti lī	ū'ti lī	ge'ne rī	i ti'ne rī
Acc. ū'ti lem	ū'ti le	ge'nus	i'ter
Voc. ū'ti lis	ū'ti le	ge'nus	i'ter
Abl. ū ti lī	ū'ti lī	ge'ne re	i ti'ne re
Plur. Nom. ū'ti lēs	ū ti'li a	Plur. ge'ne ra	Plur. i ti'ne ra
Gen. ū ti'li um	ū ti'li um	ge'ne rum	i ti'ne rum
Dat. ū ti'li bus	ū ti'li bus	ge ne'ri bus	i ti ne'ri bus
Acc. ū'ti līs (ēs)	ū ti'li a	ge'ne ra	i ti'ne ra
Voc. ū'ti lēs	ū ti'li a	ge'ne ra	i ti'ne ra
Abl. ū ti'li bus	ū ti'li bus	ge ne'ri bus	i ti ne'ri bus

Like *om'nis* decline *for'tis*, also *fi dē'lis*, whose nom. and gen. sing. are as follows : —
M. F. *fi dē'lis*, N. *fi dē'le;* M. F. and N. *fi dē'lis*, etc.

74.

1. Every class of our citizens was desiring war. 2. The Roman people were preparing faithful legions for the march. 3. Our brave legions are making the march into Gaul. 4. Brave leaders are on the march with our faithful legions. 5. The enemy will persuade every class of the Roman people. 6. Our legions will protect every class. 7. All classes of revenues are useful to the state. 8. The state desires all classes of revenues. 9. Large revenues will encourage all classes. 10. The sea is useful to many classes of men. 11. There are many brave sailors upon the sea. 12. The enemy make forced marches and come to the sea.

ADJECTIVES IN -ER (*I-STEMS* CONTINUED), THREE TERMINATIONS.

SUGGESTIONS. — 1. Ācer and celer have three forms for gender in the nom. and voc. sing.; *e.g.* masc. *dominus ācer;* fem. *famēs ācris*; neut. *frigus ācre*: masc. *equus celer;* fem. *nāvis celeris*; neut. *flūmen celere* (see 1 and 6). Otherwise the forms and declensions are similar to those of *omnis*.

2. With nouns below denoting persons translate ācer, *active;* elsewhere, *violent, bitter.*

3. Neuter stems in **or** as well as those in **er** (see Suggestion 1, Ex. 73), often have **us** in the nom. sing.; *e.g.* stem **frigor**, nom. **frigus**. The stem **flūmin** changes i to e in the nom. sing.

75.

1. Dominus ācer, famēs ācris, frigus ācre est.[1] . 2. Servī dominī ācris, famis ācris, frigoris ācris, nōn erant cupidī. 3. Līberī dominō ācrī, famī ācrī, frigorī ācrī inimīcī sunt. 4. Cīvēs dominum ācrem, famem ācrem, frigus ācre nōn postulant. 5. Hostēs dominō ācrī, fame ācrī, frigore ācrī dignī sunt. 6. Erat equus celer, nāvis celeris, flūmen celere in urbe. 7. Puer equī celeris, nāvis celeris, flūminis celeris est amīcus. 8. Faber equō celerī, nāvī celerī, flūminī celerī nōn est inimīcus. 9. Senātor equum celerem, nāvem (-im) celerem, flūmen celere laudābit. 10. Nūn-

tius equō *celerī*, nāve (-ī) *celerī*, flūmine[2] *celerī* Rōmam mīttēbātur. 11. Celeria Galliae flūmina et ācria Rhēnī frīgora nostrōs nōn dēlectābant. 12. Gallī flūminibus celeribus, Germānī
frīgoribus ācribus dēlectābantur. 13. Perīcula celerium Galliae
flūminum et ācrium Germāniae frīgorum Caesarem monent.
14. Gallī flūminibus celeribus Germāniae et frīgoribus ācribus nōn
student.

DIRECTION. — Learn A. & G.: [1]**205**, *d.* [2]**258**, *g*; Rule 48.
II.: [1]**463**, I. [2]Rule XXV.

ācer, *active;* stem **ācrī-**

	M.	F.	N.
Sing. Nom.	ā'cer	ā'cris	ā'cre
Gen.	ā'cris	ā'cris	ā'cris

Continue like *om'nis.*

celer, *swift;* stem **celerī-**

	M.	F.	N.
Sing.	ce'ler	ce'le ris	ce'le re
	ce'le ris	ce'le ris	ce'le ris

Continue like *ū'ti lis.*

flūmen, *a river;* stem **flūmin-**

	Sing.	Plur.
Nom.	flū'men	flū'mi na
Gen.	flū'mi nis	flū'mi num
Dat.	flū'mi nī	flū mi'ni bus
Acc.	flū'men	flū'mi na
Voc.	flū'men	flū'mi na
Abl.	flū'mi ne	flū mi'ni bus

frigus, *cold;* stem **frigor-**

	Sing.	Plur.
Nom.	frī'gus	frī'go ra
	frī'go ris	frī'go rum
	frī'go rī	frī go'ri bus
	frī'gus	frī'go ra
	frī'gus	frī'go ra
	frī'go re	frī go'ri bus

76.

1. A brave scout with a swift messenger was sent to the river
Rhone. 2. A swift ship bore the faithful companions to the province. 3. The active scout has a swift boat. 4. The dangers of
the many swift rivers of Gaul will warn the commander. 5. The
faithful friends with the boat cross many swift rivers. 6. Swift
ships will drive the enemy's fleets from rivers and seas. 7. The
cold of Germany is bitter (active). 8. Many unfortunate men
are not protected from the bitter cold. 9. Our legions are not
desirous of cold and hunger. 10. Our forces [do] not praise the
bitter cold weather of Germany. 11. The bitter cold weather of
Germany [does] not assist our cause. 12. The soldiers are
not encouraged by bitter cold weather.

RECAPITULATION, WITH NEW NOUNS OF THE THIRD DECLENSION.

SUGGESTION. — In-fert means *he brings upon;* fert, *he brings,* governs the *accusative,* and, in composition with in, *upon,* the dative (see 2, 10, 12).

77.

1. Est coniūrātiō nova in Galliā. 2. Calamitās māgna populō[1] Rōmānō coniūrātiōne īnfertur. 3. Māgnitūdō coniūrātiōnis cīvitātem monēbat. 4. Lēgātus cum explōrātōre, comite dīgnō, in Galliam mittēbātur. 5. Explōrātor cum lēgātō ʻGenāvam venit. 6. Lēgātus fidēlis salūtī sociōrum studēbit et obsidēs postulābit. 7. Prīnceps ab Galliae nātiōnibus supplex Genāvam mittitur. 8. Supplex indīguus est perfuga et sēdem in Galliā habet. 9. Perfuga miser lēgātō erit nōtus et ad mortem dūcētur. 10. Hostēs cīvitātī calamitātem māgnam īnferunt. 11. Explōrātōrēs fortēs māgnitūdinem calamitātis dēmōnstrant. 12. Mors explōrātōrum prōvinciae calamitātēs novās īnfert. 13. Supplicēs omnēs multīs cum comitibus Rōmam veniēbant. 14. Supplicēs et comitēs sēdibus novīs in prōvinciā studēbant. 15. Cīvitās et supplicibus et comitibus sēdīs (-ēs) novās dabit. 16. Salūs supplicum et comitum cīvitātem dēlectat.

DIRECTION. — Learn A. & G. : [1] 228 ; Rule 23.
II. : [1] 386.

Decline *ex plō rā'tor,* gen. *ex plō rā tō'ris,* like *ō rā'tor* (Ex. 43) ; *con iūrā'ti ō,* gen. *con iū rā ti ō'nis,* like *nā'ti ō* (Ex. 45) ; *ca la'mi tās,* gen. *ca lami tā'tis,* like *cī'vi tās* (Ex. 47) ; *mā gni tū'dō,* gen. *mā gni tū'di nis,* like *for ti tū'dō* (Ex. 49) ; *co'mes,* gen. *co'mi tis,* like *ob'ses* (Ex. 55); *sa'lūs,* gen. *sa lū'tis,* like *vir'tūs* (Ex. 57) ; *sē'dēs,* gen. *sē'dis,* like *cae'dēs* (Ex. 61) ; *mors,* gen. *mor'tis,* like *urbs* (Ex. 61). *Sup'plex* has gen. *sup'pli cis,* dat. *sup'pli cī,* etc.

78.

1. A great conspiracy brings war upon the province. 2. War is a misfortune of great magnitude. 3. Our faithful companions and allies are driven from Gaul by the misfortunes of war.

4. The state is warned by the magnitude of its misfortunes.
5. The state arms its brave cohorts and brings safety to its
allies. 6. Leading men of Gaul were coming [as] suppliants to
Rome. 7. The suppliants were desirous of safety and were giving
hostages. 8. There was with the suppliants a wounded scout.
9. The unfortunate scout, a companion of the suppliants, was a
robber. 10. The populace will demand the death of the robber.
11. The state is encouraged by the death of the conspiracy and
the safety of our allies.

RECAPITULATION, WITH NEW NOUNS, PROPER NAMES.

SUGGESTION. — Translate in with the name of a people, *e.g.* in **Sêquanôs**,
into the country of the Sequanī.

79.

1. Dumnorix,[1] frāter Divitiacī, Helvētiīs [2] favēbit. 2. Helvētiī
Dumnorigem lēgātum ad Caesarem mīttent. 3. Fīlia Orgetorigis
Dumnorigī in mātrimōnium dabātur. 4. Caesar Divitiacō, fidēlī
Dumnorigis frātrī, erat amīcus. 5. Orgetorix Dumnorigī persuādē-
bit. 6. Potestās [1] Ariovistī māgna erat. 7. Germānī ā Sēquanīs
in Galliam vocābantur. 8. Germānī in Sēquanōs ab Ariovistō
dūcēbantur. 9. Ariovistus, rēx Germānōrum, sēdīs (-ēs) multās
in Belgīs habet. 10. Rhēnus Belgās ā Germānīs dīvidit. 11. Belgae suōs omnēs Rhēnum trānsdūcēbant et Germānīs bellum īnferē-
bant. 12. Agrī Haeduōrum ā Helvētiīs vastābantur. 13. Rhodanus prōvinciam nostram ab Helvētiīs dīvidit. 14. Caesar multās
legiōnēs fortīs (-ēs) in Haeduōs mīttet. 15. Nostrī omnēs
Rhodanum trānsībunt et Genāvam, oppidum Allobrogum, venient. 16. Helvētiī Allobrogibus nōn persuādēbunt.

DIRECTION. — Learn A. & G.: [1] **75**, 1 and 3. [2] **76**, 1 and 3, last sentence.
88, *a*.
II.: [1] **130**, I., 1) and 2). [2] **441**.

Orgetorix; stem Orgetorig.	Allobrogēs; stem Allobrog·	Divitiacus; stem Divitiaco·
Sing. Nom. Or ge′to rix (x = g-s)	Plur. Al lo′bro gēs	Sing. Di vi ti′a cus
Gen. Or ge to′ri gis	Al lo′bro gum	Di vi ti′a cī
Dat. Or ge to′ri gi	Al lo bro′gi bus	Di vi ti′a cō
Acc. Or ge to′ri gem	Al lo′bro gēs	Di vi ti′a cum
Voc. Or ge′to rix	Al lo′bro gēs	Di vi ti′a ce
Abl. Or ge to′ri ge	Al lo bro′gi bus	Di vi ti′a cō

Like *Or ge′to rix* decline *Dum′no rix*, gen. *Dum no′ri gis*. *A ri o vi′stus* has gen. *A ri o vi′stī*, dat. *A ri o vi′stō*, etc. *Bel′gae* is declined like the plural of *nau′ta*. Decline the following adjectives: *Hel vē′ti us* and *Hae′du us* (like *sau′ci us*, Ex. 25); *Ger mā′nus* (like *a mi′cus*, Ex. 29); *Sē′qua nus* (like *cu′pi dus*, Ex. 27). Their masc. plurals are used as nouns. Decline new nouns of the first, second, and third declensions whenever introduced.

80.

1. Dumnorix was a brother of Divitiacus. 2. Dumnorix was unworthy of his brother Divitiacus. 3. The unworthy brother has a wife, the daughter of Orgetorix, from the Helvetii. 4. Orgetorix gives his daughter in marriage to Dumnorix. 5. Ours (our forces) are not assisted by Dumnorix. 6. A multitude of men was summoned by Orgetorix from the fields. 7. Ambassadors were sent to Ariovistus. 8. Faithful messengers will be sent to the state of the Haedui. 9. The Roman people call the Haedui brothers. 10. Caesar was leading all his [forces] across the Rhine into the territory of the Allobroges. 11. Our [forces] were led across the Rhine into the [country of the] Allobroges. 12. The Allobroges will cross the Rhone, the Germans the Rhine. 13. The Germans make war upon the Belgae. 14. The Rhine separates the Germans from the Helvetii.

BELLUM HELVĒTIŌRUM.

SUGGESTION. — Com-mīttit for cum-mīttit means *with-sends, sends together;* i.e. *joins.* Translate proelium committit, *he joins battle.* In fugam dat means *he gives in flight;* i.e. *he puts to flight.*

81.

Orgetorix, prīnceps Helvētiōrum, potestātis cupidus et agrōrum novōrum, coniūrātiōnem nōbilitātis omnis facit. Coniūrātiō cīvitātī accepta est et multitūdō hominum cum uxōribus et līberīs ad Rhodanum venit. Nostrī sociī fidēlēs sunt Rhodanō fīnitimī et perīculum prōvinciae magnum est. Caesar Orgetorigem prō hoste habet et bellum parat. Nostrae legiōnēs fortēs amīcīs et sociīs auxilium dant et hostēs Rhodanum nōn trānseunt. Helvētiī agrīs Rhodanō fīnitimīs expelluntur et ad fīnīs (-ēs) Sēquanōrum veniunt. Sēquanī Helvētiīs nōn sunt īgnōtī. Dumnorix est plēbī Sēquanōrum acceptus. Orgetorix est Dumnorigī amīcus, et fīlia Orgetorigis est Dumnorigis uxor. Dumnorix magnam in cīvitāte suā potestātem habet et Orgetorigī et Helvētiīs favet. Sēquanī et Helvētiī coniūrātiōnem faciunt, suōs in Haeduōs, amīcōs populī Rōmānī, dūcunt, agrōs sociōrum nostrōrum vastant. Caesar multīs cum legiōnibus fortibus Haeduīs auxilium fert et ad Ararim venit. Helvētiī miserī suōs Ararim trānsdūcunt. Caesar proelium cum Helvētiīs committit et hostīs (-ēs) in fugam dat et hominēs multī pereunt. Pars Haeduōrum causae nostrae inimīca est et Caesarem nōn iuvat. Dumnorix est Haeduōrum inimīcōrum prīnceps. Caesar Dumnorigem monet, suōs cōnfirmat, proelium cum Helvētiīs committit, hostīs (-ēs) magnā cum caede expellit. Multitūdō hostium in fugā perit et fīlia Orgetorigis et fīlius in Caesaris potestātem veniunt.

THE WAR WITH ARIOVISTUS.

82.

Ariovistus, king of the Germans, has many friends in the territory of the Sequani. Desirous of power, the active king demands new fields from the Sequani. The states adjacent to the Sequani [do] not favor Ariovistus, and leading men come to Caesar and desire aid. Caesar sends ambassadors to Ariovistus, and demands the liberty and safety of all our allies. The ambassadors [do] not make peace, and Caesar leads his [forces] into the ter ritory of the Germans. There are in Gaul many forests well-known to the enemy. The magnitude of the forests brings danger to our cohorts. Caesar shows his soldiers the danger of flight and the glory of our cause, and encourages the cohorts. Caesar has a faithful legion of brave men. The faithful legion, worthy of its leader, assists Caesar and persuades the unfortunate cohorts. Caesar joins battle with the enemy and puts the soldiers of Ariovistus to flight. The wives of Ariovistus and a daughter perish in the flight. Ariovistus is driven from the territory of the Sequani, and crosses the Rhine. The Rhine separates Gaul from Germany.

ADJECTIVES IN -X, ONE TERMINATION.

83.

1. Erat lēgātus *audāx*, phalanx *audāx*,* praesidium *audāx*, in prōvinciā. 2. Calamitās lēgātī *audācis*, phalangis *audācis*, imperī *audācis* māgna erat. 3. Cīvitās lēgātō *audācī*, phalangī *audācī*, praesidiō *audācī* laudem dabit. 4. Caesar lēgātum *audācem*, phalangem *audācem*, praesidium *audāx* Rōmam mittet. 5. Sociī lēgātō *audācī (-e)*, phalange *audācī (-e)*, praesidiō *audācī (-e)* dignī sunt. 6. Sunt praefectī *audācēs*, cohortēs *audācēs*, auxilia *audācia* in Galliā. 7. Virtūs praefectōrum *audācium*, cohortium *audācium*, auxiliōrum *audācium* erat māgna. 8. Salūs praefectīs *audācibus*, cohortibus *audācibus*, auxiliīs *audācibus* est accepta. 9. Cōnsul praefectōs *audācīs (-ēs)*, cohortīs (-ēs) *audācīs (-ēs)*, auxilia *audācia* vocābat. 10. Fuga praefectīs *audācibus*, cohorti-bus *audācibus*, auxiliīs *audācibus* est indīgna. 11. Ō audāx faci-nus et indīgnum! 12. Vulgus audācī *(-ē)* Sullae facinore dēlectā-tur. 13. Facinora audācia nātiōnem māgnam in perīculum saepe dūcunt. 14. Sulla calamitātem māgnam cīvitātī facinoribus suīs īnferet.

DIRECTION. — Read A. & G. : •85 and Note.
       II. : •156, foot-note 1.

audāx, *daring;* stem, audāc·

	M. F.	N.	M. F.	N.
Sing. Nom.	au'dāx (*x* = *c* s)		Plur. au dā'cēs	au dā'ci a
Gen.	au'dā'cis			au dā'ci um
Dat.	au'dā'cī			au dā'ci bus
Acc.	au dā'cem	au'dāx	au dā'cīs (ēs)	au dā'ci a
Voc.	au'dāx		au dā'cēs	au dā'ci a
Abl.	au dā'cī *or* au'dā ce		au dā'ci bus	

Decline *fa'ci nus*, gen. *fa ci'no ris*, like *fri'gus* (Ex. 75).

84.

1. A daring citizen is elected commander of a new legion.
2. The brave commander is sent into Gaul to our faithful allies.
3. Men friendly to daring crime encourage a conspiracy. 4. The well-known commander perishes by a daring crime. 5. The death of the daring commander was a great misfortune. 6. Enemies of the Roman people are the friends of conspiracy and crime. 7. Faithful citizens [do] not encourage crime. 8. The robbers of Italy are not unfriendly to daring crimes. 9. A multitude of daring crimes warn the citizens. 10. The daring crimes of robbers drive many people from the city. 11. Unworthy men were encouraging daring crimes. 12. Faithful citizens were not encouraged by the daring crimes of unworthy men.

ADJECTIVES AND PARTICIPLES IN -*NS*, ONE TERMINATION.

85.

1. Erat tribūnus *dīligēns*, cohors *dīligēns*, agmen *dīligēns* in urbe. 2. Māgna tribūnī *dīligentis*, cohortis *dīligentis*, agminis *dīligentis* erat virtūs. 3. Cīvitās tribūnō *dīligentī*, cohortī *dīligentī*, agminī *dīligentī* fidēlis erat. 4. Nātiō tribūnum *dīligentem*, cohortem *dīligentem*, agmen *dīligēns* postulābat. 5. Ītalia tribūnō *dīligentī* (-*e*), cohorte *dīligentī* (-*e*), agmine *dīligentī* (-*e*) dīgna est.

6. Tribūnī *diligentēs,* cohortēs *diligentēs,* agmina *diligentia* cīvitātī sunt ūtilēs. 7. Comitēs tribūnōrum *diligentium,* cohortum *diligentium,* agminum *diligentium* virī dīgnī sunt. 8. Plēbs tribūnīs *diligentibus,* cohortibus *diligentibus,* agminibus *diligentibus* laudem māgnam dat. 9. Vulgus tribūnōs *diligentīs (-ēs),* cohortēs *diligentīs (-ēs),* agmina *diligentia* laudat. 10. Lībertās ā tribūnīs *diligentibus,* cohortibus *diligentibus,* agminibus *diligentibus* servābātur. 11. Homō potēns erat Ariovistus, rēx Germānōrum. 12. Calamitās māgna Haeduīs ā rēge potentī (-e) īnferēbātur. 13. Auxilia nostra fortia sunt et potentia. 14. Cōnsul ducēs fidēlīs (-ēs) et potentīs (-ēs) dēliget. 15. Hostēs nostrī suīs cum ducibus multīs et potentibus pereunt.

potēns, *powerful ;* stem, **potent-**

	M. F.	N.		M. F.	N.
Sing. Nom.	po'tēns		Plur.	po ten'tēs	po ten'ti a
Gen.	po ten'tis			po ten'ti um	
Dat.	po ten'tī			po ten'ti bus	
Acc.	po ten'tem	po'tēns		po ten'tīs (ēs)	po ten'ti a
Voc.	po'tēns			po ten'tēs	po ten'ti a
Abl.	po ten'tī *or* po ten'te			po ten'ti bus	

86.

1. The Helvetii with their powerful chief were coming into the territory of the Haedui. 2. Orgetorix, the powerful chief, is diligent in war. 3. Orgetorix will give his daughter in marriage to Dumnorix, a powerful chief of the Sequani. 4. Dumnorix brings assistance to Orgetorix and encourages the diligent chief. 5. Caesar warns Dumnorix and his powerful ally. 6. Our brave legions were protecting the faithful Haedui. 7. Caesar joins battle with the allies, and many brave soldiers of the powerful chief perish. 8. Faithful consuls will demand [as] hostages the children of powerful chiefs. 9. Powerful nations were sending hostages to our diligent consuls. 10. Hostages were sent from the powerful nations adjacent to our allies. 11. The hostages were sent to Rome with faithful guards. 12. The state praises its diligent consuls.

ADJECTIVES WITH OS-STEMS, TWO TERMINATIONS.
COMPARATIVES.

SUGGESTION. — Comparatives change the stem-ending os to or, except in the nom., acc., and voc. neut. sing., where it becomes us.

87.

1. Cōnsul *melior*,ᵃ nōbilitās *melior*, *melius* cīvium genus ā cīvitāte postulātur. 2. Prīncipēs cōnsulis *meliōris*, nōbilitātis *meliōris*, *meliōris* cīvium generis erant cupidī. 3. Urbs cōnsulī *meliōrī*, nōbilitātī *meliōrī*, *meliōrī* cīvium generī nōn erat inimīca. 4. Plēbs cōnsulem *meliōrem*, nōbilitātem *meliōrem*, *melius* cīvium genus postulābit. 5. Rōma cōnsule *meliōre* (-*ī*), nōbilitāte *meliōre* (-*ī*), *meliōre* (-*ī*) cīvium genere est dīgna. 6. Cōnsulēs *meliōrēs*, mūnītiōnēs *meliōrēs*, *meliōra* cīvium genera cīvitātem dēlectābunt. 7. Potestās cōnsulum *meliōrum*, mūnītiōnum *meliōrum*, *meliōrum* cīvium generum cīvitātem servābit. 8. Honor māgnus cōnsulibus *meliōribus*, mūnītiōnibus *meliōribus*, *meliōribus* cīvium generibus dabātur. 9. Ōrātōrēs cōnsulēs *meliōrīs* (-*ēs*), mūnītiōnēs *meliōrīs* (-*ēs*), *meliōra* cīvium genera postulābant. 10. Lībertās ā cōnsulibus *meliōribus*, mūnītiōnibus *meliōribus*, *meliōribus* cīvium generibus servātur. 11. Legiō fidēlis ducis meliōris est cupida. 12. Legiō ducem meliōrem creat. 13. Auxilia habent galeās meliōris, meliōrīs equōs nostrī. 14. Galeae meliōrēs legiónibus melióribus dabantur.

DIRECTION. — Read A. & G.: **86**, *a* and *b*, last sentence.
H.: **154**, Note 1, first sentence.

melior, *better ;* stem melior- for melios-

	M. F.	N.		M. F.	N.
Sing. Nom.	me′li or	me′li us	Plur.	me li ō′rēs	me li ō′ra
Gen.	me li ō′ris			me li ō′rum	
Dat.	me li ō′rī			me li ō′ri bus	
Acc.	me li ō′rem	me′li us		me li ō′rīs (ēs)	me li ō′rā
Voc.	me′li or	me′li us		me li ō′rēs	me li ō′ra
Abl.	me li ō′rī *or* me li ō′re			me li ō′ri bus	

88.

1. The slave of Claudius is a good man, the slave of Brutus is better. 2. Claudius favors the better slave. 3. Brutus will give Claudius the better slave. 4. The consul is desirous of a better decree. 5. A better decree is demanded from the council. 6. The council is worthy of a better decree. 7. Our active sailors were desirous of better boats. 8. Faithful engineers will prepare better boats. 9. Better boats will be given to our active sailors. 10. With the better boats the sailors will cross swift rivers. 11. The army of the allies is good, our auxiliaries [are] better. 12. Caesar calls the army good, the auxiliaries better. 13. Our commanders will favor the better auxiliaries. 14. The auxiliaries are worthy of better commanders.

COMPARATIVE WITH *QUAM*, AND WITH THE ABLATIVE.

SUGGESTIONS. — 1. In the study of comparative sentences the *terms compared* should first be accurately determined. In the sentences below, from 1 to 10, inclusive, both *terms of the comparison* have the same relation to similar words; *e.g.* in 1, **Caesar** is the *subject* of **est** (expressed), and **Sulla** is the *subject* of **est** (understood); in 7, **nōbilitātem** and **plēbem** are *objects* of **habet** (expressed or understood). In such sentences **quam** may be used, with both terms in the same case (nom. or acc.), or **quam** may be omitted and the last term be put in the ablative. See sentences 1, 2, 7, 9.

2. In sentence 11, the *first term of the comparison* is **Caesar** (expressed), the *second*, **Caesar** (understood), while **legiōnum** and **auxiliōrum** are merely words having a common relation to **cupidior** (expressed or understood). In sentence 12, **morte** and **lībertāte** are not *terms of comparison*, but similar constructions, governed by **dīgnior**. In such sentences **quam** must be used.

3. Translate **habet**, *regards ;* **dūcit**, *considers.*

89.

1. Caesar[1] clārior est *quam*[2] *Sulla.*[1]   Caesar est *Sullā*[3] clārior. 2. Supplex dīgnior erat *quam perfuga.* Supplex erat *perfugā* dīgnior. 3. Divitiacus populō Rōmānō amīcior erit quam Ariovistus. 4. Virtūs est potestāte melius. 5. Legiōnēs auxiliīs dīgniōrēs

sunt. 6. Senātōrēs sociīs nostrīs amīciōrēs erant quam ōrātōrēs. 7. Caesar nōbilitātem amīciōrem *quam plēbem* habēbat. Caesar nōbilitātem amīciōrem *plēbe* habēbat. 8. Cōnsul lībertātem meliō-rem quam pācem dūcit. 9. Auxilia tribūnōs clāriōrīs (-ēs) *quam praefectōs* habēbant. Auxilia tribūnōs clāriōrīs (-ēs) *praefectīs* habēbant. 10. Populus Rōmānus Haeduōs dīgniōrīs (-ēs) quam Helvētiōs dūcēbat. 11. Caesar legiōnum fortium erat cupidior quam auxiliōrum. 12. Latrō morte dīgnior erat quam lībertāte.

DIRECTION. — Learn A. & G.: [1]247, *a.* [2]208 and *a.* [3]247; Rule 44.
H.: [1]417, 1. [2]309, 1. [3]417; Rule XXIII.

Like *me'li or* decline *a mī'ci or, clā'ri or, cu pi'di or,* and *dī'gni or.*

90.

1. The daughter is better than the son. 2. The populace was more friendly than the nobility. 3. Our cause was more worthy than yours. 4. The territory of the Haedui is better than the fields of the Germans. 5. Our consuls are more illustrious than your leaders. 6. The Haedui were more friendly than the Germans. 7. The state regards valor [as] better than bravery. 8. The common people consider the senator more illustrious than the orator. 9. The orator regards fleets [as] better than auxiliary forces. 10. The nation considers the prisoners more worthy than the deserters. 11. Our auxiliaries were more useful to the Roman people than our allies. 12. He was more faithful to the consul than to the state.

COMPARATIVES (CONTINUED).

SUGGESTIONS. — 1. Sentences 1–8, inclusive, have two forms. Translate the comparatives in sentences 9–12 by *too* or *rather*, with the positive.

2. In sentences 13 and 14 the *terms of comparison* do not sustain the same relation to the governing words; in 14, for instance, the *first term,* **mīlitibus,** is in the ablative, after **ā,** while *the second,* **auxilia,** is the subject of a proposition. In such sentences *use* **quam** *and a verb with the second term as a subject.*

91.

1. Fīliae dīligentiōrēs fīliīs sunt. 2. Fīliī audāciōrēs sunt quam fīliae. 3. Tribūnī potentiōrēs praefectīs erant. 4. Legiōnēs fortiōrēs auxiliīs erant. 5. Cicerō nōtior Claudiō erat. 6. Caesar vir dīgnior erat quam Sulla. 7. Caesar legiōnēs ūtiliōrīs (-ēs) quam auxilia dūcit. 8. Cīvitās cōnsulem fidēliōrem tribūnō habet. 9. Nostrī audāciōrēs[1] erant. Mīles audācior erat. 10. Flūmen celerius est. Flūmina celeriōra sunt. 11. Dominī potentiōrēs sunt. Dominus potentior est. 12. Puer ācrior erat. Puerī ācriōrēs erant. 13. Populus Rōmānus cupidus est sociōrum fidēliōrum quam sunt Helvētiī. 14. Urbs ā mīlitibus fortiōribus, quam sunt auxilia, servābitur.

DIRECTION. — Learn A. & G. : [1]93, a.
II. : [1]444 and 1.

Like *me'li or* decline *au dā'ci or*, *dī li gen'ti or*, *fi dē'li or*, *for'ti or*, *nō'ti or*, *po ten'ti or*, and *ū ti'li or*.

92.

1. The sailor was more daring than the engineer. 2. The engineer is more diligent than the sailor. 3. The scouts were braver than the messengers. 4. The Haedui are more friendly than the Germans. 5. Peace is more acceptable to the populace than war. 6. Caesar regards the Helvetii more powerful than the Haedui. 7. The consul considers Italy more unfortunate than the province. 8. The nobility will be too powerful. The enemy will be too powerful. 9. The horse will be rather fleet (swift). The horses will be rather fleet. 10. The citizen was rather active. The citizens were rather active. 11. Rome will be full of soldiers more daring than the enemy. 12. The state will give the authority to a man more worthy than the consul.

SUPERLATIVES.

SUGGESTIONS. — 1. Superlatives are declined like **bonus**, and are translated by English superlatives, or by the *positive* with *very*.
2. **Similis** may be followed by the *genitive* or *dative*.

93.

1. Meus amīcus est vir *clārus*,[1] tuus *clārior*, amīcus Sullae *clārissimus*. 2. Servus tuus erat *fidēlis*, meus *fidēlior*, servus Caesaris *fidēlissimus*. 3. *Audāx* erit custōs, nūntius *audācior*, explōrātor *audācissimus*. 4. *Celer*[2] est Rhodanus, *celerior* Liger, Arar omnium *celerrimus*. 5. Claudius suī amīcī *similis*[3] est, frātris *similior*, fīliī *simillimus*. 6. Līberī erant comitum suōrum simillimī.[4] Oppida castrīs simillima sunt. 7. Ōrātor cōnsulem potentissimum virum et dīgnissimum appellat. 8. Praefectus fortis erat vir dīligentissimus. 9. Faber clāssem celerrimam et ūtilissimam parābat. 10. Dominus servīs fidēlissimīs et amīcissimīs laudem māgnam dabat. 11. Cōnsul mīlitēs audācissimōs et fortissimōs postulābat. 12. Cīvitās mīlitum audācissimōrum et fortissimōrum cupida erat. 13. Cīvitās mīlitibus audācissimīs et fortissimīs erat dīgna. 14. Sunt in Helvētiōrum cīvitāte flūmina multa et celerrima. 15. Nostrī mīlitēs ācerrimī flūmina celerrima saepe trānseunt.

DIRECTION. — Learn A. & G. : [1]**89**. [2]**89**, *a*. [3]**89**, *b*. [4]**93**, *b*, first sentence. H. : [1]**162** and Note. [2]**163** and 1. [3]**163** and 2. [4]**444** and 1.

Audācissimus, *most (very) daring ;* stem **audācissimo-**

	M.	F.	N.
Sing. Nom.	au dā cis'si mus	au dā cis'si ma	au dā cis'si mum
Gen.	au dā cis'si mī	au dā cis'si mae	au dā cis'si mī, etc.

Continue like *bo'nus ;* so decline all superlatives. Decline new adjectives in all degrees of comparison whenever introduced.

94.

1. The captive is worthy, the hostage more worthy, the exile most worthy. 2. The orator was powerful, the senator more powerful, the victor most powerful. 3. The wife will be diligent, the sister more diligent, the daughter most diligent. 4. The boy is active, the sailor more active, the engineer most active. 5. The common people are friendly, the council more

friendly, the garrison most friendly. 6. Our allies were brave, the nobility braver, the legion bravest. 7. The legion is worthy of a very illustrious and very faithful leader. 8. Our forces were faithful to their very worthy leader. 9. The Germans are very brave and very daring. 10. The state is desirous of very active and very diligent consuls. 11. Italy has very active and very diligent consuls. 12. The diligent engineer was preparing very useful ships. 13. The consul will give much money to the very brave and very faithful soldiers. 14. The daughter was most like her brother.

IRREGULAR COMPARISON

95.

1. Vir *bonus* est praefectus, tribūnus *melior*, cōnsul *optimus*.
2. Homō *malus* erat supplex, latrō *pēior*, perfuga *pessimus*.
3. Vir *māgnus* erit Claudius, Brūtus *māior*, Caesar *māximus*. 4. Honor servī est *parvus*, cālōnis *minor*, captīvī *minimus*.
5. Tribūnus melior erat quam praefectus, cōnsul quam tribūnus. 6. Cīvitās Caesarem meliōrem Brūtō dūcit. 7. Fīlia senātōris[1] est fēmınārum[2] optima. 8. Ōrātor honōre māximō dīgnus erat. 9. Minima erat cōpiārum nostrārum calamitās, hostium māxima. 10. Belgae sunt nātiōnibus māximīs fīnitimī. 11. Senātōrēs populī Rōmānī honōribus māximis sunt dīgnī. 12. Germānī agrōrum optimōrum cupidī sunt. 13. Sulla ad auxilium suum hominēs pessimōs vocābit. 14. Hostēs castra minima habēbunt.

DIRECTION. — Learn A. & G.: [1]**214**, *a*, 1. [2]**216**, and *a*, 2; Rule 16.
H.. [1]**396**, 1. [2]**397** and 3; Rule XVI.

96.

1. The wife of the senator is a good woman, [his] sister better, [his] daughter best. 2. The power of the commander was great, [that] of the tribune greater, of the consul greatest. 3. The province is small, the state of the Helvetii less, [that] of the Allobroges the least. 4. Our phalanxes were good, our cohorts better,

our legions best.   5. The dangers of our cohorts will be small, [those] of our phalanxes less, of our legions least.   6. Our allies were very good soldiers.   7. The consul regards our allies very good soldiers.   8. Our brave soldiers are worthy of the greatest praise.   9. The territory of Gaul is adjacent to very large seas. 10. Sulla will give a very small part of Italy to worthy men. 11. Italy is desirous of the greatest glory.

IRREGULAR AND DEFECTIVE COMPARISON.

SUGGESTIONS. — 1. Translate plūs honōris, *more (of) honor* (see 1). Proximus is followed by the *dative* or *accusative* in Caesar (see 3, 11, 12). Quam before *superlatives* makes them more emphatic (see 9 and 10) ; translate quam plūrimās, *as many as possible;* quam optimās, *the best possible.*
2. Such genitives as plūris, minōris, māgnī and parvī (4 and 5), are called *genitives of indefinite value.* In translating them, supply some such word as *value* or *worth.*

97.

1. Honor *multus* conciliō, *plūs*[1] honōris[2] senātōribus, honor *plūrimus* cōnsulibus dabātur.   2. Cōnsul *prior* dux bonus nōn erat; omnium ducum *prīmus* est Caesar.   3. Caesar est quam lēgātus suus *propior* castra[3] et *proximus* oppidum,[3] Genāvam. 4. Servus plūris[4] erat quam scapha, scapha minōris quam equus. 5. Servus māgnī est, scapha parvī.   6. Cōnsul auxilia plūra postulābat.   7. Populus Rōmānus cōnsulēs priōris (-ēs), virōs clārissimōs dūcēbat.   8. Honōrēs māximī cōnsulibus priōribus ā populō Rōmānō dabantur.   9. Cōnsulēs nāvīs (-ēs) quam plūrimās[5] parābant et nautās quam optimōs dēligēbant.   10. Praefectus castra quam māxima faciēbat.   11. Hostēs sunt in agrīs proximīs prōvinciae.   12. Belgae proximī Germānīs sunt.   13. Tribūnī suōs ad proxima oppida dūcent.

DIRECTION. — Learn A. & G.: [1]86, *b*, first sentence. [2]216, *a*, 2 and 3.
    [3]234, *e.* [4]252 and *a.* [5]93 *b*, second
    sentence.
H.: [1]165, Note 1. [2]397 and 3. [3]433, I.,
    Note 2. [4]405. [5]170, 2 (2).

Plūs, *more;* stem plūr- for plūs.

	M. F.	N.	M. F.	N.
Sing. Nom.	——	plūs	Plur. plū'rēs	plū'ra
Gen.	——	plū'ris	plū'ri um	
Dat.	——	——	plū'ri bus	
Acc.	——	plūs	plū'rīs (ēs)	plū'ra
Voc.	——	plūs	plū'rēs	plū'ra
Abl.	——	plū're	plū'ri bus	

98.

1. Much praise will be given to the cohorts, more (of) praise to the legions, most praise to our faithful commanders. 2. The former leader is a good commander, the new leader the first of soldiers. 3. The province is nearer Italy than the territory of the Allobroges, the Allobroges are nearest the Sequani. 4. Our fleet was of great [value], the fleet of the enemy of little [worth]. 5. Garrisons are of more [worth] than decrees, decrees of less [value] than a faithful populace. 6. The common people give more (of) praise to our soldiers than to our commanders. 7. The state is desirous of more allies and larger revenues. 8. The Roman people will prepare as many auxiliary [forces] as possible. 9. Caesar was arming as many legions as possible and was selecting the best possible leaders. 10. The great leaders are worthy of their former glory. 11. Of Roman soldiers, Caesar was. the first and greatest. 12. The Germans are nearest the Rhine and the Belgae.

IRREGULAR AND DEFECTIVE COMPARISON
(CONTINUED).

SUGGESTIONS. — 1. Forms from the positive īnferus and superus are used mostly as nouns.

2. Translate summus mōns (collis), *top of the mountain (hill);* īnfimus collis (mōns), *foot of the hill (mountain);* the ablatives māgnitūdine, virtūte (see 1, 2, 14), *in respect to, in;* magis idōneus, māximē idōneus, etc., *more suitable, most (very) suitable,* etc.

3. Collis and mōns are of the masculine gender.

99.

1. Mōns est māgnitūdine [1] *superior*. *Summus (suprēmus)* mōns plēnus est mīlitum. 2. Collis est māgnitūdine *inferior*. *Īnfimus (īmus)* [2] collis est in Helvētiōrum fīnibus. 3. Collis īnfimus magis [3] idōneus castrīs erat quam summus mōns. 4. Pars collis est in Sēquanōrum fīnibus, pars montis in Helvētiōrum cīvitāte. 5. Cīvitās Allobrogum collī [4] et montī est proxima. 6. Nostrī ad collem, hostēs ad montem, castra faciēbant. 7. Erant sub īnfimō monte et summō in collī (-e) silvae māximae. 8. Montēs Sēquanōrum sunt māiōrēs et arduiōrēs quam collēs Allobrogum. 9. Fīnēs Helvētiōrum flūminum celerium, montium māximōrum, collium arduōrum plēnae sunt. 10. Sēquanī montibus multīs et collibus sunt fīnitimī. 11. Helvētiī sēdīs (-ēs) ad [a] montīs (-ēs) et collīs (-ēs) arduissimōs habent. 12. Sunt sub arduīs montibus et summīs in collibus hostēs multī. 13. Summus collis nōn est arduissimus et castrīs māximē [3] idōneus est. 14. Cōnsulēs hostīs (-ēs) multitūdine hominum superiōrīs (-ēs), īnferiōrīs (-ēs) virtūte habēbant.

DIRECTION. — Read A. & G.: **258, *c*, 2, Note 1.

              H.: **433, I. ad (2).

    Learn A. & G.: [1]**253**; Rule 53. [2]**193**; Rule 5. [3]**89**, *d*.

                    [4]**234** and *a*; Rule 28.

        H.: [1]**424** and Note 1; Rule XXIX. [2]**440, 2**, Notes 1, 2. [3]**169, 2**; **170**. [4]**391** and I.; Rule XIV.

100.

1. The consul is superior in power. 2. The highest safety of the state summons the consul to Rome. 3. The mountain is not inferior in magnitude. 4. The foot [of] the mountain was more suitable for a camp than the top [of] the hill. 5. The sea is very near the foot [of] the hill and the mountain. 6. Ours (our forces) have the foot [of] the mountain; the enemy, the top [of] the hill. 7. Our camp was protected by a mountain and a very rugged hill. 8. The tops [of] the hills and mountains are not suitable for a camp. 9. Faithful legions are the guards of our mountains and hills. 10. Ours (our forces) come to the mountains and hills of

the Sequani.   11. The enemy are driven from the mountains and
hills into the territory of the Helvetii.   12. The Helvetii will
summon as many auxiliaries as possible.

IRREGULAR AND DEFECTIVE COMPARISON
(CONTINUED).

SUGGESTIONS.— 1. **Senex** and **iuvenis** are adjectives, with the comparatives **senior** and **iūnior**, but they are mostly used as nouns. For their
adjective use, see 1 and 2, below.
2. **Invītus** has no comparative; **laetus** has regular comparison. Translate the forms of these words in the sentences below *as adverbs ;* e.g. **invītus**
unwillingly ; **laetissimus,** *very gladly.*

101.

1. Exsul *iuvenis* est, obses *iūnior*[1] quam exsul.   2. Praefectus
senex erat, tribūnus *senior*[1] quam praefectus.   3. Senex[2] *invītus,*[3]
iuvenis[2] *invītissimus*[3] perfugam iuvābit.   4. Puer iter laetus,[3]
iuvenis laetior,[3] senex laetissimus faciet.   5. Fortitūdō senis
et virtūs iuvenis cīvitātī salūtem ferent.   6. Honor et senī et
iuvenī est acceptissimus.   7. Concilium senem laude dīgniōrem
quam ,iuvenem dūcēbat.   8. Facinus audāx sene et iuvene erat
indīgnum.   9. Senēs laetī, iuvenēs nōn invītī, captīvō auxilium
ferunt.   10. Cīvitās nōn invīta virtūtem iuvenum, fortitūdinem
senum laudābit.   11. Laudēs cīvitātis et senibus et iuvenibus
erunt acceptissimae.   12. Cīvitās ā senibus cōnfirmābātur, ā
iuvenibus servābātur.   13. Cōnsul iuvenēs bellō magis idōneōs
quam senēs dūcit.   14. Iuvenēs nostrī virtūte superiōrēs erunt,
fortitūdine senēs.

DIRECTION. — Learn A. & G.: [1]**91**, c, first sentence. [2]**188** and *a.* [3]**191**.
H.: [1]**168**, 4.   [2]**62**, V. and foot-note 3.   [3]**443**
and Note 1 (1).

Iuvenis, *a young man ;* stem iuveni-

M. (F.)

Sing. Nom.	iu've nis	Plur.	iu've nēs
Gen	iu've nis		iu've num
Dat.	iu've nī		iu ve'ni bus
Acc.	iu've nem		iu've nīs (ēs)
Voc.	iu've nis		iu've nēs
Abl.	iu've ne		iu ve'ni bus

senex, *an old man ;* stem senec- and seni-

M. (F.)

Sing. Nom.	se'nex (*x* = *c-*s)	Plur.	se'nēs
Gen.	se'nis		se'num
Dat.	se'nī		se'ni bus
Acc.	se'nem ·		se'nēs
Voc.	se'nex		se'nēs
Abl.	se'ne		se'ni bus

102.

1. The sister of the senator is young, the senator younger than [his] sister. 2. The slave was old, the master older than the slave. 3. The wife of the orator will come gladly, the daughter more gladly. 4. The consul unwillingly, the state most unwillingly was preparing war. 5. The old [man] was a friend of the youth, the youth a companion of the old [man]. 6. The children were very friendly both to the youth and to the old [man]. 7. All the children will praise the youth and the old [man]. 8. The boys were warned by the youth and by the old [man]. 9. The companions of the young [men] and the friends of the old [men] will assist the nation very gladly. 10. The nation was very faithful both to its old [men] and to its young [men]. 11. The nation was arming its young [men] and protecting its old [men]. 12. Both young and old are not inferior in valor.

COMPARISON OF ADVERBS.

SUGGESTIONS. — 1. Adverbs formed from adjectives of the first and second declensions are mostly compared like cupidē and bene (see 1 and 6) ; those formed from adjectives of the third declension, like **audācter**, **dīligenter**, and **fortiter** (see 3, 4, and 5).

2. **Ordō** is of the masculine gender; **arbor** is feminine.

103.

1. Cohors *cupidē*,[1] phalanx *cupidius*,[2] legiō *cupidissimē*[2] proelium commīttit.   2. Ītalia *saepe*,[3] prōvincia *saepius*, Gallia *saepissimē* auxilium postulābat.   3. Sociī *audācter*,[4] auxilia *audācius*, nostrī *audācissimē* fīnēs hostium vastābant.   4. Haeduī *dīligenter*, Helvētiī *dīligentius*, populus Rōmānus quam *dīligentissimē* bellum. parābat.   5. Belgae *fortiter*, Haeduī *fortius*, nostrī *fortissimē* Germānīs bellum īnferent.   6. Praefectus urbem *bene*, tribūnus *melius*, cōnsul quam *optimē* servābit.   7. Est summō in colle ōrdō mīlitum fortissimōrum.   8. Pars ordinis ducem māximē dēlectat.   9. Caesar ordinī mīlitum fidēlium auxilium acceptissimum dabat.   10. Ducēs ordinum nostrōrum proelium fortissimē commīttunt.   11. Mīlitēs multī et sauciī in ordinibus pereunt.   12. Est summō in colle arbor māxima.   13. Sunt ad arborem explōrātōrēs audācissimī.   14. Māgnitūdō arborum summō in monte minima erat.   15. Summus mōns arboribus māgnīs minimē idōneus est.   16. Erat sub īnfimō monte ad arborēs multās et māgnās ager castrīs idōneus.

DIRECTION. — Learn A. & G.: [1]**148** and *a*.   [2]**92**.   [3]**148**, *f*.   [4]**148** and *b*; **207**; Rule 10.

H.: [1]**304** and II. 2.   [2]**306**.   [3]**306**, 4.   [4]**304**, IV.; **551**; Rule LXI.

104.

1. A well-known commander bravely leads the company.   2. Ours (our forces) make the march very quickly.   3. The companies were very carefully prepared.   4. There was very near the foot of the hill a large tree.   5. Ours (our forces) were near the tree.   6. Guards were protecting the tree as carefully as possible.   7. There was in the top of the tree an active scout.   8. There were very many trees upon the hill.   9. Our companies will be protected from the enemy by the trees.

NOUNS OF THE FOURTH DECLENSION. MASCULINE GENDER.

SUGGESTION. — The case-ending of the nom. and voc. sing. is -us ; gen. -ūs ; dat. -uī (-ū) ; acc. -um ; abl. -ū. The case-ending of the nom., acc., and voc. pl. is -ūs ; gen. -uum ; dat. and abl. -ibus (-ubus).

105.

1. Senāt*us* exercit*um* quam celerrimē parābat. 2. Pars exercit*ūs* impet*um* in hostīs (-ēs) audācter facit. 3. Senāt*us* impetu*ī* (-*ū*) favet. 4. Prīncipēs senāt*ūs* exercitum laudābunt. 5. Exercitus senāt*um* impet*ū* audācissimō dēlectat. 6. Exercit*us* erit senātu*ī* (-*ū*) fidēlissimus. 7. Cīvitās et exercit*ū* et senāt*ū* quam dīligentissimē servābitur. 8. Laus exercitu*ī*(-*ū*) fortī dabātur. 9. Exercit*ūs* impet*ūs* multōs in hostīs (-ēs) ācriter facient. 10. Impet*ūs* multī exercit*ūs* hostium dīvidunt. 11. Hostēs impet*ibus* exercit*uum* nostrōrum in fugam dabantur. 12. Senāt*ūs* multī et clārissimī exercit*ibus* nostrīs laudem dabant. 13. Honor et senāt*ibus* et exercit*ibus* populī Rōmānī dabitur. 14. In senāt*ibus* senātōrēs multī impet*ibus* audācibus favēbunt. 15. Nātiōnēs fīnitimae senāt*ūs* clārissimōs habent.

senātus, *senate;* stem senātu-

M.

Sing.	Nom.	se nā'tus	Plur.	se nā'tūs
	Gen.	se nā'tūs		se nā'tu um
	Dat.	se nā'tu ī (-ū)		se nā'ti bus
	Acc.	se nā'tum		se nā'tūs
	Voc.	se nā'tus		se nā'tūs
	Abl.	se nā'tū		se nā'ti bus

impetus, *attack;* stem impetu-

M.

Sing.	Nom.	im'pe tus	Plur.	im'pe tūs
	Gen.	im'pe tūs		———
	Dat.	im pe'tu ī (im'pe tū)		im pe'ti bus
	Acc.	im'pe tum		im'pe tūs
	Voc.	im'pe tus		im'pe tūs
	Abl.	im'pe tū		im'pe ti bus

Like *im'pe tus* decline *e xer'ci tus.*

106.

1. Both the army and the senate favor an attack. 2. The attack was worthy of the army and the senate. 3. The power of the senate and the bravery of the army were very great. 4. Our leaders will be friendly to the senate and faithful to the army. 5. Leading men were desirous of an attack and were encouraging both the senate and the army. 6. Our senates are worthy of their armies. 7. Our armies by swift attacks encourage our senates. 8. The valor of the armies and the power of the senates are our glory. 9. Leaders suitable for our armies were selected by illustrious senates. 10. Brave attacks will bring safety to our senates. 11. The danger of the state summons our armies to brave attacks. 12. The leaders of our armies are desirous of daring attacks. 13. Great praise will be given to the senates and armies of the Roman people.

NOUNS OF THE FOURTH DECLENSION (CONTINUED).

SUGGESTIONS. — 1. **Domus** is of the feminine gender. **Cornū** is neuter, and its case-signs are nom., dat., acc., voc., and abl. sing. -ū ; gen. -ū (-ūs) ; nom., acc., and voc. pl. -ua ; gen. -uum ; dat. and abl. -ibus.

2. In 9 and 10 translate **domī**, *at home;* **domum**, *home;* **domō**, *from home.*

3. **Genāvae, Avaricī, Vesontiōnī (Vesontiōne),** in 11, are called *locative* forms, and are to be translated *at Geneva, at Avaricum,* etc.

107.

1. *Domus*[a] mea māior *domō* (*domū*) tuā est. 2. Praefectus *domūs* māximae cupidus erat. 3. *Domus* lēgātī *domuī* (*domō*) praefectī est fīnitima. 4. Praefectus *domum* lēgātō dēligit. 5. *Domūs* prōvinciae *domibus* nostrīs simillimae sunt. 6. Urbs *domuum* (*domōrum*) māximārum plēna erat. 7. *Domūs* nostrae lēgātōrum *domōs* (*domūs*) servant. 8. Lēgātī *domibus* suīs multitūdine hostium expellēbantur. 9. Cōnsul *domī*[3] erat, exsul *domō*[1] Rōmam[2] veniēbat. 10. Exsul *domum*[2] Rōmā mittēbātur.

11. Captīvus Genāvae,³ obses Avaricī,³ senātor Vesontiōnī³ (Vesontiōne) erat. 12. Cornū 'dextrum māgnō in perīculō erit. 13. Caesar auxilium ā sinstrō cornū ad cornū dextrum mīttet. 14. Pars cornū (-ūs) dextrī in fugā erat. 15. Auxilium cornū dextrō dabātur. 16. Cornua exercitūs flūmine et colle servābuntur. 17. Ducēs cornuum virī clārissimī erant. 18. Legiōnēs fortēs cornibus auxilium ferēbant. 19. Hostēs cornibus virtūte legiōnum expellentur.

DIRECTION. — Read A. & G.: *68; 69.
　　　　　　　　　H.: *116 and 1; 118.
　　　　　Learn A. & G.: ¹258, a. ²258, b. ³258, c, 2, both sentences; 36, c; 40, a; 62; 70, g; Rule 57.
　　　　　　　　　H.: ¹412, II. 1. ²380, II. 2, 1). ³426, 2; 48, 4; 51, 8; 66, 4; 119, 1; Rule XXX.

domus, *house;* stem domu-

	F.		F.
Sing. Nom.	do'mus	Plur.	do'mūs
Gen.	do'mūs (I)		do'mu um (ō'rum)
Dat.	do'muī (ō)		do'mi bus
Acc.	do'mum		do'mōs (ūs)
Voc.	do'mus		do'mūs
Abl.	do'mō (ū)		do'mi bus

cornu, *wing (of an army);* stem cornu-

	N.		N.
Sing. Nom.	cor'nū	Plur.	cor'nu a
Gen.	cor'nū (ūs)		cor'nu um
Dat.	cor'nū		cor'ni bus
Acc.	cor'nū		cor'nu a
Voc.	cor'nū		cor'nu a
Abl.	cor'nū		cor'ni bus

Hereafter decline all nouns of the fourth declension whenever introduced.

108.

1. The commander's house was smaller than my house. 2. A part of my house was protected by large trees. 3. The Mediterranean Sea is adjacent to my house. 4. Many large trees protect

my house. 5. The houses of the city were not like the houses of the province. 6. There is a multitude of houses in a large city. 7. The common people will regard our houses [as] very large. 8. In our houses are many faithful friends. 9. The wounded soldier will be sent home from Vesontio. 10. The scout was summoned from home and sent to Avaricum. 11. The sailor was at Geneva, the engineer at Vesontio. 12. The messenger was at home, the scout at Avaricum. 13. The left wing of the army is near the sea. 14. The commander was leading his cohort from the right to the left wing. 15. The leader of the left wing was wounded. 16. Assistance was very acceptable to the left wing. 17. The wings eagerly joined battle with the enemy. 18. The safety of the wings will encourage the army. 19. The auxiliaries are near the wings. 20. The army was protected by its wings.

NOUNS OF THE FIFTH DECLENSION. FEMININE GENDER.

SUGGESTIONS.— 1. The case-signs of this declension are sing., nom. -ēs ; gen. -ēī ; dat. -ēī ; acc. -em ; voc. -ēs ; abl. -ē ; plural, nom. -ēs ; gen. -ērum ; dat. -ēbus; acc. -ēs ; voc. -ēs ; abl. -ēbus. In the gen. and dat. sing. of rēs, ī before ē is short by exception.

2. Diēs is sometimes feminine in the singular.• Diem ex diē dūcit (see 4) means *delays from day to day;* rēs novae, *new things,* i.e. *a revolution.*

109.

1. *Diēs*• lībertātis celerrimē veniet. 2. Vulgus *diēī (diē)* māximē cupidum est. 3. Nōbilitās laeta *diēī (diē)* honōrem māgnum dabit. 4. Cōnsul indīgnus lībertātī est inimīcus et *diem ex diē* dūcit. 5. Laetī lībertātis *diēs* vulgus cōnfirmābunt. 6. Omnēs *diērum* laetissimōrum sunt cupidī. 7. Cīvitās multīs lībertātis *diēbus* cupidē studēbit. 8. Bonī *diēs* lībertātis laetōs *diēs* appellābunt. 9. Bonī *diēbus* multīs sunt dīgnī. 10. *Rēs*publica māgnō in perīculō est. 11. Māgnum est *reī*publicae perīculum. 12. Cīvēs ācrēs *reī*publicae auxilium dabunt. 13. Cōpiae nostrae *rem*publicam fortiter servābunt. 14. Hostēs lībertātis *rēpublicā* expellō-

bantur. 15. *Rēs* novae cōpiās Rōmam vocābunt. 16. Virī multī *rērum* novārum sunt cupidī. 17. Nōbilitās *rēbus* novīs studēbat. 18. Prīncipēs cīvitātis rēs novās parābant. 19. Hominēs multī et indīgnī novīs in *rēbus* pereunt.

DIRECTION. — Read A. & G.: *72 ; 73 ; 74, *c* and *d*.
II.: *120 and 1 ; 122, 1 ; 123.

rēs, *thing;* stem rē-		dies, *day;* stem diē-
F.		M. and F.
Sing. Nom. rēs (pu'bli ca)	Plur. rēs (pu'bli cae)	Sing. di'ēs
Gen. re'ī (pu'bli cae)	rē'rum (pu bli cā'rum)	di ē'ī (di'ē)
Dat. re'ī (pu'bli cae)	rē'bus (pu'bli cīs)	di ē'ī (di'ē)
Acc. rem (pu'bli cam)	rēs (pu'bli cās)	di'em
Voc. rēs (pu'bli ca)	rēs (pu'bli cae)	di'ēs
Abl. rē (pu'bli cā)	rē bus (pu'bli cīs)	di'ē

The plural of *di'ēs* has nom. *di'ēs*, gen. *di ē'rum*, etc.
Decline all nouns of the fifth declension whenever introduced.

110.

1. The day is suitable for a journey (march). 2. Caesar will make a day's journey. 3. The journey is suitable for the day. 4. The enemy [do] not make an attack, they delay from day to day. 5. The days of peace were many and joyful. 6. The common people are desirous of joyful days. 7. The orator gives praise to the joyful days. 8. The good will call the days of peace, very joyful days. 9. The good are worthy of many (and) joyful days. 10. The commonwealth will demand faithful citizens. 11. The power of the commonwealth is very great. 12. The populace gives the commonwealth great praise. 13. All praise the commonwealth. 14. The populace is assisted by the commonwealth. 15. A revolution will bring danger to the nobility. 16. The friends of the revolution were summoned to Rome. 17. The leaders of our armies will favor a revolution. 18. The nobility will not demand a revolution. 19. New power will be given to the common people by the revolution.

DEMONSTRATIVE PRONOUNS. *IS, EA, ID,* SINGULAR NUMBER.

SUGGESTIONS. — 1. **Is, ea, id** is a demonstrative, meaning *that, this; e.g.* Caesar tribūnōs in **eam** cīvitātem mīttit, Caesar sends tribunes into *this* state. 2. **Ēius cōnsulis** in 2 means *of this consul;* **eī testī**, in 3, *to this witness;* and so on. 3. Observe that the demonstrative usually precedes its noun. 4. The paradigm of **is** is given under Exercise 113.

111.

1. *Is* tribūnus et '*ea* legiō et *id* praesidium laudābantur. 2. Auctōritās *ēius* cōnsulis, *ēius* lēgātiōnis, *ēius* conciliī erat plēbī acceptior quam Caesarī. 3. *Eī* testī, *eī* fēminae, *eī* conciliō auctōritās dabātur. 4. Exercitus *eum* agrum, *eam* prōvinciam *id* flūmen trānsībat. 5. *Eō* diē, in *eā* urbe, in *eō* conciliō bellum parābātur. 6. Legiōnēs novae in eam partem Galliae mīttēbantur; ea rēs hostibus nōta erat. 7. Ad eum prīncipem Caesar lēgātiōnem mīttit; ēius lēgātiōnis Galba est dux. 8. Ēius reī[1] populus Rōmānus erat testis. 9. Id concilium plūs auctōritātis habēbit in Galliā quam[2] in eā urbe. 10. Testis eī lēgātō et eī lēgātiōnī persuādet. 11. Cōnsul est eō teste[2] melior. 12. Exercitus noster propior eam urbem erat quam Rōmam. 13. Id oppidum propius montī est quam Rōmae. 14. Senātus eō honōre dīgnior erat quam cōnsul. 15. Auctōritās senātūs plēbī acceptior erat quam cōnsulis.

DIRECTION. — Learn A. & G.: [1] 213, 1 and 2 ; 217; Rule 17. [2] 247 and *a* ;
Rule 44.
H.: [1] 396, II. and III. [2] 417 and 1 ; Rule XXIII.

112.

1. The consul will give this embassy new authority. 2. The authority of this leader was more acceptable to our soldiers than (that of) Caesar. 3. That commander will have authority by a decree of the council; of this fact the Roman people will be a witness. 4. Caesar's army crosses that swift river; this fact is

known to the enemy. 5. This river is often crossed by our army. 6. To that ambassador the senate will give more authority than to the consul. 7. Caesar is a better commander than this consul. 8. This embassy is nearer to the city than to our camp. 9. Our authority was greater in Rome than in this city.

IS, EA, ID, PLURAL NUMBER.

SUGGESTIONS. — 1. **Is, ea, id** means in the plural *those, these*.
2. Translate **reliquus**, in 8 and 9, *the rest of;* so, for such expressions as *the rest of the soldiers*, say, in Latin, not **reliquī mīlitum**, but **reliquī mīlitēs**.

113.

1. Ī (eī) mīlitēs, *eae* mūnītiōnēs, *ea* oppida in nostrā potestāte sunt. 2. Auctōritās *eōrum* cōnsulum, *eārum* cīvitātum, *eōrum* conciliōrum erat māior quam populī Rōmānī. 3. Domus *eīs* (*īs*) servīs, *eīs* (*īs*) fīliābus, *eīs* (*īs*) praesidiīs dabātur. 4. Hostēs *eōs* praefectōs, *eās* cōpiās, *ea* praesidia terrent. 5. In *eīs* (*īs*) agrīs et in *eīs* (*īs*) urbibus et in *eīs* (*īs*) oppidīs multī hostēs erant. 6. Ī (eī) mīlitēs veniēbant et ēius reī causā erat perīculum. 7. Is cōnsul in castrīs hominēs fidēlīs (-ēs) habet; ex eīs (īs) hominibus lēgātum dēliget. 8. Eōrum mīlitum fugā *reliquus*[1] exercitus terrētur. 9. Ob eam rem Caesar ad omnia ea oppida *reliqua* lēgātiōnēs mīttēbat. 10. Caesar māior est eō duce. Caesar māior est quam is dux.

DIRECTION. — Learn A. & G.: [1]**193**; Rule 5.
II.: [1]**440**, 2, Notes 1 and 2.

	M.	F.	N.		M.	F.	N.
Sing. Nom.	is	e'a	id	Plur.	Ī (eī)	e'ae	e'a
Gen.	ē'ius	ē'ius	ē'ius		e ō'rum	e ā'rum	e ō'rum
Dat.	e'ī	e'ī	e'ī		e'īs (īs)	e'īs (īs)	e'īs (īs)
Acc.	e'um	e'am	id		e'ōs	e'ās	e'a
Voc.	—	—	—		—	—	—
Abl.	e'ō	e'ā	e'ō		e'īs (īs)	e'īs (īs)	e'īs (īs)

114.

1. The enemy desire those fields, those provinces, those towns.
2. Caesar has many legions; of these he will send the largest to
Rome. 3. These soldiers come from that town to our province
and terrify the citizens. 4. The rest of the soldiers are worthy
of these leaders and these decrees. 5. The towns of the allies
are large; to these the consul will send the rest of the legions.
6. In these towns there were witnesses of these things; on this
account Caesar sends ambassadors. 7. *Practice giving in Latin:*
This man, these sailors, in those states, to (or for) this slave, of
this commander, of those towns, to (or for) these witnesses, into
that city, on account of these things, this fact, of that legion, to
(or for) this embassy, with these auxiliary [forces], this decree,
of these witnesses, in company with this witness.

HĪC, HAEC, HŌC.

SUGGESTIONS. — 1. The demonstrative **hīc, haec, hōc** means *this*, and
refers to a person or thing near at hand.

2. In the plural number, **hīc** has the case-endings of **bonus** with **haec**
(not **ha**) in the nom. and acc. neut.

115.

1. *Hīc* exercitus, *haec* phalanx, *hōc* praesidium in servitūtem
mīttēbātur. 2. Ducēs *hūius* exercitūs, *hūius* phalangis, *hūius*
praesidī Rōmam iter facient. 3. *Huic* exercituī (-ū), *huic* phalangī,
huic praesidiō Caesar persuādēbat. 4. Praefectus *hunc* exercitum, *hanc* nāvem (-im), *hōc* praesidium armābit. 5. *Hōc* honōre,
hāc spē, *hōc* dēcrētō cōnsul mīlitēs ācrīs (-ēs) cōnfirmābit. 6. Nostrī *hōc* flūmen invītī trānsībant. 7. Hīc locus ab hoste passūs [1]
sexcentōs [2] abest. 8. Īnfimus collis ab hāc urbe passūs multōs
aberat. 9. Hōc flūmen multīs locīs [3] trānsitur. 10. Hae silvae
et haec flūmina in nostrā prōvinciā sunt. 11. Haec loca ā summō
monte mīlia [4] passuum [5] VI. [6] (sex) absunt. 12. Nostrī ab hōc
locō mīlia passuum octō aberant. 13. Multitūdō hostium ācrium
omnia haec loca trānseunt. 14. Haec urbs Rōmae simillima est.

DIRECTION. — Learn A. & G. : [1]257 ; Rule 36. [2]94, *d*. [3]258, *f*, 1 and 2. [4]94, *e* and Note. [5]216, *a*, 2. [6]94, *c*. H.: [1]379 ; Rule IX. [2]177. [3]425, II. and 2. [4]178. [5]397 and 2. [6]176.

	M.	F.	N.		M.	F.	N.
Sing. Nom.	hĭc	haec	hŏc	Plur. hī	hae	haec
Gen.	hū'ius	hū'ius	hū'ius		hō'rum	hā'rum	hō'rum
Dat.	huic	huic	huic		hīs	hīs	hīs
Acc.	hunc	hanc	hŏc		hōs	hās	haec
Voc.	——	——	——		——	——	——
Abl.	hōc	hāc	hŏc		hīs	hīs	hīs

116.

1. The leader was giving helmets to this legion, to these auxiliary [forces], to this commander. 2. These citizens, these councils, these states have the greatest honors. 3. To this state, to this citizen, to this council the consul will give very great honors. 4. This place is in the hands of Romans. 5. Our soldiers very often cross these swift rivers. 6. These places are six miles distant from Rome. 7. There are many very swift rivers in this province. 8. The attack of these auxiliary [forces], of this cohort, of this leader, is more acceptable to our brave soldiers than to the enemy. 9. This legion is six hundred paces from the city. 10. These rivers are in many places known to the enemy. 11. For this reason the slave is more useful than this soldier. 12. This hope, to these places, of this cohort, of these states, in these places, to (or for) these leaders, in these cities, to (or for) this army, by means of this authority, to (or for) this witness, into this swift river, by this decree, in this place, this sea, of these decrees, into these provinces.

ILLE, ILLA, ILLUD.

SUGGESTIONS. — 1. Ille, illa, illud is a demonstrative, meaning *that*, *yonder*. It differs in declension from bonus only in the forms given in sentences 1–5.

2. **Hīc**, *this*, refers to something near at hand; **ille**, *that*, to something more remote; e.g. *Hīc* locus est in prōvinciā nostrā, *ille* in vestrā, *This* place is in our province, *that* in yours.

117.

1. *Ille* honor, *illa* glōria, *illud* imperium est Caesaris.[1] 2. Salūs *illīus* custōdis, *illīus* fēminae, *illīus* praesidī est in manibus meīs. 3. *Illī* mīlitī, *illī* cohortī, *illī* praesidiō honor dabātur. 4. *Hōc* lītus rēgem dēlectat, *illud* nōn. 5. Omnēs hominēs *illud* foedus prō facinore habēbunt. 6. Ob eam rem ducēs illīus exercitūs quam hūius fidēliōrēs erant. 7. Impetus *hūius* phalangis rēgī ūtilior erat quam *illīus*. 8. *Hīc* locus ā summō monte mīlia passuum VII. (septem) aberat, *ille* X. (decem). 9. Cōnsulēs potentēs huic iuvenī equum, galeam illī dant. 10. Latrō illā spē testīs (-ēs) reliquōs cōnfirmābit. 11. Hōc foedus ūtilius erit quam illud. 12. Hī ducēs illīs pēiōrēs sunt. 13. Cōnsul illī legiōnī meliōrem ducem quam huic dabit.

DIRECTION. — Learn A. & G.: [1]**214**, *c.*
H.: [1]**401**; Rule XVIII.

	M.	F.	N.		M.	F.	N.
Sing. Nom.	il'le	il'la	il'lud	Plur.	il'lī	il'lae	il'la
Gen.	il lī'us	il lī'us	il lī'us		il lō'rum	il lā'rum	il lō'rum
Dat.	il'lī	il'lī	il'lī		il'līs	il'līs	il'līs
Acc.	il'lum	il'lam	il'lud		il'lōs	il'lās	il'la
Voc.	——	——	——		——	——	——
Abl.	il'lō	il'lā	il'lō		il'līs	il'līs	il'līs

118.

1. With that treaty the commander will encourage the faithful soldiers. 2. On this account the senators were more friendly to this commander than to that. 3. This treaty was more useful to our soldiers than that. 4. This army will have more commanders than that. 5. The guards of yonder city were braver than [the guards] of this. 6. There are more swift ships on that shore than on this. 7. This shore is nearer to Italy than to Germany. 8. Our soldiers will be faithful to this very worthy leader. 9. On this account, the consul considers these soldiers braver than those.

10. Of this place, of those places, to (or for) that witness, by means of this authority, on these shores, those treaties, to (or for) the rest of the soldiers, of these embassies, of this very useful council, to that city, to those places, by means of that treaty, on this account.

IS, HĪC, AND *ILLE* AS SUBSTANTIVE PRONOUNS.

SUGGESTIONS. — 1. Is, hĭc, and ille are used not only as adjective pronouns modifying nouns, but also alone as substantive pronouns ; e.g. *Huic* persuādet Caesar, Caesar persuades *him* (this one).
2. Translate **terrā marīque,** in 7, *by land and sea.*

119.

1. Eī lēgātiōnī Ariovistus respondet; iterum ad *eum* Caesar lēgātōs mīttit. 2. Est flūmen *id*que[1] multīs locīs vadō[2] trānsībātur. 3. Multī flūmen vadō trānsībant; in *hīs* Ariovistus erat. 4. Caesar mīlitēs acrīs (-ēs) in urbe habet; ex *eīs (īs)* Galbam ad hostīs (-ēs) mīttet. 5. *Eōrum* fēminae līberīque in servitūtem dūcēbantur; ēius reī populus Rōmānus erat testis. 6. Ab castrīs oppidum hostium abest mīlia passuum novem; id summā vī[3] nostrī oppūgnant. 7. Ī (eī) urbīs (-ēs) nostrās terrā marīque ācriter oppūgnant. 8. Hunc Caesar prohibet ab eīs (īs) locīs. 9. Huic Ariovistus iterum iterumque respondēbat. 10. Multī illud flūmen trānsībant; illōs Caesar Rōmam mīttēbat. 11. Germānī erant fīnitimī; apud eōs erat rēx Ariovistus. 12. Apud Helvētiōs nōbilissimus erat Orgetorix; is coniūrātiōnem nōbilitātis faciēbat. 13. Cōnsul ob eam rem cālōnēs et custōdēs vocābat; hōs laudābat, monēbat illōs. 14. Ēius bellī fēmina est causa ; ea tribūnōs mīlitum in eās cīvitātēs mīttit.

DIRECTION. — Learn A. & G.: [1]156, *a.* [2]258, *g.* [3]248; Rule 46.
H.: [1]554, I., 2 and 3. [2]Rule XXV. [3]419, III. ;
Rule XXIV., III.

120.

1. Caesar storms all those towns by land and sea, and keeps the force of the enemy from his own camp. 2. The Germans

84   A STRAIGHT ROAD TO CAESAR.

were adjacent; of them the noblest were sent to Caesar.
3. These states again were sending their chiefs as ambassadors
to Rome; this was known to our soldiers.   4. The king's daughter is in Geneva; she will send a slave to Rome.   5. There is a
bridge upon that river; to it the Germans send a large army.
6. This chief again and again responds to that commander and
his soldiers.   7. Ariovistus keeps the force of the enemy from
his camp all these days.   8. Among them are deserters and
guards; these he will praise, those he will warn.   9. Caesar will
choose for his camp a more suitable place than the top of a mountain.   10. Caesar sends to the city more captives than Sulla.

IPSE, ISTE, ĪDEM.

SUGGESTION. — **Iste**, *that, that of yours,* is declined like **ille**. **Ipse,** *self,*
is similarly declined, but has the form **ipsum,** nom. and acc. sing. neut.
Īdem, *the same,* is the demonstrative **is** plus the affix **-dem** ; it has **īdem**
for *isdem,* **idem** for *iddem,* and changes **m** to **n** before **d**, as in **eundem** for
eumdem.

121.

1. *Ipse*[1] in Ītaliam māgnīs itineribus contendit.   2. Salūs tuae
cohortis *ipsīus*[2] in manibus tuīs erat.   3. Multī plūs potestātis
habēbant quam magistrātūs *ipsī*.   4. Iterum oppidum *ipsum*
nostrī oppūgnābant terrā marīque.   5. *Ipse* erat Dumnorix,
summā audāciā,[3] māgnā apud plēbem grātiā, cupidus rērum novārum.   6. Mercēs *istīus*[4] facinoris mors erit.   7. Fēmina *istī* cālōnī
miserō nōn respondēbit.   8. *Ista* mercēs exsulēs nōn cōnfirmat.
9. Magistrātūs *ipsī*, summā audāciā, māgnā grātiā, ad urbem con-
tendunt.   10. *Iste* locus testibus miserīs datur, mercēs māgnī
facinoris.   11. Exercitūs nostrī urbem *ipsam* ācerrimē oppūgnā-
bunt.   *Idem* facient sociī.   12. Caesar Rōmam contendēbat.
Īdem[5] senātōrēs vocat.   13. Caesar et Ariovistus ad *eundem*
locum contendent.   14. Magistrātūs omnēs *eārundem* mercēdum
cupidī erant.

DIRECTION. — Learn A. & G.: [1]195, *g.* [2]195, *f.* [3]251; Rule 61. [4]102, *c*, last sentence. [5]195, *e.*
H.: [1]452. [2]438 and 1. [3]419, II.; Rule XXIV., II. [4]450, 1, Note. [5]451, 3.

	M.	F.	N.	M.	F.	N.
Sing. Nom.	i'pse	i'psa	i'psum	Plur. i'psī	i'psae	i'psa
Gen.	i psī'us	i psī'us	i psī'us	i psō'rum	i psā'rum	i psō'rum
Dat.	i'psī	i'psī	i'psī	i'psīs	i'psīs	i'psīs
Acc.	i'psum	i'psam	i'psum	i'psōs	i'psās	i'psa
Voc.	i'pse	i'psa	i'psum	i'psī	i'psae	i'psa
Abl.	i'psō	i'psā	i'psō	i'psīs	i'psīs	i'psīs

	M.	F.	N.
Sing. Nom.	ī'dem	e'a dem	i'dem
Gen.		(M. F. N.) ē ius'dem	
Dat.		(M. F. N.) e ī'dem	
Acc.	e un'dem	e an'dem	i'dem
Voc.	———	———	———
Abl.	e ō'dem	e ā'dem	e ō'dem

	M.	F.	N.
Plur. Nom.	ī'dem (eī-)	e ae'dem	e'a dem
Gen.	e ō run'dem	e ā run'dem	e ō run'dem
Dat.		(M. F. N.) e īs'dem *or* īs'dem	
Acc.	e ōs'dem	e ās'dem	e'a dem
Voc.	———	———	———
Abl.		(M. F. N.) e īs'dem *or* īs'dem	

Like *il'le*, decline M. *is'te*, F. *is'ta*, N. *is'tud.*

122.

1. The honor of the witness himself was in our hands. 2. The victor [does] not respond to that slave of yours. 3. The citizen was braver than the magistrate himself; for this reason he was [a man] of great influence among the populace. 4. These citizens [do] not praise that witness of yours; this is known to the magistrate himself. 5. The same leader, [a man] of great boldness and of the highest popularity among them, was hastening to Italy itself. 6. The decree itself will have great authority among those citizens of yours. 7. The orator by the same oration was

86   A STRAIGHT ROAD TO CAESAR.

persuading the senate itself. 8. The rest of the soldiers actively
storm the town and keep the force of the enemy from the city
itself. 9. Caesar hastens into Gaul; he (the same) summons the
council. 10. All the magistrates were desirous of the same
good things.

ALIUS, NŪLLUS, ŪNUS, ALTER.

SUGGESTION. — **Alius, nūllus, ūnus,** and **alter** have the gen. sing. in **-īus**
(**alter,** in **-ius**) and the dat. sing. in **-ī,** like **ille. Alius** is also like **ille** in the
nom. and acc. neut. sing.; *e.g.* in 5.

123.

1. Exercitūs duo[1] in nostrīs fīnibus erant; mīlitēs *ūnīus*[2] audācēs erant, *alterius*[3] nōn.   2. *Nūllīus* laus populō Rōmānō acceptior
erit quam cōnsulis.   3. Galliae factiōnēs erant duae; hārum
alterius prīncipātum habēbant Haeduī, *alterius* Arvernī.   4. *Alterius* factiōnis prīncipēs sunt Haeduī, *alterius* Sēquanī.   5. *Aliud*
iter Helvētiī habent *nūllum*.   6. Erant itinera dua: *ūnum* per
Sēquanōs, *alterum* per prōvinciam nostram.   7. Cōnsul *ūnī* equum
dabit, *aliī* domum, *aliī* servum; īdem summā apud plēbem grātiā[4]
est.   8. Audācia *ūnīus* magistrātūs laudābātur, auctōritās alterius.
9. Aliī vim hostium ab hīs locīs, aliī ab illīs prohibent.   10. Plūs
honōris illī magistrātuī dabātur quam cōnsulī ipsī.   11. Tribūnus
melior erat quam praefectus.   12. Fīlia ēius senātōris erat fēminārum optima.   13. Cīvitās istōs perfugās hominēs pessimōs
habēbat.

DIRECTION. — Learn A. & G.: [1]94, *b*. [2]83 (commit list). [3]203. [4]Rule 51.
      H.: [1]175. [2]151 and 1 (commit list). [3]459.
            [4]Rule XXIV. II.

	M.	F.	N.
Sing. Nom.	ū'nus	ū'na	ū'num
Gen.		(M. F. N.) ū nī'us	
Dat.		(M. F. N.) ū'nī	
Acc.	ū'num	ū'nam	ū'num
Voc.	——	——	
Abl.	ū'nō	ū'nā	ū'nō

Complete the declension like that of *bo'nus*, Lesson 23.

	M.	F.	N.
Plur. Nom.	du'o	du'ae	du'o
Gen.	du ō'rum	du ā'rum	du ō'rum
Dat.	du ō'bus	du ā'bus	du ō'bus
Acc.	du'ōs (duo)	du'ās	du'o
Voc.	———	———	———
Abl.	du ō'bus	du ā'bus	du ō'bus

Du'o has no singular.

	a'li us, *other.*				al'ter, *the other.*		
	M.	F.	N.		M.	F.	N.
Sing. Nom.	a'li us	a'li ā	a'li ud	Sing.	al'ter	al'te ra	al'te rum
Gen.	(M. F. N.) a li'us				(M. F. N.) al te'ri us		
Dat.	(M. F. N.) a'li ī				(M. F. N.) al'te rī		
Acc.	a'li um	a'li am	a'li ud		al'te rum	al'te ram	al'te rum
Voc.	———	———	———		———	———	———
Abl.	a'li ō	a'li ā	a'li ō		al'te rō	al'te rā	al'te rō

Complete the declension like that of
    sau'ci us, Exercise 25.

Complete the declension like that of
    cu'pi dus, Exercise 27.

124.

1. There were two parties; the leader of one was known to the magistrates, [the leader] of the other [was] not. 2. To no citizen was more authority given than to Dumnorix. 3. There were two exiles in the camp; one was more friendly than the other. 4. The popularity of no friend is dearer to the consul than the liberty of the state itself. 5. To one of these daring men the leader gives a horse, to another a helmet, to another a slave. 6. Some will quickly storm this town, others that. 7. The approach of this one daring youth terrifies the magistrates. 8. Again this consul, a man of great boldness, was hastening to the city. 9. The leaders of one faction were soldiers, of the other, citizens. 10. The same man, of the same magistrates, to this one place, of the same rewards, of the state itself, to (or for) the rest of the citizens, of the other consul, to another city, in company with the king himself, of the magistrate alone.

THE REFLEXIVE SUĪ.

SUGGESTIONS. — 1. Reflexives refer to the subject of the sentence. Suī, *of himself* (*herself, itself*), is the reflexive of the third person ; *e.g.* Caesar equitātum omnem ante sē mīttit, Caesar sends all the cavalry before *him* (*self*).
2. Distinguish carefully **suī**, referring to the subject of the sentence, and is, **hīc, ille**, referring to some other person or thing. See 9 and 12. Distinguish **suī** from the genitive of the adjective **suus**.
3. The character ‿ signifies that the vowel over which it is placed — *e.g.* **sibī** in 2 — is *common* in quantity. See page 14, 3 (under quantity).

125.

1. Caesar māgnō suī[1] (gen. sing.) cum perīculō Rōmam contendet. 2. Vir bonus multa faciet nōn sibī (dat. sing.) sed aliīs. 3. Caesar sē nōn laudat, sed alterum. 4. Cicerō ā sē et ab aliīs laudābātur. 5. Nātiōnēs māgnō suī cum perīculō bellum gerunt. 6. Omnēs hominēs sibī ūtilēs sunt. 7. Hī omnēs sē victōrēs appellant. 8. Germānī et ā sē et ā populō Rōmānō fortēs appellantur. 9. Caesar ipse quam māximīs[2] itineribus ad eōs contendit equitātumque omnem ante sē mīttit. 10. Orgetorix Dumnorigī persuādet eīque fīliam suam in mātrimōnium dat. 11. Helvētiī in Haeduōrum fīnēs veniunt eōrumque agrōs vastant. 12. Haeduī sē suaque ab eīs (īs) nōn dēfendunt. 13. Caesar cum Germānīs audācter bellum gerit. 14. Omnis mīles comitēs trēs[3] sēcum[4] habēbit.

DIRECTION. — Learn A. & G.: [1]196 ; 217 ; Rule 7. [2]93, *b*, last sentence.
[3]94, *c.* [4]99, *e.*
H.: [1]396, III. ; 448 ; 449 ; Rule XXXV.
[2]170, 2, (2). [3]175. [4]184, 0.

su'ī (nom. and voc. wanting).

Gen. (both numbers), **su'ī**, of himself, of herself, of itself, of themselves.
Dat. " " **si'bī**, to " to " to " to "
Acc. " " **sē (sē'sē)**, " " " "
Abl. " " **sē (sē'sē)**, by " by " by " by "

For the Reflexive Possessive Pronoun *su'us*, see Lesson 31.

trēs, *three.*

Nom. M. F. **trēs**, N. **tri'a** ; Gen. M. F. N. **tri'um** ; Dat. and Abl. M. F. N. **tri'bus** ; Acc. M. F. **trēs (trīs)**, N. **tri'a.**

126.

1. Caesar makes himself commander of the soldiers and carries on war with the Gauls. 2. Good men do not praise themselves. 3. The master, with great danger to himself, boldly defends his slaves and their children; for this reason he has great popularity among them. 4. Sulla will hasten by the longest marches possible to his own city and send all the slaves before him. 5. Every soldier was arming himself. 6. The populace gave themselves and their property to the consuls. 7. The guard himself, a man of great boldness, makes himself a helmet. 8. Every soldier will have a helmet with him. 9. Our men hasten to the territory of the Helvetii, and carry on war with them. 10. The Haedui boldly defend themselves and their property from the Helvetii. 11. The people will give the consul his property and defend their own.

THE RELATIVE, QUĪ, QUAE, QUOD, WHO, WHICH.

SUGGESTION. — The paradigm of **Quī** is given under Exercise 129.

127.

1. Magistrātus, *quī*[1] erat in castrīs nostrīs, est vir māgnae virtūtis; fēmina, *quae*[2] erat causa hūius bellī, nōn laudātur; oppidum, *quod* est propius lacum, Genāva appellātur. 2. Magistrātus, *cūius* auctōritās est māgna; urbs, *cūius* cīvēs sunt ūtilēs; praesidium, *cūius* dux est fortis, in hōc dēcrētō laudābātur. 3. Magistrātus *cuī*, factiō *cuī*, praesidium *cuī* haec auctōritās nunc datur, māgnō in perīculō est. 4. Is *quem*, ea *quam*, id *quod* omnēs cīvēs bonī nunc laudant, ā cōnsule laudātur. 5. Is ā *quō*, legiō ā *quā*, concilium ā *quō* cīvitās nunc servātur, māgnō in honōre est. 6. In eō itinere persuādet Casticō, *cūius* pater ā senātū populī Rōmānī amīcus appellātur. 7. Eā legiōne quam sēcum habet, mūrum in altitūdinem pedum[3] sēdecim perdūcit. 8. Lacus in quem flūmen īnfluit, in fīnitimā prōvinciā est. 9. Flūmen est

Arar, quod per fīnēs Haeduōrum in Rhodanum īnfluit. 10. Caesar, ā lacū quī in flūmen Rhodanum īnfluit ad montem quī fīnēs
Sēquanōrum ab Helvētiīs dīvidit, mūrum perdūcit. 11. Ariovistus lēgātōs ad eum mīttit; in quā lēgātiōne est prōcōnsul.
12. Caesar castra movēbit ad eum locum in quō locō⁴ Germānī
sunt. 13. Potestās cuī cōnsul bonus studet in manibus populī
Rōmānī est. 14. Locus in quō Caesar bellum gerit ā castrīs nostrīs mīlia passuum V (quinque) abest.

> DIRECTION.—Learn A. & G.: ¹197, 5 (coarse print). ²198; Rule 3,
> ³215, b; 257, a. ⁴200 and a.
> H.: ¹187. ²445, Note and 1. ³396, V.;
> 419, III. 2. 1). ⁴445, 8.

128.

1. The lake which flows into the river Rhone is called Lemannus. 2. The slave to whom Brutus was giving freedom is a man
of great boldness. 3. The treaty which the ambassadors are
making is praised by many citizens. 4. The wall which Caesar
is constructing is sixteen feet in height; it is six miles distant
from the lake. 5. The sea whose shores are in Italy is called
"the great sea." 6. This woman, who praises herself, is not
praised by others. 7. The legion with which Caesar is constructing the wall is equipped with large helmets. 8. That place in
which our soldiers were, was protected by a wall sixteen feet in
height. 9. The wall which divides their province from ours is
six feet in height.

QUĪ, QUAE, QUOD, PLURAL NUMBER.

129.

1. Praefectī *quī*, legiōnēs *quae*, auxilia *quae* in hōc locō bellum
gerēbant, ā nōbilibus laudābantur. 2. Cīvēs *quōrum* agrī ā Germānīs vastābuntur, audācissimē bellum gerent; nātiōnēs *quārum*
oppida oppūgnābuntur pācem facient; auxilia *quōrum* equī hōc
flūmen trānsībunt, in metū māgnō erunt. 3. Senātōrēs *quibus*,

fēminae *quibus*, concilia *quibus* hōc dēcrētum dēmōnstrābātur, ad urbem contendēbant. 4. Agrī *quōs*, prōvinciae *quās*, flūmina *quae* nostrī trānseunt, Caesaris sunt. 5. Agrī in *quibus*, urbēs in *quibus*, oppida in *quibus* mīlitēs castra facient, in nostrā prōvinciā sunt. 6. Allobrogēs, quī trāns Rhodanum possessiōnēs habent, ad Caesarem veniunt. 7. Partem unam incolunt Belgae, aliam Aquitānī, tertiam (eī, ī) quī ipsōrum linguā Celtae, nostrā Gallī appellantur. 8. Hostēs prohibentur possessiōnibus quās sociī habent. 9. Flūmina quae nostrī trānsībant in fīnibus Galliae sunt. 10. Fēminae quīque ad bellum inūtilēs sunt, in ūnō locō conlocantur. 11. Haeduī Boiōs suīs in fīnibus conlocant; quibus illī agrōs dant. 12. Hostēs ad eum locum veniunt; quōrum pars castra movet, pars in nostrōs impetum facit. 13. Lingua Rōmā-nōrum ūtilis est. 14. Inter fīnēs Helvētiōrum et Allobrogum, quī sunt sociī nostrī, Rhodanus fluit, isque multīs locīs vadō trānsitur. 15. Flūmen est Rhodanus quod inter fīnēs Helvētiōrum et Allo-brogum fluit.

quī, who.

		M.	F.	N.		M.	F.	N.
Sing.	Nom.	quī	quae	quod	Plur.	quī	quae	quae
	Gen.	cū'ius	cū'ius	cū'ius		quō'rum	quā'rum	quō'rum
	Dat.	cuī	cuī	cuī		qui'bus	qui'bus	qui'bus
	Acc.	quem	quam	quod		quōs	quās	quae
	Voc.	———	———	———		———	———	———
	Abl.	quō	quā	quō		qui'bus	qui'bus	qui'bus

130.

1. The soldiers whose attack was delighting Caesar are [those] of the third legion. 2. The fields which our commanders desire are in the enemy's country and are six miles from our camp. 3. They who inhabit this territory are called Germans in our lan-guage. 4. This is the boundary of the places which our citizens inhabit. 5. Those nations which ·were bravely protecting their possessions in Gaul are our allies. 6. A third part of the cavalry is placed in the territory which is [the territory] of the Aedui. 7. The allies with whom Caesar is coming to Rome are terrified by the attack of the enemy. 8. The councils whose decrees are

in our hands will be praised by our citizens. 9. The people, who in their own language are called Celts, are placed in the province which is called Gaul. 10. The river which flows between the territory of the Helvetii and the Allobroges is called the Rhone.

THE INTERROGATIVES, *QUIS* AND *QUĪ, NE, NŌNNE, NUM.*

SUGGESTION. — **Praeest** is to be translated *is at the head of, is in charge of;* **praeficit** (fut. **praeficiet**), *places at the head of, places in charge of.*

131.

1. *Quis*[1] apud Helvētiōs nōbilissimus erat ? Orgetorix erat apud Helvētiōs nōbilissimus. 2. *Cūius* pater ā senātū populī Rōmānī amīcus appellābātur ? 3. *Cūi* in eō itinere persuādēbat Orgetorix ? Orgetorix persuādēbat Casticō. 4. *Quō* itinere Helvētiī domō exeunt ? Eō itinere quod per Sēquanōs dūcit. 5. *Quid* habet Caesar in manibus ? 6. *Cui* mūnītiōnī[2] Caesar Labiēnum praeficit ? Eī mūnītiōnī quae est inter lacum et montem. 7. *Quis* eīs mūnītiōnibus[2] quās Caesar nunc habet praeerat ? 8. *Quod* oppidum in potestāte rēgis nostrī est ? 9. Dūcuntne[3] Helvētiī suās copiās in Sēquanōrum fīnēs ? 10. *Nōnne*[4] est vir acceptissimus quī hanc urbem servat ? Is acceptissimus est. 11. *Num*[5] Caesar eōs laudat quī agrōs populī Rōmānī vastābant ? Caesar nōn istōs laudat. 12. Quid illī simile bellō est ? 13. Num Caesar lēgātum praeficiet eīs mīlitibus quōs sēcum habet ? 14. Nōnne Labiēnus illī exercituī praeest quī in nostrā prōvinciā est ?

DIRECTION. — Learn A. & G.: [1]**104,** *a* ; **210,** *e.*   [2]**228** ; Rule 23.   [3]**210,** *a* ; Rule 11.   [4]**210,** *c,* first sentence. [5]**210,** *c,* second sentence ; Rule 12.
H. : [1]**188,** II. and 1 ; **351** and 1.   [2]**386.**   [3]**351,** 1, Note 1.   [4]**351,** 1, Note 2.   [5]**351,** 1, Note 3.

Quis, *who ? which ? any* (used substantively).

.	M.	F.	N.	M.	F.	N.
Sing. Nom.	**quis,**	**quae,**	**quid** ;	Acc. **quem,**	**quam,**	**quid.**

Complete the paradigm with the remaining forms like those of **quī**, Exercise 120.

Quī, *which ? what ? any* (used adjectively), is declined like the relative **quī**.

132.

1. Who was the bravest leader in our army ? 2. What reward will Caesar give to these magistrates ? 3. Is Rome larger than all Italy ? 4. Was not the commander who is in Gaul in charge of that town ? 5. Is not Caesar the greatest of our generals ? 6. What is better than virtue ? 7. What fortification will be more useful than that which Labienus is in charge of ? 8. What treaty have the good with those men ? 9. What citizens were most acceptable to the faithful consul ?

THE DEPARTURE OF THE HELVETIANS.

SUGGESTION. — This exercise and the following may well be read in connection with the study of a map.

PART FIRST.

The Helvetii are superior to the rest of the Gauls in valor. For this reason they desire a larger territory than that which they now inhabit.

There are two roads which lead from the territory of the Helvetii; the one through the Sequani, the other through our province. That is difficult; this is easy. The Helvetii choose the way through our province.

Between the territory of the Helvetii and the Allobroges, who inhabit our province, flows the Rhone, and this is crossed in many places by fords. At Geneva, a city of the Allobroges, which is near the territory of the Helvetii, there is a bridge.

All these facts are known to Caesar. He leads an army from Rome and hastens to Geneva by the longest marches possible. He destroys the bridge which is near Geneva. His coming is known to the Helvetii; and they send ambassadors to him, the noblest of the state. Caesar responds to them. He does not favor them; and he does not grant them a way through our province. Caesar himself, with the (that) legion which he has with him, constructs a wall sixteen feet in height, from lake Lemannus, which flows into the river Rhone, to the mountain which separates the territory of the Sequani from the Helvetii.

PROFECTIŌ HELVĒTIŌRUM.

PARS SECUNDA.

Est alterum per Sēquanōs iter. Helvētiī lēgātōs ad Dumnorigem Haeduum mīttunt et ab eō auxilium postulant. Is māgnā apud Sēquanōs grātiā est et Helvētiīs est amīcus. Is Sēquanīs persuādet. Illī foedus cum Helvētiīs faciunt, et itinere eōs nōn prohibent.

Māgnum est perīculum prōvinciae nostrae. Ob eam causam Caesar eī mūnītiōnī, quam ille habet, Labiēnum praeficit; ipse in Ītaliam māgnīs itineribus contendit duāsque legiōnēs cōnscrībit, et trēs ē castrīs ēdūcit, et in Galliam per Alpēs cum hīs quīnque legiōnibus contendit.

Helvētiī per fīnēs Sēquanōrum suās cōpiās trādūcunt et in Haeduōrum fīnēs perveniunt eōrumque agrōs vastant. Haeduī sē suaque ab eīs nōn dēfendunt. Paene in cōnspectū exercitūs Rōmānī, agrī eōrum vastantur, līberī in servitūtem abdūcuntur, oppida expūgnantur. Haeduī Ambarrī, fīnitimī Haeduōrum, nōn facile ab oppidīs vim hostium prohibent. Allobrogēs, quī trāns Rhodanum possessiōnēs habent, fugā sē ad Caesarem recipiunt.

Flūmen est Arar, quod per fīnēs Haeduōrum et Sēquanōrum in Rhodanum īnfluit, incrēdibilī lēnitāte. Id Helvētiī trānseunt. Trēs jam partēs copiārum Helvētiōrum trāns id flūmen sunt. Quarta pars citrā flūmen Ararim reliqua est. Caesar cum legiōnibus tribus ē castrīs exit et ad eam partem pervenit quae citrā flūmen est. Māgnam partem eōrum concīdit; reliquī fugā sēse in proximās silvās recipiunt.

Caesar pontem in Arare facit atque ita exercitum trādūcit. Helvētiī lēgātōs ad eum mīttunt.

VERBS.

SUM, *I AM*, PRESENT INDICATIVE. THE PERSONAL PRO-NOUNS *EGO* AND *TŪ*. SIMPLE CONDITIONS.

SUGGESTIONS. — 1. The personal pronoun as subject of a verb is not ex-pressed in Latin unless it is emphatic: **sum** means *I am ;* **es,** *thou art ;* **sum homō,** *I am a man ;* **ego sum cōnsul,** *I am consul.*

2. There is no personal pronoun of the third person, *he, she, it,* in Latin; but the demonstratives **is** and **ille** are sometimes used.

3. The declension of **ego** and **tū** is contained in sentences 10–19. **Ego** has no vocative ; the vocative of **tū** is like the nominative in both singular and plural.

4. In the *conditional sentence,* **Sī ades, bene est,** *if you are here, it is well, sī ades* is called the *Protasis* or *Condition, bene est* the *Apodosis* or *Conclusion.*

5. In the accompanying paradigm, and others like it, the English auxili-aries in parenthesis are to be used in translation and thoroughly committed to memory in connection with the corresponding Latin forms. The first sentence, **sī adsum, nostrīs mägnō ūsuī sum,** is, therefore, to be trans-lated, *if I am here, I am of great service to our forces.* For the construction of **nostrīs** and **ūsuī,** see A. & G., **233,** *a ;* Rule 27. II., **390,** 1 ; Rule XIII.

Sī (*am*) adsum, nostrīs mägnō ūsuī (*am*) sum.
Sī (*are*) ades, hostrīs mägnō ūsuī (*are*) es.
Sī (*is*) adest, nostrīs mägnō ūsuī (*is*) est.
Sī (*are*) adsumus, nostrīs mägnō ūsuī (*are*) sumus.
Sī (*are*) adestis, nostrīs mügnō ūsuī (*are*) estis.
Sī (*are*) adsunt, nostrīs mägnō ūsuī (*are*) sunt.

6. The *apodosis* of the second sentence in all Latin Exercises from 133 to 149 is to be inflected in connection with the rest of the sentence ; *e.g.* (2, below) *Sī adest, parātus sum ; sī adest, parātus es,* etc.

133.

1. (Ego) *sum,* (tū) *es,* (is) *est ;* (nōs) *sumus,* (vōs) *estis,* (ī, eī) *sunt.* 2. Sī[1] adest,[2] parātus sum.[2] 3. Rērum novārum cupidus es.

4. In exercitū Rōmānō mīles sum.   5. Tū animō māgnō fortīque es.   6. Ille est vir māgnae virtūtis.   7. Aditū Caesaris miserī sumus.   8. Illī sunt mīlitēs quōs auxilī causā lēgātus sēcum habet. 9. Ēius exercitūs praefectī estis.   10. *Ego* graviōris aetātis sum quam˙ *tū.*   11. Tū *meī* [3] oblītus es, ego *tuī* [3] nōn.   12. Nōnne aditus prīncipis et *mihī* et *tibī* acceptus est ?   13. Prīnceps *mē* laudat, *tē* nōn.   14. Lēgātiō ā *mē* mīttitur, nōn ā *tē.*   15. *Nōs* hūius bellī causa sumus, *vōs* illīus.   16. Ūnus *nostrūm* [4] in vestrīs manibus est, ūnus *vostrūm* [4] in nostrīs.   17. Lēgātus et *nōbīs* et *vōbīs* persuādet.   18. Cōnsul *nōs* monet, laudat *vōs.*   19. Phalanx ā *nōbīs* armātur, ā *vōbīs* in bellum mīttitur.   20. Nōs *vostrī* [5] (*vestrī*) oblītī nōn sumus.

DIRECTION.— Learn A. & G. : [1] **304**, Note, *a* and *c*, first clause.   [2] **305,** *a*, 1 and example.   [3] **218**, *a* and Rule 18.   [4] **99**, *a* and *b* ; **194** and *b* ; Rule 6.   [5] **99**, *c* ; **216, 5, Objective Genitive** ; **217.**

H. : [1] **506**.   [2] **507,** I.   [3] **399,** I., 1, 2 and 3.   [4] **446**, Note 3.   [5] **396**, III. ; **399** and Note.

ego, *I.*

	Sing.	Plur.
Nom.	e'go	nōs
Gen.	me'ī	no'strūm (strī)
Dat.	mi'hī	nō'bīs
Acc.	mē	nōs
Voc.	——	——
Abl.	mē	nō'bīs

tū, *you.*

	Sing.	Plur.
Nom.	tū	vōs
Gen.	tu'ī	vo'strūm (strī), ve'strūm (strī)
Dat.	ti'bī	vō'bīs
Acc.	tē	vōs ·
Voc.	tū	vōs
Abl.	tē	vō'bīs

adsum, *am here.*

Sing.		Plur.	
1.	ad'sum	1.	ad'su mus
2.	ad'es	2.	ad es'tis
3.	ad'est	3.	ad'sunt

SUGGESTION. — The *protasis* of the second sentence in all English Exercises from 134 to 152 is to be inflected in place ; *e.g.* (2, below) *If I am in charge of the army, it is well; if you are in charge of the army, it is well,* etc.

134.

1. I am not forgetful of these citizens, who desire liberty.
2. If I am in charge of the army, it is well. 3. We are of greater age than you. 4. You (sing.) are in Rome, Italy's greatest city. 5. You are not desirous of a revolution. 6. The approach of this army is more acceptable to me than to you. 7. These ambassadors respond to us, those to you. 8. For this reason they are forgetful both of us and of you. 9. The magistrate places me in charge of this, you in charge of that, fortification. 10. One of you is a man of great boldness, the other [is] not. 11. The enemy are eight miles distant from us, twelve miles from you. 12. The lieutenant is praised by me, warned by you.

SUM, IMPERFECT INDICATIVE. SIMPLE CONDITIONS.

SUGGESTIONS. — 1. Eram means *I was;* erās, *thou wast (you were),* etc.

2. Sī (*was*) aderam, nostrīs māgnō ūsuī (*was*) eram.
Sī (*were*) aderās, nostrīs māgnō ūsuī (*were*) erās.
Sī (*was*) aderat, nostrīs māgnō ūsuī (*was*) erat.
Sī (*were*) aderāmus, nostrīs māgnō ūsuī (*were*) erāmus.
Sī (*were*) aderātis, nostrīs māgnō ūsuī (*were*) erātis.
Sī (*were*) aderant, nostrīs māgnō ūsuī (*were*) erant.

135.

1. (Ego) eram, (tū) erās, (ille) erat; (nōs) erāmus, (vōs) erātis, (illī) erant. 2. Sī aderat,[1] parātus eram. 3. Vōbīs illō diē[2] ūtilis eram. 4. Et tū[3] et ille[3] eō diē dīgnus laude omnī erātis.[3] 5. Avaricī erāmus frūmentī causā. 6. Num eōs diēs[4] omnēs Rōmae erātis? 7. Silva erat nōn māgna inter nostrum[5] atque hostium exercitum. 8. Multī vostrūm Helvētiīs amīcī erant. 9. Nōs vostrī oblītī erāmus, vōs nostrī nōn. 10. Num suī oblītī sunt? 11. Brūtusne Gallicīs nāvibus[6] praeerat?

98   A STRAIGHT ROAD TO CAESAR.

DIRECTION. — Learn A. & G.: ¹305, a, 2 and example. ²256, 1 ; Rule 55.
³205 and a. ⁴256, 2 ; Rule 55. ⁵99,
a. ⁶231, a.
H.: ¹ Rule XLIV. I. ²429 ; Rule XXXI. ⁸463,
I., II. and 1; Rule XXXVI. ⁴379 ;
Rule IX. ⁵447. ⁶386.

Sing. 1. ad'e ram	Plur. 1. ad e rā'mus
2. ad'e rās	2. ad e rā'tis
3. ad'e rat	3. ad'e rant

136.

·1. You (sing.) were in Rome on that day; now you are in
Avaricum. 2. If I was in charge of the army, it was well.
3. I was in Rome many days; now I am at home. 4. There
were two roads; one through the Sequani, the other through our
province. 5. The soldiers of this legion were forgetful of Caesar.
6. We were not forgetful of you (plur.); you were forgetful of us.
7. Caesar was in charge of the soldiers on that day. 8. All those
days we were in Avaricum, which is a town of Gaul. 9. You
were a soldier; you are now a commander. 10. The leaders are
men of great courage. 11. We are in charge of this fortification.
12. I am wretched on account of Caesar's approach.

SUM, **FUTURE INDICATIVE.**   **FUTURE CONDITIONS.**

SUGGESTIONS. — 1. In translating, use *shall* in the first person, *will* in the
second and third persons ; *e.g.* I *shall* be, you *will* be, he *will* be ; we *shall* be,
you *will* be, they *will* be.

2. The following paradigms illustrate the *Future Condition, More Vivid,*
with the *future tense* in both *protasis* and *apodosis :* —

Sī (*am*) aderō, nostrīs māgnō ūsuī (*shall be*) erō.
Sī (*are*) aderis, nostrīs māgnō ūsuī (*will be*) eris.
Sī (*is*) aderit, nostrīs māgnō ūsuī (*will be*) erit.
Sī (*are*) aderimus, nostrīs māgnō ūsuī (*shall be*) erimus.
Sī (*are*) aderitis, nostrīs māgnō ūsuī (*will be*) eritis.
Sī (*are*) aderunt, nostrīs māgnō ūsuī (*will be*) erunt.

The Latin *future* in the *protasis* is commonly translated by the English
present, but the auxiliary *shall* may be used in the *protasis* throughout.

137.

1. *Erō, eris, erit ; erimus, eritis, erunt.* 2. Sī aderit,[1] parātus erō.[1] 3. Rōmae eram, domī sum, in Germāniā erō. 4. Nōs, quī amīcī tuī sumus, hūius lēgātiōnis prīncipēs erimus. 5. Pōns quī est ad Genāvam in nostrīs manibus erit. 6. Ubī illō diē eris, amīce ? Vesontiōnī (-e) erō. 7. Quī cum cōnsule fortī illō diē erunt ? 8. Sī mihī amīcitia populī Rōmānī deerit, miser erō. 9. Equitātuī, quem auxiliō [2] Caesarī [2] Haeduī mīttunt, tū praeeris. 10. Nōnne vōs, quī novissimīs [3] auxiliō erātis, in cornū sinistrō eritis ? 11. Vōs nōbīs auxiliō māgnō estis. 12. Superiōrēs et virtūte [4] et numerō [4] erātis. 13. Nōs in numerō tuōrum amīcōrum semper erimus. 14. Decima legiō māgnō ūsuī vōbīs eōs diēs omnēs erat. 15. Sī pars exercitūs superit, nōbīs [5] erit spēs victōriae. 16. Sī decima legiō aberit, hostēs audācissimī erunt.

DIRECTION. — Learn A. & G.: [1]**305**, *b*, 1 (*a*) and example. [2]**233** and *a* ; Rule 27. [3]**188**, *c.* [4]**253** ; Rule 53. [5]**231** ; Rule 25.

II.: [1]**507**, I. ; **508**. [2]**390**, I., II. ; Rule XIII. [3]**440** ; **441**. [4]**424** ; Rule XXIX. [5]**387**.

Sing.		Plur.	
1. ad'e rō		1. ad e'ri mus	
2. ad'e ris		2. ad e'ri tis	
3. ad'e rit		3. ad'e runt	

138.

1. You who are making these plans will be known to the enemy. 2. If I am in charge of (future) the army, it will be well. 3. You who are of great assistance to us will always be in the number of our friends. 4. We were in Germany, we are now in Rome, we shall be in Vesontio. 5. You who are the leading men of that embassy will be of great use to the consul. 6. The tenth legion will be of great use to us all those days. 7. You (sing.) who are in charge of the tenth legion will be an aid to the leader. 8. Shall we not be of use to those who are making this plan? 9. If a part of the army remains (future), you will have hope of victory. 10. If the consul is (future) absent, the enemy will be more daring.

SUM, PERFECT INDICATIVE.

SUGGESTIONS. — 1. The perfect indicative is to be translated *was* or *has been*, as seems best to fit the meaning of the sentence. Many sentences will allow either meaning. In connected discourse, the context will generally decide which translation must be used.

> 2. Sī (*have been*) adfuī, nostrīs māgnō ūsuī (*have been*) fuī.
> Sī (*have been*) adfuistī, nostrīs māgnō ūsuī (*have been*) fuistī.
> Sī (*has been*) adfuit, nostrīs māgnō ūsuī (*has been*) fuit.
> Sī (*have been*) adfuimus, nostrīs māgnō ūsuī (*have been*) fuimus.
> Sī (*have been*) adfuistis, nostrīs māgnō ūsuī (*have been*) fuistis.
> Sī (*have been*) adfuērunt, nostrīs māgnō ūsuī (*have been*) fuēre.

139.

1. *Fuī, fuistī, fuit; fuimus, fuistis, fuērunt* or *fuēre.* 2. Sī adfuit,[1] parātus fuī.[1] 3. Hostis fuistī; in numerō cīvium eris. 4. Captīvus fuī; nunc in salūte sum. 5. Illa cīvitās, patrum nostrōrum memoriā, māgnā inter Belgās auctōritāte fuit. 6. Ex eō diē diēs continuōs quīnque in castrīs fuistī. 7. Hī praefectī, quī cōnsulī auxiliō fuērunt (fuēre), māgnō in honōre sunt. 8. Est mihī[2] domī pater. 9. Exercitus tibī est, et is mihī māgnō ūsuī est. 10. Nōs, quī ēius cōnsilī auctōrēs fuimus, nunc māgnā in grātiā sumus. 11. Germānīs fuit rēx, Ariovistus. 12. Flūminis erat altitūdō pedum[3] trium. 13. Quae mercēs illī erit?

DIRECTION. — Learn A. & G.: [1]**305,** *a,* 2, second example. [2]**231** and Remark. [3]**215,** *b.*
II.: [1]**507,** I.; **508** and 2. [2]**387.** [3]**396,** V.

Sing. 1. ad'fuī	Plur. 1. ad fu'i mus.
2. ad fu i'stī	2. ad fu i'stis
3. ad'fu it	3. ad fu ē'runt (·re)

140.

1. Divitiacus has been especially acceptable to the common people. 2. If I have been in charge of the army, it has been well. 3. Within the memory of your ancestors, Divitiacus was a chief

among them. 4. I was in the territory of Germany, you (sing.) were at Rome. 5. These states have been of great influence among the Belgae. 6. All the rest of the Belgae were of assistance to the rear. 7. Five successive days from that day you were at home. 8. We who are chiefs have a great reward. 9. The plan which you (plur.) have will be acceptable to the consul. 10. The armies which the consuls have will be of great use to them. 11. We have a mother at home.

SUM, PLUPERFECT INDICATIVE.

SUGGESTION. — The sign of the pluperfect in English is *had;* e.g. fueram, *I had been;* fuerās, *you had been,* etc.

141.

1. *Fueram,'fuerās, fuerat; fuerāmus, fuerātis, fuerant.* 2. Ego dux illīus agminis fueram. 3. Captīvī in castrīs hostium fuerātis. 4. Praefectō vestrō semper nōtus fueram. 5. Illī agminī praefuerās. 6. Hūius lēgātiōnis Divicō prīnceps fuit, quī bellō alterō dux Helvētiōrum fuerat. 7. In urbe hostium fuerāmus; illō diē Rōmae fuimus. 8. Galba istīus profectiōnis auctor nōn fuerat. 9. Rōmae erant, in Galliā fuerant; Vesontiōne (-ī) erunt. 10. Mīlitēs decimae legiōnis, quī in castrīs fuerant, illō diē novissimō agminī auxiliō fuērunt (fuēre). 11. Haec rēs mihī māgnō ūsuī fuerat. 12. Equī·quōs prīncipēs habent illīs māgnō ūsuī fuērunt (fuēre).

Sing. 1. ad fu′e ram	Plur. 1. ad fu e rā′mus	
2. ad fu′e rās	2. ad fu e rā′tis	
3. ad fu′e rat	3. ad fu′e rant	

142.

1. You (sing.) who had been in the ship were in great peril. 2. You (plur.) who have been in the Roman army are worthy of all praise. 3. We had been companions of senators; on that day we were exiles. 4. The authority of this state had been very great. 5. One thing was of greatest use to the state. 6. The

soldiers of the tenth legion, who had been of assistance to the rear rank, were on that day in camp. 7. You had been chief of an embassy in another war. 8. I had been in charge of that fortification.

SUM, FUTURE PERFECT INDICÀTIVE. FUTURE CONDITIONS, MORE VIVID.

SUGGESTIONS. — 1. The sign of the future perfect in English is *shall have*, in first persons; *will have*, in second and third; *e.g.* **fuerō**, *I shall have been;* **fueris**, *you will have been*, etc.

2. Sī (*am*) ad**fuerō**, nostrīs mūgnō ūsuī (*shall be*) erō.
Sī (*are*) ad**fueris**, nostrīs māgnō ūsuī (*will be*) eris.
Sī (*is*) ad**fuerit**, nostrīs mūgnō ūsuī (*will be*) erit.
Sī (*are*) ad**fuerimus**, nostrīs māgnō ūsuī (*shall be*) erimus.
Sī (*are*) ad**fueritis**, nostrīs māgnō ūsuī (*will be*) eritis.
Sī (*are*) ad**fuerint**, nostrīs māgnō ūsuī (*will be*) erunt.

The Latin *future perfect* in the *protasis* is usually translated by the English *present*, but the auxiliary *shall have been* may be used in the *protasis* throughout.

143.

1. *Fuerō, fueris, fuerit; fuerimus, fueritis, fuerint.* 2. Sī adfuerit,[1] parātus fuerō.[1] 3. Reliquus in illā urbe fuerit nēmō. 4. Nōs amīcīs nostrīs ūsuī fuerimus. 5. Sī vobīs amīcitia populī Rōmānī dēfuerit, miserrimī eritis. 6. Mīlitibus illīs multae difficultātēs fuerint. 7. Cīvēs vestrī lēgātiōnī ūtilēs fuērunt. 8. Post eius mortem ad eam rem Helvētiī parātī erant. 9. Dumnorix, māgnā apud plēbem grātiā, cupidus rērum novārum fuit. 10. Ego itinere longō dēfessus fuerō. 11. Urbs Rōma ornāmentō cīvitātī erit. 12. Inter novissimum hostium agmen et nostrum prīmum nōn amplius sēnīs mīlibus[2] passuum interest.

DIRECTION. — Learn A. & G.: [1]**307**, 2, *a*, Note and *c*, first clause. [2]**94**, *e* and Note.
H.: [1]**507**, I.; **508**. [2]**178** and Note.

Sing.		Plur.	
1. ad **fu'e rō**		1. ad **fu e'ri mus**	
2. ad **fu'e ris**		2. ad **fu e'ri tis**	
3. ad **fu'e rit**		3. ad **fu'e rint**	

144.

1. You will have been witnesses of these things. 2. If I am in charge (fut. perfect) of the army, it will be (fut. perfect) well. 3. Great will have been the authority of the friendly states. 4. You (sing.) will have been braver than these citizens. 5. All these states will have been in the power of the Roman people. 6. Our city is not more than six thousand paces distant from your territory. 7. Between our rear rank and the front rank of the enemy is the river Rhone. 8. This place was a thousand paces distant from the enemy. 9. If our cavalry is absent (fut. perfect), the enemy will be more daring. 10. If a part of the cavalry remains (fut. perfect), I shall have hope of victory.

SUM, PRESENT SUBJUNCTIVE. FUTURE CONDITIONS, LESS VIVID.

SUGGESTION. — The following form of conditional sentence is called a *Future Condition, Less Vivid :* —

Sī (*should*) ad**sim**, nostrīs māgnō ūsuī (*should*) **sim**.
Sī (*should*) ad**sīs**, nostrīs māgnō ūsuī (*would*) **sīs**.
Sī (*should*) ad**sit**, nostrīs māgnō ūsuī (*would*) **sit**.
Sī (*should*) ad**sīmus**, nostrīs māgnō ūsuī (*should*) **sīmus**.
Sī (*should*) ad**sītis**, nostrīs māgnō ūsuī (*would*) **sītis**.
Sī (*should*) ad**sint**, nostrīs māgnō ūsuī (*would*) **sint**.

145.

1. Sī praesēns *sim*, sī praesēns *sīs*, sī praesēns *sit;* sī praesentēs *sīmus*, sī praesentēs *sītis*, sī praesentēs *sint*. 2. Sī adsit,[1] parātus sim.[1] 3. Sī haec rēs hostibus nōta sit, māgnō in metū sītis. 4. Sī ab hostium castrīs nōn longius mille passibus absīs, māgnō in perīculō sīs. 5. Sī prope castra hostium sīmus, māgnō in perīculō sīmus. 6. Sī Helvētiī ad eam rem parātī sint, ducēs eōrum laetī sint.

DIRECTION. — Learn A. & G.: [1]305, *b*, 2 (*a*) and example ; 307, 2 and *b*. H.: [1]507, II. ; Rule XLIV. II. ; 509 and Note 1.

Sing. 1. ad'sim	Plur. 1. ad sī'mus
2. ad'sīs	2. ad sī'tis
3. ad'sit	3. ad'sint

146.

1. If I should be ready, if you should be ready, if he should be ready; if we should be ready, if you should be ready, if they should be ready. 2. If I should be in charge of the army, it would be well. 3. If the crops should be ripe, the soldiers would be glad. 4. If the king should be present, we should be ready for these things. 5. If you (sing.) should be in great fear, this would be known to the enemy. 6. If I should be in charge of this fortification, you (plur.) would have hope of victory.

SUM, IMPERFECT SUBJUNCTIVE. CONDITIONS CONTRARY TO FACT, PRESENT TIME.

SUGGESTION. — The conditional sentence with the *Imperfect Subjunctive* in both *protasis* and *apodosis* is known as *a supposition contrary to fact, in present time.*

Sī (*were*) adessem, nostrīs māgnō ūsuī (*should*) essem.
Sī (*were*) adessēs, nostrīs māgnō ūsuī (*would*) essēs.
Sī (*were*) adesset, nostrīs māgnō ūsuī (*would*) esset.
Sī (*were*) adessēmus, nostrīs māgnō ūsuī (*should*) essēmus.
Sī (*were*) adessētis, nostrīs māgnō ūsuī (*would*) essētis.
Sī (*were*) adessent, nostrīs māgnō ūsuī (*would*) essent.

147.

1. Sī praesēns *essem*, sī praesēns *essēs*, sī praesēns *esset;* sī praesentēs *essēmus*, sī praesentēs *essētis*, sī praesentēs *essent*.
2. Sī adesset,[1] parātus essem.[1] 3. Sī Caesar praesēns esset, in salūte essēmus. 4. Sī sub monte essem, māgnō in perīculō essētis. 5. Sī Cōnsidius reī[2] mīlitāris perītus esset, nōn essēs in exercitū Sullae. 6. Sī summus mōns in manibus Labiēnī esset, spēs esset victōriae. 7. Sī nōn essent nōbīs ducēs perītī, māgnae essent difficultātēs.

DIRECTION. — Learn A. & G.: [1]305, *c*, 1 and example. [2]218, *a*; Rule 18.
H.: [1]507, III.; 510 and Note 1. [2]399, I., 1, 2 and 3; Rule XVII.

Sing.	1. ad es'sem		Plŭr.	1. ad es sē'mus
	2. ad es'sēs			2. ad es sē'tis
	3. ad es'set			3. ad es'sent

148.

1. If I were ready, if you were ready, if he were ready; if we were ready, if you were ready, if they were ready. 2. If I were in charge of the army, it would be well. 3. If we were upon the top of the hill, we should be in [a place of] safety. 4. If you (plur.) were ready for battle, you would not be in great fear of an attack. 5. If you (sing.) were upon the summit of the mountain, you would be in sight of the enemy. 6. If the coming of Caesar were known to the enemy, they would be in great fear.

SUM, PERFECT SUBJUNCTIVE. FUTURE CONDITIONS, LESS VIVID.

SUGGESTIONS. — 1. The Perfect Subjunctive is inflected like the Future Perfect Indicative, substituting only **fuerim** for **fuerō**. See Exercise 143.

2. The following form of conditional sentence illustrates the *Future Condition, Less Vivid*, with the Perfect Subjunctive in protasis : —

Sī (*should*) adfuerim, nostrīs māgnō ūsuī (*should*) sim.
Sī (*should*) adfueris, nostrīs māgnō ūsuī (*would*) sīs.
Sī (*should*) adfuerit, nostrīs māgnō ūsuī (*would*) sit.
Sī (*should*) adfuerimus, nostrīs māgnō ūsuī (*should*) sīmus.
Sī (*should*) adfueritis, nostrīs māgnō ūsuī (*would*) sītis.
Sī (*should*) adfuerint, nostrīs māgnō ūsuī (*would*) sint.

The Latin perfect subjunctive in the *protasis* is commonly translated as above, but the auxiliary *should have* may be used in the *protasis* throughout.

149.

1. Sī cautus *fuerim*, sī cautus *fueris*, sī cautus *fuerit;* sī cautī *fuerimus*, sī cautī *fueritis*, sī cautī *fuerint*. 2. Sī adfuerit,[1] parātus sim.[1] 3. Sī illō diē Avaricī fuerim, cupidus sim rērum novārum. 4. Sī māximē plēbī acceptus fueris, māgnō in honōre sīmus. 5. Sī Caesar fuerit Sullā clārior, bene sit. 6. Sī sub monte fuerimus, māgnō in perīculō sīmus. 7. Sī in exercitū Sullae fueritis,

reī mīlitāris perītī sītis. ˘8. Sī in exercitū Cōnsidī fuerint explōrātōrēs, eī Caesarī ūsuī sint. 9. Sī fortēs fueritis, in hōc bellō
victōrēs fuerimus.

DIRECTION. — Learn A. & G.: [1] **305**, *b*, 2 (*β*) and example.
H.: [1] **509** and Note 1.

Sing.		Plur.	
1.	ad fu'e rim	1.	ad fu e'ri mus
2.	ad fu'e ris	2.	ad fu e'ri tis
3.	ad fu'e rit	3.	ad fu'e rint

150.

1. If I should be diligent, if you should be diligent, if he
should be diligent; if we should be diligent, if you should be
diligent, if they should be diligent. 2. If I should (have been)
be in charge of the army, it would be well. 3. We should (have
been) be ready for battle, if there should be leaders in camp.
4. If the enemy should (have been) be in sight, you (sing.)
would be in great danger. 5. If I should (have been) be ready
for an attack, there would be great hope of victory. 6. If you
(plur.) should not be braver than the consul, great would be the
disaster of the Roman people.

SUM, PLUPERFECT SUBJUNCTIVE. CONDITIONS CONTRARY TO FACT, PAST TIME.

SUGGESTION. — The following form of the Conditional Sentence with the
Pluperfect Subjunctive in both *protasis* and *apodosis*, is known as *a Supposition Contrary to Fact in Past Time :* —

Sī (*had*) adfuissem, nostrīs māgnō ūsuī (*should have*) fuissem.
Sī (*had*) adfuissēs, nostrīs māgnō ūsuī (*would have*) fuissēs.
Sī (*had*) adfuisset, nostrīs māgnō ūsuī (*would have*) fuisset.
Sī (*had*) adfuissēmus, nostrīs māgnō ūsuī (*should have*) fuissēmus.
Sī (*had*) adfuissētis, nostrīs māgnō ūsuī (*would have*) fuissētis.
Sī (*had*) adfuissent, nostrīs māgnō ūsuī (*would have*) fuissent.

151.

1. Sī praesēns *fuissem*, sī praesēns *fuissēs*, sī praesēns *fuisset;*
sī praesentēs *fuissēmus*, sī praesentēs *fuissētis*, sī praesentēs *fuis-*

sent. 2. Sī adfuisset,[1] parātus fuissem.[1] 3. Sī cautus fuissem, sī cautus fuissēs, sī cautus fuisset; sī cautī fuissēmus, sī cautī fuissētis, sī cautī fuissent. 4. Sī cupidus rērum novārum fuisset, dux coniūrātiōnis fuisset. 5. Sī eō diē Rōmae fuissēmus, hostēs fortissimī fuissent. 6. Sī prope hostium castra fuissem, pūgna fuisset. 7. Sī proximī Germānis fuissētis, māgnō in perīculō fuissētis. 8. Sī fortis fuissēs, spēs victōriae fuisset.

DIRECTION. — Learn A. & G. : [1]305, *c*, 2 and example.
H. : [1]510, and Note 1.

Sing.	1. ad fu is'sem	Plur.	1. ad fu is sē'mus
	2. ad fu is'sēs		2. ad fu is sē'tis
	3. ad fu is'set		3. ad fu is'sent

152.

1. If I had been ready, if you had been ready, if he had been ready; if we had been ready, if you had been ready, if they had been ready. 2. If I had been in charge of the army, it would have been well. 3. If I had been diligent, if you had been diligent, if he had been diligent; if we had been diligent, if you had been diligent, if they had been diligent. 4. If you (sing.) had been in Rome all those days, I should not have been in great fear. 5. If this matter had been your care, you (plur.) would have been safe. 6. If we had been men of great boldness, they would not have been desirous of a revolution.

RECAPITULATION OF CONDITIONAL SENTENCES.

SUGGESTION. — The sentences in Exercise 153 are to be classified and translated, after completing and translating the paradigms indicated below: —

SIMPLE CONDITIONS.

Present Time : Sī *adest,* parātus *sum,* etc.
Past Time : Sī *aderat,* parātus *eram,* etc.
Past Time : Sī *adfuit,* parātus *fuī,* etc.

Future Time: Sī *aderit,* parātus *erō,* etc.
Future, Protasis Completed: Sī *adfuerit,* parātus *erō,* etc.
Future, Completed: Sī *adfuerit,* parātus *fuerō,* etc.

FUTURE CONDITIONS, LESS VIVID.

Future Time: Sī *adsit,* parātus *sim,* etc.
Future, Protasis Completed: Sī *adfuerit,* parātus *sim,* etc.
Future, Completed: Sī *adfuerit,* parātus *fuerim,* etc.

CONDITIONS CONTRARY TO FACT.

Present Time: Sī *adesset,* parātus *essem,* etc.
Past Time: Sī *adfuisset,* parātus *fuissem,* etc.

153.

1. Sī Divicō prīnceps sit, laetī nōn sītis.　2. Sī nōbīs equitātus fuisset, tū in potestāte hostium nōn fuissēs.　3. Sī meī nōn oblītus es, laetus sum.　4. Sī nostrī in castrīs fuerint, in salūte erimus.　5. Sī Divicō prīnceps fuerit (ind.), laetī nōn fueritis (ind.).　6. Sī meī nōn oblītus fuistī, laetus fuī.　7. Sī nostrī in castrīs fuerint (subj.), in salūte fuerimus (subj.).　8. Sī nōbīs equitātus esset, tū in potestāte hostium nōn essēs.　9. Sī meī nōn oblītus erās, laetus eram.　10. Sī Divicō prīnceps fuerit, laetī nōn sītis.　11. Sī nostrī in castrīs erunt, in salūte erimus.

RECAPITULATION CONTINUED.

SUGGESTIONS. — The paradigms indicated below are to be completed and translated into Latin.

SIMPLE CONDITIONS.

Present Time: If I *am* in charge of the army, it *is* well, etc.
Past Time: If I *was* in charge of the army, it *was* well, etc.
Past Time: If I *have been* in charge of the army, it *has been* well, etc.

FUTURE CONDITIONS, MORE VIVID.

Future Time: If I *am* (*shall be*) in charge of the army, it *will be* well, etc.
Future, Protasis Completed: If I *am* (*shall have been*) in charge of the army, it *will be* well, etc.

Future, Completed: If I am (*shall have been*) in charge of the army, it *will be* (*will have been*) well, etc.

FUTURE CONDITIONS, LESS VIVID.

Future Time: If I *should be* in charge of the army, it *would be* well, etc.
Future, Protasis Completed: If I *should be* (*should have been*) in charge of the army, it *would be* well, etc.
Future, Completed: If I *should be* (*should have been*) in charge of the army, it *would be* (*would have been*) well, etc.

CONDITIONS CONTRARY TO FACT.

Present Time: If I *were* in charge of the army, it *would be* well, etc.
Past Time: If I *had been* in charge of the army, it *would have been* well, etc.

154.

1. If we *are* (*shall be*) faithful all those days, we *shall be* of great service to the consul. 2. If you (plur.) *are* here, it *is* well. 3. We *should be* in great peril, if we *were* near the camp of the enemy. 4. If the consul *should be* here, we *should be* better prepared for all these things. 5. If you *have been* here, it *has been* well. 6. If we *are* (*shall have been*) faithful all those days, we *shall be* of great service to the consul. 7. We *should have been* in great peril, if we *had been* near the camp of the enemy. 8. If the consul *should be* (*should have been*) here, we *should be* better prepared for all these things. 9. If we *are* (*shall have been*) faithful all these days, we *shall be* (*shall have been*) of great service to the consul. 10. If you (plur.) *were* here, it *was* well. 11. If the consul *should be* (*should have been*) here, we *should be* (*should have been*) better prepared for all these things.

SUM, IMPERATIVES, INFINITIVES, PARTICIPLE.

SUGGESTIONS. — 1. IMPERATIVE :

Present, Sing. 2, **es**, *be* (*thou, you*) ; Plur. 2, **este**, *be* (*ye, you*).
Future, Sing. 2, **estō**, *you shall be, thou shalt be ;* Plur. 2, **estōte**, *ye* (*you*) *shall be.*

2. INFINITIVE :

Present, **esse**, to be; Perfect, **fuisse**, to have been; Future, **futūrus esse**
(**fore**), to be about to be.

3. PARTICIPLE :

Future, **futūrus**, about to be (declined like **bonus**).

4. a. **Ego parātus sum** becomes,
with a verb of saying,

> { (*Dīcit*) **sē parātum esse**,
> { (*He says*) that he is ready.

   b. **Ego parātus eram** (**fuī, fu-
        eram**) becomes

> { (*Dīcit*) **sē parātum fuisse**,
> { (*He says*) that he was (has been,
>   had been) ready.

   c. **Ego parātus erō** (**fuerō,
        sim, fuerim**) becomes

> { (*Dīcit*) **sē parātum futūrum esse**,
> { (*He says*) he will be (will have been,
>   would be, would have been) ready.

   d. **Ego parātus essem** (**fuis-
        sem**) becomes

> { (*Dīcit*) **sē parātum futūrum esse**,
> { (*He says*) that he would be (would
>   have been) ready.

155.

1. Mihī amīcus es.[1] Amīcīs vestrīs este fidēlēs. Dīligēns
cotīdiē estō. Fortēs semper estōte. 2. Ego sum parātus. Dīcit [2]
sē [3] esse [3] parātum.[4] 3. Ego eram (fuī, fueram) parātus. Dīcit sē
fuisse parātum. 4. Ego erō (fuerō, sim, fuerim) parātus. Dīcit
sē futūrum [4] esse parātum. 5. Dīcit sē esse nostrīs māgnō ūsuī.
6. Dīcit [5] sē fuisse [5] nostrīs māgnō ūsuī. 7. Dīcit sē futūrum esse
nostrīs māgnō ūsuī. 8. In potestāte populī Rōmānī sumus, neque
cum Belgīs reliquīs in coniūrātiōne fuimus, parātīque erimus sociī
fidēlēs esse populī Rōmānī; reliquī omnēs Belgae in armīs sunt,
māgnusque est eōrum furor. 9. Remī dīcunt sē in potestāte
populī Rōmānī esse, neque sē cum Belgīs reliquīs in coniūrātiōne
fuisse, parātōsque futūrōs esse sociōs fidēlēs esse populī Rōmānī;
reliquōs omnēs Belgās in armīs esse, māgnumque esse eōrum
furōrem.

DIRECTION. — Learn A. & G. : [1] **269**. [2] **336**, 1. [3] **272** ; 336, 2, first sen-
               tence ; Rule 60. [4] Rule 2. [5] **336**, A
               and Note 1.
          H. : [1] **487** ; Rule 40. [2] **535**, I., 1 and 2. [3] **522** ;
             523, I.; Rule LIII. I. [4] Rule XXXIV.
             [5] **537**.

IMPERATIVE MOOD.	INFINITIVE MOOD.
Present Tense.	*Perfect Tense.*
Sing. 2. ad'es	ad es'se
Plur. 2. ad e'ste	*Present Tense.*
	ad fu is'se
Future Tense.	
Sing. 2 and 3. ad e'stō	*Future Tense.*
Plur. 2. ad e stō'te	ad fu tū'rus es'se
Plur. 3. ad sun'tō	*or*
	ad'fo re

The future participle of ad'sum is ad fu tū'rus.

156.

1. Be (sing.) very brave. Be (plur.) very faithful to the Roman people. You (sing.) shall be very diligent every day. You (plur.) shall always be daring. 2. He says that he is in great fear. 3. He says that he was, has been, had been in great fear. 4. He says that he will be, will have been, would be, would have been in great fear. 5. He says that he would be, would have been in great fear.

SYNOPSIS.

At this point thoroughly commit and recite synopses of the verb sum; e.g. *sum, eram, erō, fuī, fueram, fuerō, sim, essem, fuerim, fuissem; es, erās, eris, fuistī, fuerās, fueris, sīs, essēs, fueris, fuissēs, es;* and so on through all the different persons. Compare A. & G., pp. 82, 83; H., pp. 84, 85.

FIRST CONJUGATION, ACTIVE AND PASSIVE VOICES, INDICATIVE MOOD, PRESENT TENSE.

SUGGESTIONS. — 1. In connection with sentences 1 and 8, learn the Personal Endings of Verbs, as follows : —

ACTIVE VOICE.		PASSIVE VOICE.	
Sing.	*Plur.*	*Sing.*	*Plur.*
1. -m (-ō or -ī)	-mus	-r	-mur
2. -s	-tis	-ris or -re	-minī
3. -t	-nt	-tur	-ntur

2. Verb-stems of the First Conjugation end in -ā- ; e.g. *laudā-* (stem of *laudō*), *mirā-* (stem of *mīror*). In the present tense, the personal endings are joined directly to the verb-stem, -ā- final becoming (see 1 and 8) -a- before -t, -nt, and -ntur. *Laudō* is for *laudā-m* and *mīror* for *mīrā-r*.

3. *Mīror, I wonder at,* is a *Deponent Verb ;* i.e. it has the passive form only, with an active meaning.

4. In Latin Exercises from 157 to 173, illustrating the first conjugation, sentences numbered 2 may be developed for practice in verb inflection and translation, as follows : —

Sī hōc spērō, errō ;

Sī hōc spērās, errās, etc.

157.

1. *Laudō, laudās, laudat; laudāmus, laudātis, laudant.* 2. Sī hōc spērō, errō. 3. Ego tē tuā virtūte laudō. 4. Interim cotīdiē Haeduōs[1] frūmentum[1] flāgitāmus. 5. Tū quī[2] Caesaris amīcus es,[2] concilium prīncipum convocās. 6. Servōs bonōs magnā vōce laudātis. 7. Caesar Liscum, quī summō magistrātuī praeest quem[3] "vergobretum"[3] appellant Haeduī, quī creātur annuus[4] et vītae necisque in suōs habet potestātem, graviter accūsat. 8. *Laudor, laudāris* or *laudāre, laudātur; laudāmur, laudāminī, laudantur.* 9. Et tū et ille magnā vōce laudāminī.[5] 10. Et nōs et vōs virtūte laudāmur.[5] 11. Urbemne mīrāris[6]? Māgnitūdinem urbis mīror.[6] 12. Nostrī, quī māgnō in perīculō erant, ā legiōnibus multīs fortibusque nunc iuvantur. 13. Nōnne laudibus vulgī cōnfirmāre (-ris)? 14. Num prōditiōnis[7] accūsāmur? 15. Nōs, quī amīcī populī Rōmānī appellāmur, prōditiōnis nōn accūsāmur.

DIRECTIONS. — 1. Learn A. & G. : [1] 239, 2 and *c* ; Rule 34. [2] 204 and *a* ; Rule 4. [3] 239, 1 and *a*. [4] 191. [5] 205, *a* and *b*. [6] 135. [7] 220 ; Rule 20.

II.: [1] 374 ; Rule VII. [2] 373 and 1 ; Rule VI. [4] 443. [5] 463, I., II., and 1. [6] 231 ; 465, 2. [7] 409, II. ; Rule XX. II.

2. Inflect all verbs of the conjugation illustrated in any given Exercise as suggested by the accompanying paradigms and commit thoroughly to memory.

Vocō, *I summon.*

ACTIVE VOICE, INDICATIVE MOOD, PRESENT TENSE.

Sing.		Plur.	
1. vo'cō		1. vo cā'mus	
2. vo'cās		2. vo cā'tis	
3. vo'cat		3. vo'cant	

PASSIVE VOICE, INDICATIVE MOOD, PRESENT TENSE.

Sing. 1. vo'cor	Plur. 1. vo cā'mur
2. vo cā'ris (re)	2. vo cā'mi nī
3. vo cā'tur	3. vo can'tur

SUGGESTION.— In English Exercises 158 to 174, sentences numbered 2 may be developed for translation as follows : *If I am assisting the nobility, I am strengthening the conspiracy; if you are assisting the nobility, you are strengthening the conspiracy,* etc. Sentence 9 in the same Exercises may be similarly developed by inflecting the *apodosis*.

158.

1. I summon, you summon, he summons; we summon, you summon, they summon. 2. If I am assisting the nobility, I am strengthening the conspiracy. 3. Are we strengthening the conspiracy? 4. I demand grain [of] you. 5. The undertaking is not difficult, if you (plur.) all approve. 6. The consul gives many rewards to all who assist him in the undertaking. 7. You (sing.) do not often assist a better cause. 8. I am summoned, you are summoned, he is summoned; we are summoned, you are summoned, they are summoned. 9. If there is need, I wonder at it. 10. We are protected, if the city is occupied by our legions. 11. If you (plur.) are armed, the camp is well protected. 12. I am protected, and you (sing.) are encouraged.

FIRST CONJUGATION, ACTIVE AND PASSIVE VOICES. INDICATIVE MOOD, IMPERFECT TENSE.

SUGGESTIONS. — 1. In this tense the personal endings are connected with the verb-stem by the tense-sign -bā-. Notice in 1 that -bā- in some situations becomes -ba-.

2. The Imperfect is to be translated by expressions denoting *continuance;* e.g. **laudābam,** *I was praising, I used to praise, I was wont to praise, I was in the habit of praising,* often simply *I praised.*

3. The stem of **dō** is da- (short -a-).

4. Translate **suō mōre,** *in accordance with his custom;* **quicquam potes-tātis,** *any power.*

159.

1. *Laudābam, laudābās, laudābat; laudābāmus, laudābātis, lau-dābant.* 2. Sī hōc spērābam, errābam. 3. Suō mōre[1] māgna patrum foedera laudābat. 4. Mercēdēs multās iuvenibus fidēlibus dabās. 5. Cūr quicquam potestātis[2] trāns Rhōnum postulābāmus? 6. Hominēs inimīcō animō agrōs vastābant. 7. Haeduōs auxilium flāgitābātis. 8. *Laudābar, laudābāris* or *laudābāre, laudābātur; laudābāmur, laudābāminī, laudābantur.* 9. Et ego et tū saepe laudābāmur. 10. Et vōs et illī iūre laudābāminī. 11. Ego Genāvā vocābar et cōnsul[3] creābar. 12. Tū cōnsul creābāris (-re), quam rem[4] nēmō mīrābātur. 13. Prōditiōnīs accūsābantur, id quod[4] omnēs mīrābantur.

DIRECTIONS. — 1. Learn A. & G. : [1]253 and Note, first sentence ; Rule 53. [2]216, *a*, 3 ; Rule 16. [3]176, *a* and *b*. [4]200, *e*.

II. : [1]424 and Note 1 ; Rule XXIX. [2]397 and 3 ; Rule XVI. [3]362, 1 and 2, 1) and 2) ; Rule I.

2. Notice that the Voice, Mood, and Tense of the paradigms given are suggested by the headings of Exercises.

Sing. 1. vo cā'bam	Plur. 1. vo cā bā'mus
2. vo cā'bās	2. vo cā bā'tis
3. vo cā'bat	3. vo cā'bant

Sing. 1. vo cā'bar	Plur. 1. vo cā bā'mur
2. vo cā bā'ris (-re)	2. vo cā bā'mi nī
3. vo cā bā'tur	3. vo cā ban'tur

160.

1. I used to summon, you used to summon, he used to summon; we used to summon, you used to summon, they used to summon. 2. If I was assisting the nobility, I was strengthening the conspiracy. 3. We were wont to demand chariots of the consul. 4. If you were expecting chariots from him, you were mistaken. 5. The soldiers were not in the habit of praising a consul who was not assisting them. 6. I was showing the danger to the consul, you were demanding of him assistance. 7. Why were you expecting any assistance from him ? 8. I was summoned,

you were summoned, he was summoned; we were summoned, you were summoned, they were summoned. 9. If there was need, I was wondering at it. 10. Both he and I used often to be summoned to Rome. 11. I was not assisted by the consul, a thing at which you (plur.) were all wondering. 12. You (sing.) were being overpowered by the enemy, a thing at which no one was wondering.

FIRST CONJUGATION, ACTIVE AND PASSIVE VOICES.

INDICATIVE MOOD, FUTURE TENSE.

161.

1. *Laudābō, laudābis, laudābit; laudābimus, laudābitis, laudābunt.* 2. Sī hōc spērābō,[1] errābō. 3. Tū cōnsulem aliquod[2] bonum (aliquid[2] bonī) flāgitābis. 4. Quod nāvium[3] in eō locō fuerit, armābit. 5. Sī Caesar perfugam condōnābit, eum līberābō. 6. Sī nōs cohortēs omnīs comportābimus, vōs urbem expūgnābitis. 7. Iūs lēgātōrum servō et servābam et servābō. 8. *Laudābor, laudāberis* or *laudābere, laudābitur; laudābimur, laudābiminī, laudābuntur.* 9. Nōs prōditiōnis accūsāmur et Rōmam vocābimur. 10. Tū māgnitūdinem Rōmae mīrābāre (-ris), potestātem ēiusdem mīrāberis (-re). 11. Vōs ā nostrīs legiōnibus iuvābiminī et ā hostibus nōn superābiminī. 12. Illī Rōmam vocābuntur et nōs superābimur. 13. Prōditiōnis accūsābar, id quod omnēs mīrābuntur.

DIRECTION. — Learn A. & G. : [1]**278**, and *b.* [2]**105**, *d* and paradigm. [3]**216**, *a*, 3.
    H. : [1]**470**, 2. [2]**190**, 2, 1), Notes 1 and 2. [3]**397** and 3.

Sing. 1. vo cā'bō
    2. vo cā'bis
    3. vo cā'bit

Plur. 1. vo cā'bi mus
    2. vo cā'bi tis
    3. vo cā'bunt

Sing. 1. vo cā'bor
    2. vo cā'be ris (-re)
    3. vo cā'bi tur

Plur. 1. vo cā'bi mur
    2. vo cā bi'mi nī
    3. vo cā bun'tur

162.

1. I shall summon, you will summon, he will summon; we shall summon, you will summon, they will summon. 2. If I assist the nobility, I shall strengthen the conspiracy. 3. If we bring our legions together, the State will assist us. 4. I shall demand assistance of the State. 5. You (plur.) were protecting and will protect the rights of all the citizens. 6. Some will set the slaves free, others will arm the allies. 7. You (sing.) will encourage the auxiliaries. 8. I shall be summoned, you will be summoned, he will be summoned; we shall be summoned, you will be summoned, they will be summoned. 9. If there is need, I shall wonder at it. 10. If we are conquered, you (plur.) will be accused of treason. 11. If I am set free, you (sing.) will be pardoned. 12. If our forces are brought together, the city will be captured.

FIRST CONJUGATION, ACTIVE AND PASSIVE VOICES.

INDICATIVE MOOD, PERFECT TENSE.

SUGGESTIONS. — 1. The Perfect Stem of *laudō* is *laudāv-*. The tense-sign of the perfect active is **-vi-**. Notice in sentence 1 that the perfect active has certain special personal-endings: Sing. 2, **-stī**; Plur. 2, **-stis**; 3, **-ērunt** or **-ēre**.

2. This tense is translated (1) as a *Perfect Definite*, e.g. *laudāvī, I have praised;* or (2) as a *Historical Perfect*, e.g. *laudāvī, I praised*. Carefully distinguish (2) from *I praised*, meaning *I was praising* and expressed by **laudābam**. Translate perfects in 163 both as historical perfects and perfect definites.

3. The Perfect Passive is a compound tense formed by using the Perfect Passive Participle, e.g. *laudātus, having been praised* (declined like *bonus*), with the present tense of **sum**.

4. *Iuvō* has an irregular perfect, inflected as follows: *iūvī, iūvistī, iūvit; iūvimus, iūvistis, iūvērunt* or *iūvēre*. Its perfect participle is *iūtus*.

163.

1. *Laudāvī, laudāvistī, laudāvit; laudāvimus, laudāvistis, laudāvērunt* or *laudāvēre*. 2. Sī hōc spērāvī, errāvī.ˋ 3. Agrōs Helvētiō-

rum ferrō īgnīque vastāvimus. 4. Timor exercitum occupāvit.
5. Sī vōs exsulēs iūvistis, errātis. 6. Sociī nostrī duo itinera dē-
mōnstrāvērunt (-ēre). 7. Ego hōs mīlitēs, quī urbem servābant,
iūvī, tū eōsdem māgnopere cōnfirmāvistī. 8. *Laudātus* (-*a*) (-*um*)
sum, laudātus (-*a*) (-*um*) *es, laudātus* (-*a*) (-*um*) *est; laudātī* (-*ae*)
(-*a*) *sumus, laudātī* (-*ae*) (-*a*) *estis, laudātī* (-*ae*) (-*a*) *sunt*. 9. Cōnsul laudātus est. Legiō laudāta est. Concilium laudātum est.
10. Iuvenēs iūtī et servātī sunt. Fēminae iūtae et servātae sunt.
Auxilia iūta et servāta sunt. 11. Vōs, quī iūtī estis, in locō
idōneō collocātī estis. 12. Agrī, quī vastābantur, nōn servātī
sunt.

Sing.		Plur.	
1.	vo cā'vī	1.	vo cā'vi mus
2.	vo cā vi'stī	2.	vo cā vi'stis
3.	vo cā'vit	3.	vo cā vē'runt (-re)

Sing.		Plur.	
1.	vo cā'tus sum	1.	vo cā'tī su'mus
2.	vo cā'tus es	2.	vo cā'tī e'stis
3.	vo cā'tus est	3.	vo cā'tī sunt.

164.

1. I (have) summoned, you (have) summoned, he (has) summoned; we (have) summoned, you (have) summoned, they (have)
summoned. 2. If I have assisted the nobility, I have strengthened the conspiracy. 3. We have equipped the ships which you
pointed out. 4. I have assisted the citizens who liberated the
slaves. 5. The fear which took possession of the army has assisted the enemy. 6. You (plur.) have encouraged the enemy,
and they have laid waste our fields. 7. Why did you (sing.)
encourage the enemy? 8. I have been (was) summoned, you
have been (were) summoned, he has been (was) summoned;
we have been (were) summoned, you have been (were) summoned, they have been (were) summoned. 9. If there has been
need, I have wondered at it. 10. You (sing.) have been very
much harassed, if your cities have been laid waste. 11. You
(plur.) have been pardoned, and we have been set free. 12. The
prisoner has been set free, a thing which I have very much
wondered at.

118   A STRAIGHT ROAD TO CAESAR.

FIRST CONJUGATION, ACTIVE AND PASSIVE VOICES.
INDICATIVE MOOD, PLUPERFECT TENSE.

SUGGESTIONS.—1. The Pluperfect Active is formed by connecting the verb-stem and the personal-endings by means of the tense-sign -verā-. Its forms may easily be remembered by thinking of them as made up of the *imperfect tense* of **sum** joined to the *perfect stem ;* e.g. *laudāv*-**eram,** *laudāv*-**erās,** etc.

2. The Pluperfect Passive is formed by using the Perfect Passive Participle with the imperfect tense of **sum** ; e.g. *laudātus* **eram,** *I had been praised.*

165.

1. *Laudāveram, laudāverās, laudāverat; laudāverāmus, laudā-*
• *verātis, laudāverant.*   2. Ego hōc spērāveram sed errābam.
3. Sevēritātem lēgum laudāverātis.   4. Nōs praefectōs saepe cōnfirmāverāmus ; sed eī nōs nunquam iūverant.   5. Cōpiās, quae bonō in populum Rōmānum animō nōn erant, domum vocāverās.
6. Haeduōs frūmentum flāgitāveram.   7. Ōrātor Caesarem mā-gnum appellāverat.   8. *Laudātus (-a) (-um) eram, laudātus (-a)
(-um) erās, laudātus (-a) (-um) erat; laudātī (-ae) (-a) erāmus,
laudātī (-ae) (-a) erātis, laudātī (-ae) (-a) erant.*   9. Cōnsul iūtus erat.   Legiō iūta erat.   Concilium iūtum erat.   10. Iuvenēs vocātī erant.   Fēminae vocātae erant.   Auxilia vocāta erant.   11. Lau-dibus cīvium bonōrum saepe cōnfirmātī erāmus.   12. Ego amīcus populī Rōmānī appellātus eram, tū prōditiōnis accūsātus erās.
13. Vōs, quī vocātī estis, ūnō in locō collocātī erātis.

Sing. 1. vo cā've ram   Plur. 1. vo cā ve rā'mus
      2. vo cā've rās   2. vo cā ve rā'tis
      3. vo cā've rat   3. vo cā've rant

Sing. 1. vo cā'tus e'ram   Plur. 1. vo cā'tī e rā'mus
      2. vo cā'tus e'rās   2. vo cā'tī e rā'tis
      3. vo cā'tus e'rat   3. vo cā'tī e'rant

166.

1. I had summoned, you had summoned, he had summoned; we had summoned, you had summoned, they had summoned.   2. I

had assisted the nobility, but I had not strengthened the conspiracy.   3. The strictness of the laws had especially assisted our cause.   4. You (sing.) had encouraged my friends, and I had protected yours.   5. We laid waste the fields, but you (plur.) had captured the cities of the enemy.   6. How quickly have we conquered the troops which they had brought together!   7. We had prepared for a great war.   8. I had been summoned, you had been summoned, he had been summoned; we had been summoned, you had been summoned, they had been summoned.   9. There has been need, but I had not wondered at it.   10. I had been accused of treason, but you (sing.) had been called a friend of the Roman people.   11. The city had been captured, and the prisoners set free.   12. We had not expected assistance, but you (plur.) had quickly brought together large forces.

FIRST CONJUGATION, ACTIVE AND PASSIVE VOICES.

INDICATIVE MOOD, FUTURE PERFECT TENSE.

SUGGESTIONS. — 1. The tense-sign of the Future Perfect Active is -veri-. Notice that this tense has the perfect stem, and that the remaining part of the verb is inflected like the future of **sum**, except that in Plur. 3, -i- is retained before -nt.

2. This-tense is used with great exactness in Latin; in English, its place is often supplied by the future or even the present tense.

3. The Future Perfect Passive is formed by using the Perfect Passive Participle with the future tense of **sum**; e.g. *laud*ātus erō, *I shall have been praised.*

167.

1. *Laudāverō, laudāveris, laudāverit; laudāverimus, laudāveritis, laudāverint.*   2. Sī hōc spērāverō, errāverō.   3. Facilis tum erit rēs, cum omnēs probāverimus.   4. Nōs tum in salūte erimus, cum in ūnō locō legiōnēs collocāveritis.   5. Ut sociōs iūveris, ita tū laude dīgnus eris.   6. Errābō, sī in hīs locīs cōpiās nōn collocāverō.   7. Ut hīc cīvīs servāverit, ita sē cīvēs servābunt.   8. *Laudātus (-a) (-um) erō, laudātus (-a) (-um) eris, laudātus (-a) (-um)*

erit; laudātī (*-ae*) (*-a*) *erimus, laudātī* (*-ae*) (*-a*) *erilis, laudātī*
(*-ae*) (*-a*) *erunt.* 9. Pōns servātus erit. Urbs iūta erit. Iter
parātum erit. 10. Fīnēs nostrī servātī erunt. 11. Vōs tum fortitūdinem hostium mīrāberis, cum ab illīs superātī eritis. 12. Sī
nōs prōditiōnis accūsātī erimus, amīcī populī Rōmānī nōn appellā-
bimur.

Sing. 1. vo cā've rō   Plur. 1. vo cā ve'rī mus
2. vo cā've ris   2. vo cā ve rī tis
3. vo cā've rit   3. vo cā've rint

Sing. 1. vo cā'tus e'rō   Plur. 1. vo cā'tī e'rī mus
2. vo cā'tus e'ris   2. vo cā'tī e'ri tis
3. vo cā'tus e'rit   3. vo cā'tī e'runt

168.

1. I shall have summoned, you will have summoned, he will
have summoned; we shall have summoued, you will have summoned, they will have summoned. 2. If I assist (shall have
assisted) the nobility, I shall strengthen (shall have strengthened) the conspiracy. 3. When we shall have given the scout
suitable assistance, then will he be more daring. 4. Then will
you (sing.) praise the strictness of the laws, when the nobility
shall have attempted a revolution. 5. If you shall have conquered the nobility, you will liberate Italy from great fear.
6. As you (plur.) shall have brought together great armies, so
will you assist the cause of liberty. 7. As I shall have harassed
the enemy, so will the undertaking be easy. 8. I shall have been
summoned, you will have been summoned, he will have been summoned; we shall have been summoned, you will have been summoned, they will have summoned. 9. If there is (shall have
been) need, I shall wonder at it. 10. The young men will have
been assisted. The troops will have been assisted. The auxiliaries
will have been assisted. 11. As the Mediterranean Sea shall
have been protected, so will our revenues be safe. 12. If we
shall be (shall have been) encouraged by large revenues, I shall
be prepared for war.

FIRST CONJUGATION, ACTIVE AND PASSIVE VOICES.
SUBJUNCTIVE MOOD, PRESENT TENSE.

SUGGESTION.— The Present Subjunctive in both voices changes final -ā- of the verb-stem to -ē-, which becomes -e- before the endings -m, -t, -nt ; -r, -ntur.

169.

1. Sī *laudem,* sī *laudēs,* sī *laudet;* sī *laudēmus,* sī *laudētis,* sī *laudent.* 2. Sī hōc spērem, errem. 3. Sī mē iuvētis, pecūniam multam vōbīs dem. 4. Hīc servōs līberet, sī omnēs probent. 5. Servī sint fidēlēs, sī eōs līberēmus. 6. Sī mīlitēs fortīs dextrō in cornū collocēmus, hostēs nostrōs superēmus. 7. Sī Caesar perfugam condōnet, laetus sim. 8. *Sī lauder, sī laudēris* or *laudēre, sī laudētur; sī laudēmur, sī laudēminī, sī laudentur.* 9. Sī nōs armēmur, vōs nōn superēminī. 10. Sī hostēs superentur, eōs servem.

Sing.	1. vo'cem		Plur.	1. vo cē'mus
	2. vo'cēs			2. vo cē'tis
	3. vo'cet			3. vo'cent
Sing.	1. vo'cer		Plur.	1. vo cē'mur
	2. vo cē'ris (-re)			2. vo cē'mi nī
	3. vo cē'tur			3. vo cen'tur

170.

1. If I should summon, if you should summon, if he should summon; if we should summon, if you should summon, if they should summon. 2. If I should assist the nobility, I should strengthen the conspiracy. 3. If we should assist the nobility, you (plur.) would not approve. 4. If you (sing.) should encourage the exiles, you would go wrong. 5. If Caesar should demand aid of me, I should bring together all our forces. 6. If I should pardon the treachery of Dumnorix, he would be very glad. 7. If they should approve the undertaking, they would not go wrong. 8. If I should be summoned, if you should be summoned, if he should be summoned; if we should be summoned, if you should be summoned, if they should be summoned. 9. If there should

be need, I should wonder at it.   10. If you (sing.) should be prepared for war, the citizens would be delighted.   11. If you (plur.) should be assisted, I should be especially encouraged.   12. If a bad man should be elected consul, we should be greatly harassed.

FIRST CONJUGATION, ACTIVE AND PASSIVE VOICES.
SUBJUNCTIVE MOOD, IMPERFECT TENSE.

SUGGESTION. — The connecting tense-sign of the Imperfect Tense in both voices is -rē-. This becomes -re- before the endings, -m, -t, -nt; -r, -ntur.

171.

1. Sī *laudārem,* sī *laudārēs,* sī *laudāret;* sī *laudārēmus,* sī *laudārētis,* sī *laudārent.*   2. Sī hōc spērārem, errārem.   3. Sī mē auxilium flāgitārētis, legiōnēs fortēs in nostrā urbe collocārem.   4. Sī eōs iuvārēmus, nōbīs pecūniam multam darent.   5. Sī omnēs probārētis, auxilia dextrō in cornū collocārem.   6. Auxilia in sinistrō cornū collocārēmus, sī adessētis.   7. Laetus essem, sī tū cornū dextrum iuvārēs.   8. Sī *laudārer,* sī *laudārēris,* or *laudārēre,* sī *laudārētur;* sī *laudārēmur,* sī *laudārēminī,* sī *laudārentur.*   9. Sī nōs armārēmur, vōs nōn superēminī.   10. Sī tū cōnsul creārēris, ego ā multīs virīs fortibus iuvārer.   11. Omne imperium cōnsulī nostrō nōn darētur, sī nōs ā virīs fortissimīs iuvārēmur.

Sing. 1. vocā'rem	Plur. 1. vocārē'mus
2. vocā'rēs	2. vocārē'tis
3. vocā'ret	3. vocā'rent
Sing. 1. vocā'rer	Plur. 1. vocārē'mur
2. vocārē'ris (-re)	2. vocārē'minī
3. vocārē'tur	3. vocāren'tur

172.

1. If I were summoning, if you were summoning, if he was summoning; if we were summoning, if you were summoning, if they were summoning.   2. If I were assisting the nobility, I should strengthen the conspiracy.   3. If we were liberating the slaves, the populace would not approve.   4. If all were approv-

ing, I should assist the exile. 5. If I were ready, I should set the captives free. 6. We should assist the unfortunate men, if we were present. 7. If I were elected consul, I should strengthen the cause of liberty. 8. If I were summoned, if you were summoned, if he were summoned; if we were summoned, if you were summoned, if they were summoned. 9. If there were need, I should wonder at it. 10. Good men would be encouraged, if you (sing.) were assisted. 11. If we were armed, you (plur.) would not be conquered. 12. If I were summoned, he would be protected.

FIRST CONJUGATION, ACTIVE AND PASSIVE VOICES. SUBJUNCTIVE MOOD, PERFECT AND PLUPERFECT TENSES.

SUGGESTIONS. — 1. The Perfect Subjunctive Active is inflected like the Future Perfect Indicative with this exception, that in Sing. 1 final -i- of the tense-sign is unchanged and the personal-ending -m is retained.

2. The Pluperfect Subjunctive has the tense-sign -vissē-. Its final -ē- becomes -e- before the personal-ending -m, -t, and -nt. The inflection of this tense may easily be remembered by thinking of its forms as made up of the perfect stem, prefixed to the imperfect subjunctive of **sum** with its initial vowel changed from e to i throughout; e.g. *laudāv-***essem** becomes *laudāv-***issem**.

3. The Perfect and Pluperfect Passive are formed by using with the perfect participle the present and imperfect subjunctive of **sum**; e.g. Perfect, *laudā***tus sim**, etc.; Pluperfect, *laudā***tus essem**, etc.

173.

1. (*a*) Sī *laudāverim*, sī *laudāveris*, sī *laudāverit;* sī *laudāverimus*, sī *laudāveritis*, sī *laudāverint.* (*b*) Sī *laudāvissem*, sī *laudāvissēs*, sī *laudāvisset;* sī *laudāvissēmus*, sī *laudāvissētis*, sī *laudāvissent.* 2. (*a*) Sī hōc spērāverim, errem. (*b*) Sī hōc spērāvissem, errāvissem. 3. Sī eam rem ēnūntiāverim, mē graviter accūsēs. 4. Sī cīvēs frūmentum flāgitāvissēmus, id comportāvissent. 5. Sī perfidiam Dumnorigis condōnāvissem, Caesar mē graviter accūsāvisset. 6. Sī eōs iūvissēmus, urbem expūgnāvissent. 7. Sī perfidiam Dumnorigis condōnāvissēs, cōnsilia Caesaris hostibus ēnūntiāvis-

sēs. 8. (a) Sī *laudātus* (-*a*) (-*um*) *sim*, etc. (b) Sī *laudātus* (-*a*) (-*um*) *essem*, etc. 9. Sī lēgātus superātus sit, ego māgnopere mīrer. 10. Sī tū condōnātus essēs, nēmō mīrātus esset. 11. Sī nostrae urbēs vastātae essent, concilium prīncipum convocāvissēmus. 12. Sī nōs ā legiōnibus veterānīs iūtī essēmus, vōs nōn superātī essētīs.

Sing. 1. vo cū've rim   Plur. 1. vo cū ve'ri mus
      2. vo cū've ris   2. vo cū ve'ri tis
      3. vo cū've rit   3. vo cū've rint

Sing. 1. vo cū vis'sem   Plur. 1. vo cū vis sē'mus
      2. vo cū vis'sēs   2. vo cū vis sē'tis
      3. vo cū vis'set   3. vo cū vis'sent

Sing. 1. vo cā'tus sim   Plur. 1. vo cā'tī sī'mus
      2. vo cā'tus sīs   2. vo cā'tī sī'tis
      3. vo cā'tus sit   3. vo cā'ti sint

Sing. 1. vo cā'tus es'sem Plur. 1. vo cā'tī es sē'mus
      2. vo cā'tus es'sēs   2. vo cā'tī es sē'tis
      3. vo cā'tus es'set   3. vo cā'tī es'sent

174.

1. (a) If I should summon (should have summoned), if you should summon, if he should summon; if we should summon, if you should summon, if they should summon. (b) If I had summoned, if you had summoned, if he had summoned; if we had summoned, if you had summoned, if they had summoned. 2. (a) If I should assist (should have assisted) the nobility, I should strengthen the conspiracy. (b) If I had assisted the nobility, I should have strengthened the conspiracy. 3. If you (sing.) should pardon treachery, the consul would severely censure you. 4. If I had revealed your plans, you (sing.) would never have pardoned me. 5. If we had summoned the scout, he would have revealed your plans. 6. If you (sing.) should capture the camp, we all should approve. 7. If the commander had approved, we should have protected the bridge. 8. (a) If I should be summoned, etc. (b) If I had been summoned, etc. 9. (a) If there should be (should have been) need, I should wonder at it. (b) If there had been need, I should have wondered at it.

FIRST CONJUGATION. IMPERATIVES, INFINITIVES.

SUGGESTIONS. — 1. The Imperative endings are as follows : —
ACTIVE VOICE. *Present :* Sing. 2. —, e.g. *parā, prepare (thou, you) ;* Plur.
2. -te, e.g. *parāte, prepare (ye, you).* *Future :* Sing. 2. -tō, e.g. *parātō, you
shall (thou shalt) prepare ;* Sing. 3. -tō, e.g. *parātō, he shall prepare ;* Plur.
2. -tōte, e.g. *parātōte, you (ye) shall prepare ;* Plur. 3. -ntō, e.g. *parantō,
they shall prepare.*
PASSIVE VOICE. *Present :* Sing. 2. -re, e.g. *parāre, be (thou, you) prepared ;* Plur. 2. -minī, e.g. *parāminī, be (you) prepared.* *Future :* Sing. 2.
-tor, e.g. *parātor, you shall (thou shalt) be prepared ;* Sing. 3. -tor, e.g. *parātor, he shall be prepared ;* Plur. 3. -ntor, e.g. *parantor, they shall be prepared.*

2. The Infinitive endings are as follows : —
ACTIVE VOICE. *Present :* -re, e.g. *līberāre, to set free ;* *Perfect :* -visse, e.g.
līberāvisse, to have set free ; *Future :* -tūrus (-tūra, -tūrum) esse, e.g. *lībe-
rātūrus esse, to be about to set free.*
PASSIVE VOICE. *Present :* -rī, e.g. *līberārī, to be set free ;* *Perfect :* -tus (-ta,
-tum) esse, e.g. *līberātus esse, to have been set free ;* *Future :* -tum īrī, e.g.
līberātum īrī, to be about to be set free.

3. In the change to the infinitive mood, after verbs such as **respondet**,
he replies,

a. **Errat** becomes
{ (*Respondet*) **eum errāre.**
{ (*He replies*) *that he is going wrong.*

b. **Errāvit (errābat, errāve·
rat) becomes**
{ (*Respondet*) **eum errāvisse.**
{ (*He replies*) *that he went or has gone (was
going, had gone) wrong.*

c. **Errāverit (errābit, erret,
errāverit) becomes**
{ (*Respondet*) **eum errātūrum esse.**
{ (*He replies*) *that he will have gone (will go,
would go, would have gone) wrong.*

d. **Errāret (errāvisset) becomes**
{ (*Respondet*) **eum errātūrum fuisse.**
{ (*He replies*) *that he was going (had gone)
wrong.*

e. **Mīrātur id** becomes
{ (*Respondet*) **eum id mīrārī.**
{ (*He replies*) *that he wonders at it.*

f. **Mīrātus est id (mīrābātur, mīrātus erat) be-
comes**
{ (*Respondet*) **eum id mīrātum esse.**
{ (*He replies*) *that he (has) wondered, (was
wondering, had wondered) at it.*

175.

1. *Laudā,*[1] *laudāte; laudātō, laudātō, laudātōte, laudantō. Laudāre,*[1] *laudāminī; laudātor, laudātor, laudantor.* 2. *Laudāre. Laudāvisse. Laudātūrus (-tūra, -tūrum) esse. Laudārī. Laudātus (-ta, -tum) esse. Laudātum īrī.* 3. Praeterita[2] Divitiacō frātrī condōnō. Caesar dīcit praeterita sē Divitiacō frātrī condōnāre.[3] 4. Tūtum iter per fīnēs nostrōs dabimus. Respondent sē tūtum iter per fīnēs suōs datūrōs esse.[3] 5. Cīvitātem cōnsuētūdine meā cōnservāvī. Dīcit sē cīvitātem cōnsuētūdine suā cōnservāvisse.[3] 6. Minus dubitātiōnis mihī datur. Caesar respondet sibī minus dubitātiōnis[4] darī. 7. Nostra cōnsilia hostibus sunt ēnūntiāta. Liscus prōpōnit nostra cōnsilia hostibus ēnūntiāta esse.[3]

DIRECTION. — Learn A. & G. : [1]110, *c* ; 112, *c.* [2]188 and Remark. [3]335 ; 336, 1, and 2 first sentence ; 336, A, and NOTE 1 first sentence. [4]216, *a*, 2.

H.: [1]487, 1 and 2 ; Rule XL. [2]441 and 1. [3]522 and 1 ; 523 and 1 ; Rule LIII. I. [4]397 and 3.

IMPERATIVE MOOD.

ACTIVE VOICE.	*Present Tense.*	**PASSIVE VOICE.**
Sing. 2. vo'cā		Sing. 2. vo cā're
Plur. 2. vo cā'te		Plur. 2. vo cā'minī

Future Tense.

Sing. 2 and 3. vo cā'tō		Sing. 2 and 3. vo cā'tor
Plur. 2. vo cā tō'te		Plur. 2. ——
Plur. 3. vo can'tō		Plur. 3. vo can'tor

INFINITIVE MOOD.

ACTIVE VOICE.	*Present Tense.*	**PASSIVE VOICE.**
vo cā're		vo cā'rī

Perfect Tense.

vo cā vis'se		vo cā'tus es'se

Future Tense.

vo cā tū'rus es'se		vo cā'tum ī'rī
		(vo cā'tus fo're)

176. *

1. Summon (thou, you), summon (ye, you); you shall (thou shalt) summon, he shall summon, you (ye) shall summon, they shall summon. Be (thou, you) summoned, be (ye, you) summoned; you shall (thou shalt) be summoned, he shall be summoned, they shall be summoned. 2. To summon. To have summoned. To be about to summon. To be summoned. To have been summoned. To be about to be summoned. 3. We pardon the past for [the sake of] our friend. They say that they pardon the past for [the sake of] their friend. 4. I have given [them] a safe passage through my territory. He replies that he had given [them] a safe passage through his territory. 5. We shall spare the state in accordance with our custom. They say that they will spare the state in accordance with their custom. 6. Less [of] doubt was given to us. They reply that to themselves less [of] doubt was given. 7. Our plans are disclosed to the enemy. Liscus represents that our plans are disclosed to the enemy.

FIRST CONJUGATION. PARTICIPLES, ABLATIVE ABSOLUTE.

SUGGESTIONS. — 1. The following tables show the corresponding Latin and English participles, also the Latin endings: —

ACTIVE VOICE.

LATIN.		ENGLISH.
Pres.	**-ns,** *Probāns.*	*Approving.*
Perf.	——, (*Wanting*).	*Having approved.*
Fut.	**-tūrus,** *Probātūrus.*	(*Wanting.*)

PASSIVE VOICE.

LATIN.		ENGLISH.
Pres.	——, (*Wanting*).	(*Being*) *approved.*
Perf.	**-tus,** *Probātus.*	*Having been approved.*
Fut.	**-ndus,** *Probandus.*	(*Wanting.*)

2. In the declension of *probāns*, -ā- becomes -a- before -nt-. Decline it, using *dīligēns*, Exercise 85, as a model. The other participles are declined like *bonus.*

3. The Present Active, and Perfect Passive, Participles are much used in the construction called the *Ablative Absolute:* thus in the phrase **monte occupātō**, *monte* is in the ablative case, and *occupātō* agrees with it. A. & G., Rules 2 and 64; II., Rules XXXIV. and XXXII. It may be variously translated: e.g. (literally) *the mountain having been occupied;* (by the missing participles) *the mountain being occupied, having occupied the mountain;* (by a clause) *when, (since, as) the mountain had been occupied, when he had occupied the mountain;* (by a phrase) *after occupying the mountain,* etc. So **mē praesente** may be translated (literally, *I being present*), *when I was present; in my presence,* etc.

177.

1. Haec, mē [1] praesente,[1] dīcit. 2. Lēgātus, quī equitātuī praeest, tertium aciem labōrantibus nostrīs subsidiō mittit. 3. Gallia est omnis dīvīsa[2] in partēs trēs. 4. Caesar, suōs cohortātus,[3] proelium committit. 5. Caesar, cum[4] oppidum expūgnāvit, centuriōnēs vehementer incūsat. 6. Dum[4] paucōs diēs ad Vesontiōnem morātur,[5] timor māgnus omnem exercitum occupāvit. 7. Caesar, occupātō[6] oppidō, ibī praesidium conlocat. 8. Hostēs, datō sīgnō, ex omnibus portīs ērumpunt. 9. Obsidibus datīs, Caesar ibī castra pōnit. 10. Ambarrī, dēpopulātīs agrīs, nōn facile ab oppidīs suīs vim hostium prohibent. 11. Datā[7] facultāte,[7] hostēs ab iniūriā nōn temperābunt. 12. Mē[8] invītō,[8] iter per prōvinciam temptāvistis. 13. Orgetorix, M. (Mārcō) Messālā[8] et M. Pīsōne[8] cōnsulibus,[8] coniūrātiōnem nōbilitātis facit.

DIRECTION. — Learn A. & G. : [1] **255** ; Rule 54. [2] **291**, *b*. [3] **135**, *a* and *b* ;
        290, *d*, 1. [4] **290**, *c*. [5] **276**, *e*. [6] **290**,
        d, 2. [7] **310**, *a*. [8] **255**, *a*.
    H. : [1] **431**; Rule XXXII. [2] **471**, 6, Note 1 ;
        550, Note 2. [3] **195**, II. 2; **231**.
        [4] **550**, Note 5. [5] **467**, 4. [6] **550**, Note 4.
        [7] **549**, 2. [8] **431**, 4.

PARTICIPLES.

ACTIVE VOICE, *Pres.* vo'cāns ; *Fut.* vo cā tū'rus.
PASSIVE VOICE, *Perf.* vo cā'tus ; *Fut.* vo can'dus.

	M. F.	N.		M. F.	N.
Sing. Nom.	vo'cāns		Plur. vo can'tēs	vo can'tī a	
Gen.	vo can'tis			vo can'tī um	
Dat.	vo can'tī			vo can'tī bus	
Acc.	vo can'tem	vo'cāns		vo can'tīs (ēs)	vo can'tī a
Voc.	vo'cāns			vo can'tēs	vo can'tī a
Abl.	vo can'tī *or* vo can'te			vo can'tī bus	

Decline *vo cā'tus* and *vo cā tū'rus* like *a mī'cus* and *in i mī'cus*, Exercise 29.

SUGGESTION. — Italicized clauses and phrases below are to be translated by the ablative absolute.

178.

1. He says this *in the presence of many witnesses*. 2. The centurion brings assistance to his struggling soldiers. 3. The hill is occupied by legions which are of service to the rear rank. 4. Caesar, *having encouraged the soldiers*, gives a signal for the fight. 5. *When the enemy have occupied the town*, we shall be in great danger. 6. *While we delay many days on the march*, the enemy capture the town. 7. Caesar, *after occupying the towns of the enemy*, sends his legions into winter [quarters]. 8. Our forces *at a given signal* break forth from camp. 9. *Many hostages having been given*, Caesar leads his army into Gaul by as long marches as possible. 10. *Since the fields have been devastated*, the enemy betake themselves into the forests. 11. *If an opportunity should be given*, the enemy would not refrain from violence. 12. The Helvetii, *against Caesar's will*, attempt a march through the territory of the Sequani. 13. The Helvetii prepare themselves for the journey *in the consulship of L. (Lucius) Piso and A. (Aulus) Gabinius*.

FIRST CONJUGATION. THE GERUNDIVE.

SUGGESTION. — The Future Passive Participle has a peculiar adjective use in which it is known as a *Gerundive*. In the Gerundive construction, such a phrase as *for transporting the legions* takes the Latin form *ad legiōnēs trāns-portandās*, in which *legiōnēs* is the accusative after *ad*, and *trānsportandās* agrees with *legiōnēs*. Notice that the nearest approach to a literal translation of this Latin phrase is the expression *for the about-to-be-transported legions*. THIS CONSTRUCTION IS VERY COMMON.

179.

1. Gallī vītandī¹ aestūs causā² plērumque silvārum āc flūminum propinquitātēs petunt.   2. Gallī subitō proeliī³ renovandī⁴ cōnsilium capiunt.   3. Germānī māgnam nāvium cōpiam ad trānsportandum⁴ exercitum⁵ mīttunt.   4. Caesar C. (Cāium) Trebōnium cum legiōnibus tribus ad eam regiōnem dēpopulandam mīttit. 5. Caesar in hīs locīs nāvium parandārum causā morātur.   6. Tempus rēbus⁶ administrandīs⁴ nōn dabātur.   7. Caesar ad hostīs cōnsectandōs equitātum mīttit.   8. Tempus ad īnsīgnia accommodanda dēfuit.

DIRECTION.— Learn A. & G. : ¹**297**; **298**. ²**245**, *c*. ⁸ Rule 14.   ⁴ Rule 2.
. ⁵**152**. ⁶ Rule 21.
H. : ¹**543** and Note. ²**416** and foot-note 2.
⁸ Rule XVI. ⁴ Rule XXXIV. ⁵**432**;
433. ⁶ Rule XII. I.

THE GERUNDIVE (Fut. Pass. Participle).

	M.	F.	N.
Sing. Nom.	vo can'dus	vo can'da	vo can'dum
Gen.	vo can'dī	vo can'dae	vo can'dī
Dat.	vo can'dō	vo can'dae	vo can'dō
Acc.	vo can'dum	vo can'dam	vo can'dum
Voc.	vo can'de	vo can'da	vo can'dum
Abl.	vo can'dō	vo can'dā	vo can'dō

Complete the plural as suggested by the singular.

180.

1. Caesar chooses the plan of renewing the war.   2. We delay in the province to prepare (for the sake of preparing) an army. 3. The consul sends ships to transport (for transporting) our legions.   4. The consul sends two legions to devastate (for devastating) the fields of the enemy.   5. Time was not given for (dative) putting on our helmets.   6. Caesar sends soldiers to pursue (for pursuing) the deserters.   7. Time is lacking for executing our plans.

FIRST CONJUGATION. THE GERUND.

SUGGESTIONS. — 1. The Gerund is a verbal noun of the second declension, neuter gender. Its plural and nominative singular are wanting, and it is declined as follows : —

Gen. *postulandī, of demanding.* Acc., *postulandum, demanding.*
Dat., *postulandō, to* (or *for*) *demanding.* Abl., *postulandō, by demanding.*

2. Sentences 1, 2, 3, 4, and 5 show the common use of the gerund. When the gerund would have an object, the gerundive construction has preference, but such constructions as those in 6, 7, 8, and 9 are not uncommon. Compare them with sentences 1, 2, 5, and 6 in the preceding exercise.

3. The Supines are verbal nouns of the fourth declension, in the acc. and abl. singular ; e.g. *rogātum, rogātū, to ask.*

4. Notice that gerundives, gerunds, and supines denote a purpose. *The infinitive must not be used in Latin to express a purpose, as in English.*

181.

1. Spēs praedandī[1] studiumque bellandī[2] hostīs ab agricultūrā revocābat. 2. Animus hostium ad dīmicandum[3] parātus est. 3. Germānī in Galliam praedandī causā veniunt. 4. Caesar hostibus potestātem pūgnandī facit. 5. Caesar in hīs locīs legiōnem hiemandī causā conlocat. 6. Gallī vītandī aestum causā plērumque silvārum āc flūminum propinquitātēs petunt. 7. Gallī subitō bellum renovandī cōnsilium capiunt. 8. Caesar in hīs locīs nāvīs parandī causā morātur. 9. Tempus rēs administrandō[4] nōn dabātur. 10. Facultās suī[5] līberandī hostibus nōn datur. 11. Haeduī lēgātōs ad Caesarem mīttunt rogātum[6] auxilium.

DIRECTION. — Learn A. & G.: [1]295. [2]298. [3]300. [4]299 and *a.*
[5]298, *a.* [6]302 ; Rule 66.
H.: [1]541. [2]542 and I. [3]542 and III.
[4]542 and II. [5]542, Note 1. [6]545, and Note 2 ; 546 ; Rule LIX.

THE GERUND.

N. Gen. vo can'dī ; Dat. vo can'dō ; Acc. vo can'dum ; Abl. vo can'dō.

THE SUPINES.

Former Supine, vo cā'tum ; Latter Supine, vo cā'tū.

182.

1. The enemy cross the line to plunder (for the sake of plundering). 2. An opportunity of fighting is given to the enemy. 3. Caesar leads his army into [the country of] the Sequanī to pass (for the sake of passing) the winter. 4. The time is suitable for (ad) renewing the battle. 5. We prepared for (ad) [decisive] fighting. 6. The enemy delay many days for the sake of preparing war. 7. Caesar remains in the same place to avoid (for the sake of avoiding) danger. 8. The enemy have an opportunity of freeing themselves. 9. Ambassadors are sent to Caesar to ask aid.

PRINCIPAL PARTS.

Verbs which, like **laudō**, have -ā- before -re in the present infinitive (*lau-dā-re*) are of the First Conjugation. To inflect a verb throughout it is necessary to know (1) to what conjugation it belongs, and (2) its three stems. The Principal Parts of a verb are therefore : —

1. The *Present Indicative*, showing the *present stem*.
2. The *Perfect Indicative*, showing the *perfect stem*.
3. The *Supine* or *Perfect Participle*, showing the *supine stem*.
4. The *Present Infinitive*, showing the *conjugation*.

Thus, *laudō, laudāvī, laudātum, laudāre*.

Learn, from the Vocabulary, the principal parts of the following verbs of the first conjugation: *appellō, armō, collocō, comportō, condōnō, cōnfirmō, convocō, creō, dēlectō, dēmōnstrō, ēnūntiō, errō, exīstimō, expūgnō, flāgitō, imperō, laudō, līberō, occupō, oppūgnō, parō, postulō, probō, pūgnō, servō, spērō, superō, temptō, vastō, vexō, vocō;* and of the irregular verbs *dō, iuvō.* Repeat these till they are mastered.

Sum is an irregular verb. Its principal parts are *sum, fuī, futūrus, esse.*

SYNOPSES.

Give synopses of the above verbs, in all persons, throughout both voices.

SECOND CONJUGATION, ACTIVE AND PASSIVE VOICES, INDICATIVE MOOD. TENSES WITH PRESENT STEM.

SUGGESTIONS. — 1. Verb-stems of the Second Conjugation end in -ē-; e.g. *monē-* (stem of *moneō, I warn*), *verē-* (stem of *vereor, I fear*). Notice that in the forms *moneō* and *vereor*, -ē- is shortened and retained before -ō and -or ; otherwise the changes of -ē- correspond to those of final -ā- in verb-stems of the first conjugation.

2. The paradigms begun in sentence 1 in this and the following Latin Exercises, are to be completed, compared with A. & G. 130, pp. 96 ff., or II. 207, pp. 90 ff., and translated. Sentences 2 and 3 may be developed in the various tenses for practice in verb inflection. For the synopsis of *vereor*, see A. & G. 135, II.

183.

1. *Moneō. Monēbam. Monēbō. Moneor. Monēbar. Monēbor.*
2. Sī collem teneō, hostīs pābulātiōne prohibeō. 3. Sī hostīs vereor, amīcus populī Rōmānī nōn habeor. 4. Nātiōnēs multae ea, quae ad effēminandōs animōs [1] pertinent, important. 5. Caesar aliās cīvitātēs territandō,[2] aliās cohortandō,[2] in officiō tenēbat. 6. Lēgātus, quī locī nātūrā continētur, mūnītiōne prohibēbitur. 7. In castrīs remanēbāmus, quod [3] (*because*) mīlitēs paucōs habēbātis. 8. In Italiā remanēbimus, quod īnsuētī nāvigandī [4] mare timēmus. 9. Inopia frūmentī est, quod agricultūrā prohibēmur. 10. Caesar inopiam verēbātur, quod Germānī agricultūrae nōn student. 11. Vim hostium ab oppidō nōn prohibēbam, quod nostrae nāvēs tempestātibus dētinēbantur. 12. Hostēs oppidō remanēbunt, quod pābulātiōne prohibentur. 13. Monte occupātō, hostīs nōn verēbimur. 14. Hostīs videō, et mihī [5] parātī ad pūgnandum nōn videntur.

DIRECTION. — Learn A. & G.: [1] 296 ; 300 and NOTE. [2] 301 (1). [3] 321 ; Rule 77, first clause. [4] Rule 18. [5] 232, c.

    H.: [1] 543 ; 544, I. [2] 542 and IV. [3] 516, I. ; Rule XLVII. I. [4] Rule XVII. [5] 384, I. ; Rule XII. I.

VIdeō, *I see* (Passive, *I seem*).

ACTIVE VOICE, INDICATIVE MOOD.

PRESENT TENSE.

Sing. 1. vi'deō   Plur. 1. videʹmus
   2. vi'dēs   2. videʹtis
   3. vi'det   3. vi'dent

IMPERFECT TENSE.

Sing. 1. vidē'bam   Plur. 1. vidē bā'mus
2. vidē'bās   2. vidē bā'tis
3. vidē'bat   3. vidē'bant

FUTURE TENSE.

Sing. 1. vidē'bō   Plur. 1. vidē'bi mus
2. vidē'bis   2. vidē'bi tis
3. vidē'bit   3. vidē'bunt

PASSIVE VOICE, INDICATIVE MOOD.

PRESENT TENSE.

Sing. 1. vi'de or   Plur. 1. vidē'mur
2. vidē'ris (-re)   2. vidē'mi nī
3. vidē'tur   3. viden'tur

IMPERFECT TENSE.

Sing. 1. vidē'bar   Plur. 1. vidē bā'mur
2. vidē bā'ris (-re)   2. vidē bā'mi nī
3. vidē bā'tur   3. vidē ban'tur

FUTURE TENSE.

Sing. 1. vidē'bor   Plur. 1. vidē'bi mur
2. vidē'be ris (-re)   2. vidē bi'mi nī
3. vidē'bi tur   3. vidē bun'tur

184.

1. I see. I was seeing. I shall see. I seem. I seemed. I shall
seem. 2. If you (sing.) remain in the army, the enemy will be
kept from our territory. 3. Many things tend to enfeeble our
minds. 4. You (sing.) are hemmed in by very rugged mountains. 5. The mountains will be held by our forces. 6. You
(plur.) will keep the enemy from foraging and from fortifying.
7. I shall not remain at home, because I am afraid of danger.
8. All the Helvetii were desiring a revolution. 9. You (sing.)
were detained at home by a storm. 10. We were kept from
foraging, because the enemy were in sight. 11. If an opportunity of fighting is given (abl. abs.), I shall not be afraid of
the enemy. 12. The victor seems to me worthy of all honor.

SECOND CONJUGATION, ACTIVE AND PASSIVE VOICES.
REMAINING TENSES OF THE INDICATIVE MOOD.

SUGGESTIONS. — 1. The perfect stem of *moneō* is *monu-*. The active tense-signs are as follows: perf., *-uī*; pluperf., *-uerā-*; fut. perf., *-ueri-*. The tenses of the passive voice are formed as in the first conjugation.

2. The following have irregular perfects, and perfect participles; *remaneō*, perf., *remānsī*, perf. part. wanting; *persuādeō*, perf., *persuāsī*, perf. part., *persuāsus*; *faveō*, perf., *fāvī*, perf. part. wanting; *removeō*, perf., *removī*, perf. part., *remōtus*; *respondeō*, perf., *respondī*, perf. part., *respōnsus*; *videō*, perf., *vidī*, perf. part., *vīsus*. The principal parts of *audeō* (semi-deponent, see A. & G. **136**; H. **268**, 3) are *audeō, ausus sum, audēre*.

185.

1. *Monuī. Monueram. Monuerō. Monitus (-a) (-um) sum. Monitus (-a) (-um) eram. Monitus (-a) (-um) erō.* 2. Sī collem tenuī, hostīs pābulātiōne prohibuī. 3. Sī hostīs veritus sum, amīcus populī Rōmānī nōn habitus sum. 4. Nostrīs persuāsī, et ī castra hostium oppūgnāre [1] ausī sunt. 5. Helvētiīs propter adfīnitātem fāverās. 6. Lēgibus paruerāmus et novīs rēbus nōn studuimus. 7. Sī equōs ex cōnspectū remōverimus, timidī vidēbimur. 8. Neque equōs ex cōnspectū remōvimus neque timidī vīsī sumus. 9. Sī in castrīs remānseris, timidus vidēberis. 10. Sī mūnītiōne prohibitī erimus, hostīs māgnō opere verēbimur. 11. Praefectus territus est quod commeātū prohibitus erat. 12. Nōs multōs diēs iter morāmur [2] quod commeātū prohibitī erāmus. 13. Castra commeātūs parandī (commeātum parandī) causā remōta erant. 14. Hostēs, datā facultāte, castra sex passuum mīlia ab oppidō remōverant.

DIRECTION. — Learn A. & G.: [1]**271**; Rule 59. [2]**276**, *a* and NOTE 1, first sentence.

H.: [1]**533**, and I. 1 and 2; Rule LVI. [2]**467**, III. 2.

ACTIVE VOICE, INDICATIVE MOOD.

PERFECT TENSE.

	Sing.		Plur.	
1.	vī'dī	1.	vī'dimus	
2.	vī di'stī	2.	vī di'stis	
3.	vī'dit	3.	vī dē'runt (-re)	

PLUPERFECT TENSE.

Sing. 1. vī'de ram   Plur. 1. vī de rā'mus
2. vī'de rās   2. vī de rā'tis
3. vī'de rat   3. vī'de rant

FUTURE PERFECT TENSE.

Sing. 1. vī'de rō   Plur. 1. vī de'ri mus
2. vī'de ris   2. vī de'ri tis
3. vī'de rit   3. vī'de rint

PASSIVE VOICE, INDICATIVE MOOD.

PERFECT TENSE.

Sing. 1. vī'sus sum   Plur. 1. vī'sī su'mus
2. vī'sus es   2. vī'sī e'stis
3. vī'sus est   3. vī'sī sunt

PLUPERFECT TENSE.

Sing. 1. vī'sus e'ram   Plur. 1. vī'sī e rā'mus
2. vī'sus e'rās   2. vī'sī e rā'tis
3. vī'sus e'rat   3. vī'sī e'rant

FUTURE PERFECT TENSE.

Sing. 1. vī'sus e'rō   Plur. 1. vī'sī e'ri mus
2. vī'sus e'ris   2. vī'sī e'ri tis
3. vī'sus e'rit   3. vī'sī e'runt

186.

1. I saw (have seen). I had seen. I shall have seen. I seemed. I had seemed. I shall have seemed. 2. You (sing.) had persuaded the legions, and they have dared to storm the enemy's camp. 3. You (sing.) have favored the Helvetii on account of relationship. 4. You (plur.) had not obeyed the laws, and you (plur.) have desired a revolution. 5. They will have seemed cowardly, if they shall have removed the horses out of sight. 6. Neither had they seemed cowardly, nor had they removed the horses. 7. They have been regarded [as] brave because they have not seemed cowardly. 8. If I shall have been kept from foraging, I shall greatly fear hunger. 9. I

had feared greatly, because I had been kept from supplies.
10. I have delayed (pres.) in town many days, because I have
been kept from fortifying. 11. The fields having been devastated,
I have had no supplies. 12. Our allies have remained in camp
for the sake of avoiding danger.

SECOND CONJUGATION, ACTIVE AND PASSIVE VOICES, SUBJUNCTIVE MOOD. SEQUENCE OF TENSES. CLAUSES OF PURE PURPOSE.

SUGGESTIONS. — 1. Notice that, in the present subjunctive, final -ē- of the verb-stem becomes -eā-, which is shortened to -ea- before -m, -t, -nt; -r and -ntur.

2. The sentence **remaneō, ut laudem et moneam**, may be variously translated; e.g. *I remain*

    (a) *that (in order that) I may praise and warn;*
    (b) *to (in order to) praise and warn;*
    (c) *for the purpose of praising and warning.*

The sentence **remanēbam ut laudārem et monērem** is similarly translated, using *might* for *may* if form (a) is employed.

The ut-clauses in these sentences, also those in 4 to 10, are called *Clauses of Pure Purpose*. The singular of the verbs in these sentences should be inflected in place.

3. *When the verb of a subordinate clause is in the subjunctive, the tense to be used is determined by a preceding verb with which the clause is connected;* thus in suggestion 2, above, **remaneō**, *present indicative*, is followed by **laudem** and **moneam**, *present subjunctives;* **remanēbam**, *imperfect indicative*, by **laudārem** and **monērem**, *imperfect subjunctives*. This principle is called *Sequence of Tenses.*

187.

1. *Sī moneam. Sī monērem. Sī monuerim. Sī monuissem. Sī monear. Sī monērer. Sī monitus (-a) (-um) sim. Sī monitus (-a) (-um) essem.* 2. Sī collem teneam, hostīs pābulātiōne prohibeam. 3. Sī hostīs verear, amīcus populī Rōmānī nōn habear. 4. Remaneō[1] (remanēbō, remānserō) ut[2] laudem[3] et moneam. 5. Remānsī[4] ut laudem et moneam. 6. Remānsī (remanēbam,

138   A STRAIGHT ROAD TO CAESAR.

remānseram) ut laudārem et monērem. 7. Castra removeō (removēbō, removerō) ut timōris suspiciōnem vītem. 8. Castra removēbam (removī, removeram) ut timōris suspiciōnem vītārem. 9. Legiōnem in hīs locīs collocō (collocābō, collocāverō) nē pābulātiōne prohibear. 10. Legiōnem in hīs locīs collocāveram (collocābam, collocāvī) nē pābulātiōne prohibērer.

DIRECTION. — Learn A. & G.: [1]**285**, 1 and 2. [2]**317** and 1; Rule 74. [3]**286**, also Note and Remark, Rule 62. [4]**287**, *a*.

II.: [1]**198**, I. 1, 2, 3, and 4, II. 1, 2, and 3; **490**; **491**. [2]**497**, II. ; Rule XLII. II. [3]**491**; Rule XLI. [4]**495**, I. ; **492**, 2, Note 1.

ACTIVE VOICE, SUBJUNCTIVE MOOD.

PRESENT TENSE.

Sing. 1. vi'de am
2. vi'de ās
3. vi'de at

Plur. 1. vi de ā'mus
2. vi de ā'tis
3. vi'de ant

IMPERFECT TENSE.

Sing. 1. vi dē'rem
2. vi dē'rēs
3. vi dē'ret

Plur. 1. vi dē rē'mus
2. vi dē rē'tis
3. vi dē'rent

PERFECT TENSE.

Sing. 1. vī'de rim
2. vī'de ris
3. vī'de rit

Plur. 1. vī de'ri mus
2. vī de'ri tis
3. vī'de rint

PLUPERFECT TENSE.

Sing. 1. vī dis'sem
2. vī dis'sēs
3. vī dis'set

Plur. 1. vī dis sē'mus
2. vī dis sē'tis
3. vī dis'sent

PASSIVE VOICE, SUBJUNCTIVE MOOD.

PRESENT TENSE.

Sing. 1. vi'de ar   Plur. 1. vi de ā'mur
2. vi de ā'ris (-re)   2. vi de ā'mi nī
3. vi de ā'tur   3. vi de an'tur

IMPERFECT TENSE.

Sing. 1. vi dē'rer   Plur. 1. vi dē rē'mur
2. vi dē rē'ris (-re)   2. vi dē rē'mi nī
3. vi dē rē'tur   3. vi dē ren'tur

PERFECT TENSE.

Sing. 1. vī'sus sim   Plur. 1. vī'sī sī'mus
2. vī'sus sīs   2. vī'sī sī'tis
3. vī'sus sit   3. vī'sī sint

PLUPERFECT TENSE.

Sing. 1. vī'sus es'sem   Plur. 1. vī'sī es sē'mus
2. vī'sus es'sēs   2. vī'sī es sē'tis
3. vī'sus es'set   3. vī'sī es'sent

SUGGESTION. — Sentences 2 to 8 inclusive may be inflected in the plural, in both English and Latin. Watch carefully the sequence of tenses, and use nē to express a negative purpose, not ut nōn.

188.

1. If I should see. If I were seeing. If I should see (should have seen). If I had seen. If I should seem. If I were seeming. If I should seem (should have seemed). If I had seemed. 2. We remain (shall remain, shall have remained) that we may praise and warn. 3. We remained (were remaining, have remained, had remained) to praise and warn. 4. We shall move (are moving, shall have moved) camp in order to avoid suspicion of fear. 5. We were moving (moved, have moved, had moved) camp that we might avoid suspicion of fear. 6. We shall have located (are locating, shall locate) a legion in these places that

we may not be kept from foraging. 7. We had located (were locating, located, have located) a legion in these places lest we should be kept from foraging.

PURPOSE CLAUSES, RELATIVE AND SUBSTANTIVE. ABRIDGED CONDITIONS. SEQUENCE OF TENSES.

SUGGESTIONS. — 1. Sentences 1 and 2 are *Relative Clauses of Purpose.* Sentences 3 to 8 inclusive are *Substantive Clauses of Purpose.* Sentences 9 to 12 inclusive are *Abridged Conditional Sentences.*

2. Translate **quō** in 2 like **ut**; **ut** after adverb of *fearing*, e.g. 7, below, *that not;* **nē**, 8, *that* or *lest.* Translate **adsit** and **adesset**, 9 and 11, *were here;* **adfuerit** and **adfuisset**, 10 and 12, *had been here.* The Latin treats such conditions as *Conditions Less Vivid,* the English as *Suppositions Contrary to Fact.* Translate **operam dederant**, 6, *had taken pains.*

3. *Purpose clauses as a rule use only the present and imperfect subjunctive.*

189.

1. Caesar equitēs habet quī[1] impetum hostium sustineat.[1] 2. Cōnsul lēgātō legiōnem dedit quō[2] impetum Gallōrum sustinēret.[2] 3. Caesar tribūnīs mīlitum imperābit ut[3] equitēs pūgnā prohibeant.[3] 4. Exsulēs ōrant ut sē iuvētis. 5. Caesar huic reī studēbit ut[4] ad urbem cum imperātōre remaneās.[4] 6. Lēgātī operam dederant ut[5] custōdēs quam māximē amīcōs habērent.[5] 7. Timēmus ut[6] (nē nōn) satis praesidī habeās.[6] 8. Timēbant nē[6] hostēs exercitum māgnum habērent.[6] 9. Horreō (horrēbō, horruī, horruerō) velut sī Ariovistus adsit. 10. Horreō (horrēbō, horruī, horruerō) velut sī Ariovistus adfuerit. 11. Horrēbam (horruī, horrueram) velut sī Ariovistus adesset. 12. Horrēbam (horruī, horrueram) velut sī Ariovistus adfuisset.

DIRECTION. — Learn A. & G.: [1]317 and 2; Rule 74. [2]317, *b* and Note 2. [3]331. [4]331 and *b.* [5]331, *e*, 1. [6]331, *f* and Note.

H.: [1]497, I.; Rule XLII. I. [2]497, II. 2, first sentence. [3,4]498 and I. [5]498 and II. [6]498, III. and Note 1.

190.

1. We had cavalry to (quī) sustain the attack of the enemy. 2. The consul gives the lieutenant a legion in order that (quō) he may sustain the attack of the Gauls. 3. Caesar was commanding us that we keep the cavalry from battle. 4. The wounded men were entreating us to assist them (that we assist them). 5. We desire this thing, that you remain near town with auxiliaries. 6. I shall take care that you have as friendly companions as possible. 7. We shall fear that you will not have sufficient protection. 8. The enemy were fearing that we had had a large army. 9. We shall shudder (shudder, have shuddered, shall have shuddered) as if Ariovistus were here. 10. We shall have shuddered (shall shudder, shudder, have shuddered) as if Ariovistus had been here. 11. We had shuddered (were shuddering, shuddered) as if Ariovistus were here. 12. We had shuddered (were shuddering, shuddered) as if Ariovistus had been here.

SECOND CONJUGATION, BOTH VOICES, IMPERATIVE AND INFINITIVE MOODS, PARTICIPLES, GERUNDS AND SUPINES.

SUGGESTIONS. — 1. The Imperatives, Infinitives, Participles, Gerund, and Supines of this conjugation are formed by joining the endings already given (Exercise 175) to the proper stem.

2. The table below exhibits the use of the infinitive when the apodoses of the Latin sentences numbered 2 and 3 from Exercises 183 to 187 are made dependent on any past tense of a verb of *Saying, Thinking, Telling, Perceiving.*

a. **Prohibēmus hostīs,** etc., becomes { (*Respondērunt*) **eōs hostīs prohibēre,** etc.
{ (*They replied*) *that they were keeping,* etc.

b. **Prohibuimus hostīs,** etc., becomes { (*Respondērunt*) **eōs hostīs prohibuisse,** etc.
{ (*They replied*) *that they had kept,* etc.

c. **Prohibēbimus hostīs, etc., becomes**
{ (*Respondērunt*) **eōs hostīs prohibiturōs esse, etc.**
((*They replied*) *that they would keep, etc.*

d. **Prohibērēmus hostīs, etc., becomes**
{ (*Respondērunt*) **eōs hostīs prohibitūrōs fuisse, etc.**
((*They replied*) *that they would have kept, etc.*

e. **Habēmur, etc., becomes**
{ (*Respondērunt*) **eōs habērī, etc.**
((*They replied*) *that they were considered, etc.*

f. **Habitī sumus, etc., becomes**
{ (*Respondērunt*) **eōs habitōs esse, etc.**
((*They replied*) *that they had been considered, etc.*

191.

1. *Monē. Monētō. Monēre. Monētor.* 2. *Monēre, monuisse, monitūrus (-tūra)· (-tūrum) esse ; monērī, monitus (-ta) (-tum) esse, monitum īrī.* 3. Ego eās rēs memoriā teneō. Caesar dīcit sēsē[1] eās rēs memoriā tenēre. 4. Ob eam causam tacuī. Liscus prōpōnit sēsē ob eam causam tacuisse. 5. Amōre frāternō commoveor. Divitiacus dīcit sē amōre frāternō commovērī. 6. Ego obsidibus nōn tenēbar. Divitiacus respondit sē obsidibus nōn tentum esse. 7. Fuga Gallōrum nōs nōn movēbit. Respondērunt fugam Gallōrum sē nōn mōtūram esse. 8. Nostrī, in castrīs manentēs,[2] hostīs nōn verentur. 9. Dumnorix summam in spem per Helvētiōs regnī obtinendī venit. 10. Cupiditās haec habendī nostrōs cōnfirmāvit. 11. Vultus barbarōrum nostrīs nōn erat facilis vīsū.[3]

Direction. — Learn A. & G.: [1]336, I. and I. *a*, 1. [2]292. [3]303 and Remark; Rule 67.

H.: [1]523, I.; Rule LIII. I. [2]549, 2 and 4. [3]547 and 2, first sentence; Rule LX.

IMPERATIVE MOOD.

ACTIVE VOICE.	*Present Tense.*	PASSIVE VOICE.
Sing. 2. vi'dē		Sing. 2. vi dē're
Plur. 2. vi dē'te		Plur. 2. vi dē'mi nī

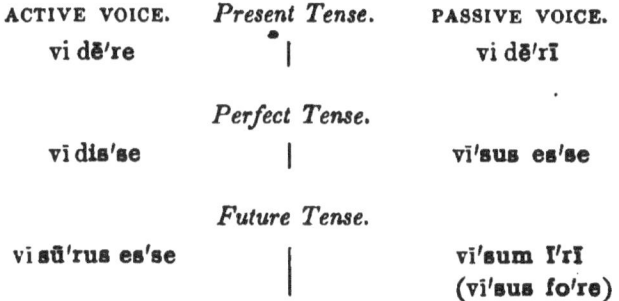

Future Tense.

Sing. 2 and 3. vi dē'tō

Plur. 2. vi dē tō'te

Plur. 3. vi den'tō

Sing. 2 and 3. vi dē'tor

Plur. 2. ——

Plur. 3. vi den'tor

INFINITIVE MOOD.

ACTIVE VOICE.   *Present Tense.*   PASSIVE VOICE.

vi dē're | vi dē'rī

Perfect Tense.

vī dis'se | vī'sus es'se

Future Tense.

vi sū'rus es'se | vī'sum ī'rī

(vī'sus fo're)

PARTICIPLES.

ACTIVE VOICE, *Present*, vi'dēns; *Future*, vī sū'rus.

PASSIVE VOICE, *Perfect*, vī'sus; *Future*, vi den'dus (Gerundive).

Decline *vi'dēns* like *po'tēns*, Exercise 85; the other participles as suggested by Exercises 177 and 179.

THE GERUND AND SUPINES.

N. Gen. vi den'dī, Dat. vi den'dō, Acc. vi den'dum, Abl. vi den'dō. Former Supine, vī'sum; Latter Supine, vī'sū.

192.

1. See (thou, you). See (ye, you). Seem (do thou, you). Seem (do ye, you). 2. To see. To have seen. To be about to see. To seem. To have seemed. To be about to seem. 3. We hold our friends in memory. They say that they are holding their friends in memory. 4. We shall be silent for a good reason. They represent that they will be silent for a good reason. 5. He had been influenced by fraternal love. 6. Divitiacus says that he had been influenced by fraternal love. We are not bound (held) by hostages. They reply that they are not bound by

hostages. 7. The flight of the Gauls has not moved us. They replied that the flight of the Gauls had not disturbed (moved) them. 8. While remaining in camp, I shall not fear the enemy. 9. I have the greatest hope (have come into the greatest hope) of obtaining assistance (gerundive). 10. I have the greatest hope of obtaining assistance (gerund). 11. The expression-of-the-countenance is not always pleasant (easy to see).

•

RESULT CLAUSES.

SUGGESTIONS. — 1. Sentences 1 and 2 are *Pure Clauses of Result*; sentence 3 is a *Relative Clause of Result.* Translate **quī (ut is)**, 3, *that he;* **quīn (quī nōn)**, 4, *that not* or *but that;* **quōminus (ut eō minus**, *that the less by this*) **pārēret**, 5, *from obeying.* Sentences 6, 7, and 8 are *Clauses of Characteristic.*

2. *Result and Characteristic Clauses take all tenses of the subjunctive.*

3. Teachers will note remark in Preface, page vii., at middle.

193.

1. Tantus[1] timor omnēs occupāvit, ut[1] nostrī in castrīs remanērent.[1] 2. Sīc fortūna versat ut alter alterī inimīcus auxiliō salūtīque sit. 3. Nēmō est tam clārus quī[2] honōribus māiōribus nōn studuerit.[3] 4. Nēmō ad bellum tam parātus erat quīn[4] pācis cupidus esset. 5. Mors cōnsulem clārissimum nōn dēterrēbat quōminus[5] lēgibus pārēret. 6. Sunt quī[6] cīvitātī fidēlēs sint. 7. Quis est quī[6] nōn gaudeat? 8. Tū es sōlus quī[7] nōn gāvīsus sīs. 9. Dīgnus est quī[8] imperet.

DIRECTION. — Learn A. & G.: [1]319 and 1, also 3, Remark. [2]319 and 2. [3]287, *b.* [4]319, *d.* [5]319, *c*; Rule 75. [6]320 and *a.* [7]320, *b.* [8]320, *f*; Rule 76.

II.: [1]500, II. and Note 1; Rule XLIII. II. [2]500, and I.; Rule XLIII. I. [3]492, 1 and 2. [4]504 and I. [5]505, II. 1. [6]503, I. [7]503, II. 1. [8]503, II. 2.

194.

1. So great terror seizes all, that our [forces] remain in camp. 2. Fortune so turned that one rival assisted and protected the other (was to the other for assistance and safety). 3. No one was so illustrious that he [did] not (who would not) desire greater honors. 4. No one is so ready for war but that he is desirous of peace. 5. Death [does] not hinder the illustrious consul from obeying (the less by which he should obey) the laws. 6. There were those who had been faithful to the state. 7. Who was [there] that had not rejoiced? 8. We were the only [persons] who did not rejoice. 9. You (plur.) were worthy to command (who should command).

PRINCIPAL PARTS AND SYNOPSES.

At this point write and give orally the principal parts and synopses of all verbs of the second conjugation, thus far used. See Principal Parts, page 132.

THIRD CONJUGATION, BOTH VOICES, INDICATIVE MOOD, TENSES WITH PRESENT STEM.

SUGGESTIONS. — 1. Verb-stems of the Third Conjugation end in -e-; e.g. *tege-* (stem of *tegō, I conceal*), *seque-* (stem of the deponent *sequor, I follow*). Learn the inflection of *tegō* in A. & G., pp. 98 and 99, or of *regō* in H., pp. 94 ff.

2. Sentence 1 in 195, 197, 199, may be developed in the common conditional forms.

195.

1. Sī hostīs sequor, eōs vincō. 2. Silva māgna hostīs tegit. 3. Duās legiōnēs in citeriōre Galliā cōnscrībēbam. 4. Oppida nostra omnia, vīcōs, reliqua prīvāta aedificia incendēs. 5. Gallī cum Germānīs bella multa gerēbant. 6. Multōs annōs[1] dē potentātū contendēmus. 7. Num Dumnorigī[2] custōdēs pōnitis? 8. Ego Caesarem ex urbe amīcitiae causā sequor. 9. Tū fīnibus patriīs expellēbāris (-re). 10. Galliā pācātā, noster exercitus in

Britanniam mīttētur. 11. Nōs ad oppidum expūgnandum dēligimur. 12. Alacritāte[3] māgnā et studiō ūtēminī. 13. Eō itinere vix singulī carrī dūcēbantur.

DIRECTION. — Learn A. & G.: [1]256; Rule 55. [2]225; Rule 21.
[3]249; Rule 49.
II.: [1]379; Rule IX. [2]384, II.; Rule XII.
II. [3]421, I.; Rule XXVI. I.

Pōnō, *I place* (Passive, *I am placed*).

ACTIVE VOICE, INDICATIVE MOOD.

PRESENT TENSE.

Sing.		Plur.	
1.	pō'nō	1.	pō'ni mus
2.	pō'nis	2.	pō'ni tis
3.	pō'nit	3.	pō'nunt

IMPERFECT TENSE.

Sing.		Plur.	
1.	pō nē'bam	1.	pō nē bā'mus
2.	pō nē'bās	2.	pō nē bā'tis
3.	pō nē'bat	3.	pō nē'bant

FUTURE TENSE.

Sing.		Plur.	
1.	pō'nam	1.	pō nē'mus
2.	pō'nēs	2.	pō nē'tis
3.	pō'net	3.	pō'nent

PASSIVE VOICE, INDICATIVE MOOD.

PRESENT TENSE.

Sing.		Plur.	
1.	pō'nor	1.	pō ni mur
2.	pō'ne ris (-re)	2.	pō ni'mi nī
3.	pō'ni tur	3.	pō nun'tur

IMPERFECT TENSE.

Sing.		Plur.	
1.	pō nē'bar	1.	pō nē bā'mur
2.	pō nē bā'ris (-re)	2.	pō nē bā'mi nī
3.	pō nē bā'tur	3.	pō nē ban'tur

FUTURE TENSE.

Sing. 1. pō'nar   Plur. 1. pō në'mur
     2. pō në'ris (-re)   2. pō në'mi nī
     3. pō në'tur   3. pō nen'tur

196.

1. I shall place a guard over Dumnorix. 2. You (sing.) will contend many days for the chief command. 3. He is waging war˙with the Gauls. 4. By this route we draw our wagons with difficulty, one by one. 5. Will you (plur.) not select the tenth legion for capturing the stronghold? 6. They were driving us out from our ancestral territory. 7. You (sing.) were concealed by large forests. 8. I shall employ great activity. 9. A new legion was being enrolled in Hither Gaul. 10. We are following Caesar for friendship's sake. 11. Our villages were all being burned. 12. You (plur.) will be sent into Britain when Gaul is subdued.

THIRD CONJUGATION, BOTH VOICES, INDICATIVE MOOD, REMAINING TENSES.

197.

1. Sī hostīs secūtus sum, eōs vīcī. 2. Caesar suōs cohortātus,[1] proelium commīsit. 3. Helvētiī in servitūtem līberōs Haeduōrum abdūxērunt. 4. Locum idōneum castrīs dēlēgerāmus. 5. Summum montis iugum ascendī. 6. Vīrōs multōs et fortissimōs ēdūxerās. 7. Tertiam Galliae partem incolueritis. 8. Multitūdō Germānōrum trāns Rhēnum trānsdūcta est. 9. Nōs ad flūmen hiemandī causā collocātī sumus. 10. Studiō māgnō et alacritāte ad hostīs cōnsectandōs ūsus eram. 11. Tū Dumnorigī custōdem positus eris. 12. Helvētiī cum omnibus carrīs secūtī erant. 13. Vōs cum legiōne decimā cōnscrīptī eritis.

DIRECTION. — Learn A. & G.: [1]111, b; 135, a and b.
           H.: [1]195, II. 2, and foot-note, first sentence.

ACTIVE VOICE, INDICATIVE MOOD.

PERFECT TENSE.

Sing. 1. po'su ī   Plur. 1. po su'i mus
      2. po su i'stī   2. po su i'stis
      3. po'su it   3. po su ē'runt (-re)

PLUPERFECT TENSE.

Sing. 1. po su'e ram   Plur. 1. po su e rā'mus
      2. po su'e rās   2. po su e rā'tis
      3. po su'e rat   3. po su'e rant

FUTURE PERFECT TENSE.

Sing. 1. po su'e rō   Plur. 1. po su e'ri mus
      2. po su'e ris   2. po su e'ri tis
      3. po su'e rit   3. po su'e rint

PASSIVE VOICE, INDICATIVE MOOD.

PERFECT TENSE.

Sing. 1. po'si tus sum   Plur. 1. po'si tī su'mus
      2. po'si tus es   2. po'si tī e'stis
      3. po'si tus est   3. po'si tī sunt

PLUPERFECT TENSE.

Sing. 1. po'si tus e'ram   Plur. 1. po'si tī e rā'mus
      2. po'si tus e'rās   2. po'si tī e rā'tis
      3. po'si tus e'rat   3. po'si tī e'rant

FUTURE PERFECT TENSE.

Sing. 1. po'si tus e'rō   Plur. 1. po'si tī e'ri mus
      2. po'si tus e'ris   2. po'si'tī e'ri tis
      3. po'si tus e'rit   3. po'si tī e'runt

198.

1. The Helvetii having encouraged their (men) had joined battle. 2. The children of the Haedui have been led away into servitude by the Helvetii. 3. A suitable place will have been selected for a camp. 4. We shall have ascended the highest ridge of the hill. 5. I have led out many legions from winter

quarters. 6. You (plur.) have inhabited one part of Gaul. 7. You (plur.) will have been led over the bridge in company with the remaining forces. 8. We had been located among the Belgae for the sake of spending the winter. 9. I had employed the same leaders for pursuing the enemy. 10. You (sing.) will have placed a guard over Dumnorix. 11. You (sing.) have followed the enemy to the fortifications. 12. Caesar had enrolled three new legions.

THIRD CONJUGATION, BOTH VOICES, SUBJUNCTIVE, IMPERATIVE, AND INFINITIVE MOODS, PARTICIPLES, GERUNDS, AND SUPINES.

SUGGESTIONS. — 1. The verbs in sentences 2 to 6 inclusive (except petunt, 4) may be inflected in place.
2. The Sequence of Tenses should be carefully studied.

199.

1. Sī hostīs sequar, eōs vincam. 2. Vereor nē[1] Divitiacī animum offendam. 3. Verēbar nē Divitiacī animum offenderem. 4. Haeduī petunt ut clēmentiā in Bellovacōs ūtar. 5. Vereor ut[1] clēmentiā dīgnā māiestāte populī Rōmānī ūsus sim. 6. Verēbar ut clēmentiā ūsus essem. 7. Dūc[2] tēcum reliquōs obsidēs. 8. Caesar, petentibus Haeduīs,[3] ut Boiōs in fīnibus suīs collocent, concēdit. 9. Galba, castellīs complūribus hostium expūgnātīs, mīssīs ad eum undique lēgātīs, obsidibusque datīs, cohortēs duās in Nantuātibus collocāre cōnstituit. 10. Divitiacus Haeduus dīxit Haeduōs[4] omnem nōbilitātem āmīsisse et sē[4] Rōmam ad senātum mīssum esse auxilium postulātum.[5] 11. Caesar dīcit sē hostīs sequī et Haeduōrum iniūriās nōn neglēctūrum (esse).[6] 12. Summa alacritās et cupiditās bellī gerendī (bellum gerendī) innāta est.

DIRECTION. — Learn A. & G.: [1]331, *f* and Note. [2]128, *c.* [3]Rule 21. [4]272; Rule 60. [5]302; Rule 66. [6]293, *a.*
H.: [1]498, III. and Note 1. [2]238. [3]Rule XII. [4]Rule LIII. I. [5]546; Rule LIX. [6]534, Note.

ACTIVE VOICE, SUBJUNCTIVE MOOD.

PRESENT TENSE.

Sing. 1. pō'nam
2. pō'nās
3. pō'nat

Plur. 1 pō nā'mus
2. pō nā'tis
3. pō'nant

IMPERFECT TENSE.

Sing. 1. pō'ne rem
2. pō'ne rēs
3. pō'ne ret

Plur. 1. pō ne rē'mus
2. pō ne rē'tis
3. pò'ne rent

PERFECT TENSE.

Sing. 1. po su'e rim
2. po su'e ris
3. po su'e rit

Plur. 1. po su e'ri mus
2. po su e'ri tis
3. po su'e rint

PLUPERFECT TENSE.

Sing. 1. po su is'sem
2. po su is'sēs
3. po su is'set

Plur. 1. po su is sē'mus
2. po su is sē'tis
3. po su is'sent

PASSIVE VOICE, SUBJUNCTIVE MOOD.

PRESENT TENSE.

Sing. 1. pō'nar
2. pō nā'ris (-re)
3. pō nā'tur

Plur. 1. pō nā'mur
2. pō nā'mi nī
3. pō nan'tur

IMPERFECT TENSE.

Sing. 1. pō'ne rer
2. pō ne rē'ris (-re)
3. pō ne rē'tur

Plur. 1. pō ne rē'mur
2. pō ne rē'mi nī
3. pō ne ren'tur

PERFECT TENSE.

Sing. 1. po'si tus sim
2. po'si tus sīs
3. po'si tus sit

Plur. 1. po'si tī sī'mus
2. po'si tī sī'tis
3. po'si tī sint

PLUPERFECT TENSE.

Sing. 1. po'si tus es'sem   Plur. 1. po'si tī es sē'mus
2. po'si tus es'sēs   2. po'si tī es sē'tis
3. po'si tus es'set   3. po'si tī es'sent

IMPERATIVE MOOD.

ACTIVE VOICE.	*Present Tense.*	PASSIVE VOICE.
Sing. 2. pō'ne		Sing. 2. pō'ne re
Plur. 2. pō'ni te		Plur. 2. pō ni'mi nī

Future Tense.

Sing. 2 and 3. pō'ni tō		Sing. 2 and 3. pō'ni tor
Plur. 2. pō ni tō te		Plur. 2. ——
Plur. 3. pō nun'tō		Plur. 3. pō nun'tor

INFINITIVE MOOD.

ACTIVE VOICE.	*Present Tense.*	PASSIVE VOICE.
pō'ne re		pō'nī

Perfect Tense.

po su is'se		po'si tus es'se

Future Tense.

po'si tū'rus es'se		po'si tum ī'rī
		(po'si tus fo're)

PARTICIPLES.

ACTIVE VOICE, *Pres.* pō'nēns; *Fut.* po si tū'rus.
PASSIVE VOICE, *Perf.* po'si tus; *Fut.* pō nen'dus (Gerundive).

THE GERUND AND SUPINES.

N. Gen. pō nen'dī, Dat. pō nen'dō, Acc. pō nen'dum, Abl. pō nen'dō.
Former Supine, po'si tum; Latter Supine, po'si tū.

200.

1. Caesar fears that he has hurt the feelings (sing.) of Divitiacus. 2. Caesar feared that he had hurt the feelings of Divitiacus. 3. I have often asked that you (sing.) exercise

kindness worthy the majesty of the Roman people. 4. I used
to fear that you (plur.) [did] not exercise kindness towards
the Helvetii. 5. Place (plur.) faithful guards over Dumnorix
(dative). 6. Caesar has granted at my request (to me asking)
that we locate the Boii in our territory. 7. Caesar, many towns
of the Gauls having been captured, determined to wage war with
the Germans. 8. Divitiacus says that the state is losing all
the nobility and that he is sent to Rome to ask (supine) assistance. 9. Caesar said that he had not neglected the wrongs of
the Haedui and that he would follow the enemy. 10. The leading men said that they were quite ready for (ad) waging war.

VERBS IN -IŌ, THIRD CONJUGATION.

SUGGESTIONS.— 1. These verbs differ from other verbs of this conjugation in certain tenses formed from the present stem.
2. The inflection of *capiō* is to be carefully committed from A. & G.,
page 100; II., Sections 218, 219.
3. Translate **sēmentēs faciam**, 2, *I shall sow;* **cōnsilium facient,** 7,
will adopt the plan; **terga vertunt,** 8, *turn and flee.*

201.

1. Sī Caesarem interficiō, nōbilibus grātum faciō. 2. Sēmentēs quam māximās faciam. 3. Allobrogēs quī trāns Rhodanum
vīcōs possessiōnēsque habent, fugā sē[1] ad Caesarem recipiunt.
4. Nōs et Haeduīs[2] et Allobrogibus satisfaciēbāmus. 5. Hostēs
fugientēs[3] capiuntur et in catēnis cōniciuntur. 6. Cōnantēs
dīcere in catēnīs cōniciēbāmur. 7. Helvētiī cōnsilium itineris
faciendī (iter faciendī) per prōvinciam capient. 8. Hostēs multa
volnera accipiunt tum cum[4] terga vertunt. 9. Praefectus, cum
trīduum[5] iter fēcimus, locum idōneum castrīs dēligit. 10. Praefectus, cum iter facerēmus, locum idōneum castrīs dēlēgit. 11. Praefectus, cum trīduum iter fēcissēmus, locum idōneum castrīs dēlēgit. 12. Postrīdiē ēius diēī[6] Caesar, priusquam[7] sē hostēs ex
terrōre āc fugā reciperent, in fīnīs Suessiōnum exercitum dūxit.
13. Prīncipēs Britanniae id optimum factū dūxērunt.

DIRECTION. — Learn A. & G. : ¹196; Rule 7. ²227, *e*, 2. ³292. ⁴325;
Rule 78. ⁵Rule 55. ⁶223, *c*. ⁷327.
II.: ¹448; 449. ²384, 4, Note 1. ³549, I.
⁴521, I.; Rule LII. I. ⁵Rule IX.
⁶398, 5. ⁷520, I.1; Rule LI. I.1.

Recipiō, *I take back* (Passive, *is taken back*).

ACTIVE VOICE, INDICATIVE MOOD.

PRESENT TENSE.

Sing. 1. re ci'piŏ   Plur. 1. re ci'pi mus
    2. re'ci pis   2. re ci'pi tis
    3. re'ci pit   3. re ci'pi unt

IMPERFECT TENSE.

Sing. 1. re ci pi ē'bam   Plur. 1. re ci pi ē bā'mus
    2. re ci pi ē'bās   2. re ci pi ē bā'tis
    3. re ci pi ē'bat   3. re ci pi ē'bant

FUTURE TENSE.

Sing. 1. re ci'pi am   Plur. 1. re ci pi ē'mus
    2. re ci'pi ēs   2. re ci pi ē'tis
    3. re ci'pi et   3. re ci'pi ent

PERFECT TENSE.

Sing. 1. re cē'pĭ   Plur. 1. re cē'pi mus
    2. re cē pi'stĭ   2. re cē pi'stis
    3. re cē'pit   3. re cē pē'runt (-re)

PLUPERFECT TENSE.

Sing. 1. re cē'pe ram   Plur. 1. re cē pe rā'mus
    2. re cē'pe rās   2. re cē pe rā'tis
    3. re cē'pe rat   3. re cē'pe rant

FUTURE PERFECT TENSE.

Sing. 1. re cē'pe rŏ   Plur. 1. re cē pe'ri mus
    2. re cē'pe ris   2. re cē pe'ri tis
    3. re cē'pe rit   .3. re cē'pe rint

Passive Voice, Indicative Mood.

Present Tense.

Sing. 1. re ci'pi or   Plur. 1. re ci'pi mur
2. re ci'pe ris (-re)   2. re ci pi'mi nī
3. re ci'pi tur   3. re ci pi un'tur

Imperfect Tense.

Sing. 1. re ci pi ē'bar   Plur. 1. re ci pi ē bā'mur
2. re ci pi ē bā'ris (-re)   2. re ci pi ē bā'mi nī
3. re ci pi ē bā'tur   3. re ci pi ē ban'tur

Future Tense.

Sing. 1. re ci'pi ar   Plur. 1. re ci pi ē'mur
2. re ci pi ē'ris (-re)   2. re ci pi ē'mi nī
3. re ci pi ē'tur   3. re ci pi en'tur

Perfect Tense.

Sing. 1. re cep'tus sum   Plur. 1. re cep'tī su'mus
2. re cep'tus es   2. re cep'tī e'stis
3. re cep'tus est   3. re cep'tī sunt

Pluperfect Tense.

Sing. 1. re cep'tus e'ram   Plur. 1. re cep'tī e rā'mus
2. re cep'tus e'rās   2. re cep'tī e rā'tis
3. re cep'tus e'rat   3. re cep'tī e'rant

Future Perfect Tense.

Sing. 1. re cep'tus e'rō   Plur. 1. re cep'tī e'ri mus
2. re cep'tus e'ris   2. re cep'tī e'ri tis
3. re cep'tus e'rit   3. re cep'tī e'runt

Active Voice, Subjunctive Mood.

Present Tense.

Sing. 1. re ci'pi am   Plur. 1. re ci pi ā'mus
2. re ci'pi ās   2. re ci pi ā'tis
3. re ci'pi at   3. re ci'pi ant

IMPERFECT TENSE.

Sing. 1. re ci'pe rem   Plur. 1. re ci pe rē'mus
      2. re ci'pe rēs   2. re ci pe rē'tis
      3. re ci'pe ret   3. re ci'pe rent

PERFECT TENSE.

Sing. 1. re cē'pe rim   Plur. 1. re cū pe'ri mus
      2. re cē'pe ris   2. re cē pe'ri tis
      3. re cē'pe rit   3. re cē'pe rint

PLUPERFECT TENSE.

Sing. 1. re cē pis'sem   Plur. 1. re cē pis sē'mus
      2. re cē pis'sēs   2. re cē pis sē'tis
      3. re cē pis'set   3. re cē pis'sent

PASSIVE VOICE, SUBJUNCTIVE MOOD.

PRESENT TENSE.

Sing. 1. re ci'pi ar   Plur. 1. re ci pi ā'mur
      2. re ci pi ā'ris (-re)   2. re ci pi ā'mi nī
      3. re ci pi ā'tur   3. re ci pi an'tur

IMPERFECT TENSE.

Sing. 1. re ci'pe rer   Plur. 1. re ci pe rē'mur
      2. re ci pe rē'ris (-re)   2. re ci pe rē'mi nī
      3. re ci pe rē'tur   3. re ci pe ren'tur

PERFECT TENSE.

Sing. 1. re cep'tus sim   Plur. 1. re cep'tī sī'mus
      2. re cep'tus sīs   2. re cep'tī sī'tis
      3. re cep'tus sit   3. re cep'tī sint

PLUPERFECT TENSE.

Sing. 1. re cep'tus es'sem   Plur. 1. re cep'tī es sē'mus
      2. re cep'tus es'sēs   2. re cep'tī es sē'tis
      3. re cep'tus es'set   3. re cep'tī es'sent

IMPERATIVE MOOD.

ACTIVE VOICE.	*Present Tense.*	PASSIVE VOICE.
Sing. 2. re'ci pe		Sing. 2. re ci'pe re
Plur. 2. re ci'pi te		Plur. 2. re ci pi'mi nĭ

Future Tense.

Sing. 2 and 3. re ci'pi tō		Sing. 2 and 3. re ci'pi tor
Plur. 2. re ci pi tō'te		Plur. 2. ———
Plur. 3. re ci pi un'tō		Plur. 3. re ci pi un'tor

INFINITIVE MOOD.

ACTIVE VOICE.	*Present Tense.*	PASSIVE VOICE.
re ci'pe re		re'ci pĭ

Perfect Tense.

re cē pis'se		re cep'tus es'se

Future Tense.

re cep tū'rus es'se		re cep'tum ĭ'rĭ
		re cep'tus fo're

PARTICIPLES.

ACTIVE VOICE, *Pres.* re ci'pi ēns ; *Fut.* re cep tū'rus
PASSIVE VOICE, *Perf.* re cep'tus ; *Fut.* re ci pi en'dus (Gerundive).

THE GERUND AND SUPINES.

N. Gen. re ci pi en'dĭ, Dat. re ci pi en'dō, Acc. re ci pi en'dum, Abl.
re ci pi en'dō.
Former Supine, re cep'tum. Latter Supine, re cep'tū.

202.

1. The enemy are making as long marches as possible.
2. You who had possessions beyond the Rhine were betaking
yourselves to Caesar. 3. I shall make amends to Caesar.
4. The ambassadors, endeavoring to do this which they had

determined [upon], are thrown into chains. 5. Caesar adopts the plan of making a march through Gaul. 6. Then you will receive many wounds, when you turn and flee (fut. perf.). 7. The enemy, when they have made a three days' march, select a suitable place for a camp. 8. The enemy, when they had made a three days' march, selected a suitable place for a camp. 9. The lieutenants who had led their legions into the territory of the Suessiones betook themselves to Caesar before the enemy had recovered from the fright. 10. This is not easy to do (supine).

PRINCIPAL PARTS AND SYNOPSES.

At this point review and commit thoroughly the principal parts and synopses of all verbs of the Third Conjugation thus far used. Let nothing interfere with complete mastery of the verb forms.

FOURTH CONJUGATION, BOTH VOICES, INDICATIVE MOOD.

SUGGESTIONS. — 1. Verb-stems of the Fourth Conjugation end in -ī-; e.g. *audī*- (stem of *audiō*, *I hear*), *experī*- (*stem of experior, I try*). The inflection of *audiō* is to be learned from A. & G., pp. 104 and 105, H., 98 ff.

2. Sentence 1, Exercises 203, 205, may be developed in the common conditional forms.

3. Translate **nōn sōlum . . . sed etiam**, 4, *not only . . . but also;* in **contemptiōnem veniētis**, 4, *you will incur the contempt;* **quam ob rem**, 5, *why;* **per īnsidiās**, 10, *treacherously;* **frūmentum mētiar**, 12, *I shall distribute rations.*

203.

1. Sī veniō, bellī fortūnam experior. 2. Quid dē hāc rē audīs (audiēbas, audiēs, audīvistī, audīverās, audīveris)? 3. Nostrī sociī audientēs quās iniūriās hostēs faciēbant, ad Caesarem veniēbant. 4. Vōs nōn sōlum hostibus sed etiam nostrīs[1] in contemptiōnem veniētis. 5. Quam ob rem lēgātus castra nōn mūnīvit? 6. Cum ego vēnerō,[2] castra vallō fossāque mūniam. 7. Nōs iam per angustiās et fīnīs Sēquanōrum nostrās cōpiās trā-

dūxerāmus et in Haeduōrum fīnīs pervēnerāmus eōrumque agrōs populābāmur. 8. Quod³ ubī audītum est, conclāmāvit omnēs victōriam. 9. Ego cōpiās meās cum C. Fabiō partiar. 10. Nostrī per īnsidiās circumveniēbantur. 11. Tōtīus Galliae imperiō potītī sumus. 12. Cum cōpiās partītī eritis, frūmentum mētiar. 13. Quam ob rem frūmentum mīlitibus nōn mēnsus erās ?

DIRECTION. — Learn A. & G.: ¹225, *b*, 2. ²281 and Remark. ⁸201, *e*.
H.: ¹384, 4. ²473, 1. ⁸453.

Mūniō, *I fortify* (Passive, *is fortified*).

ACTIVE VOICE, INDICATIVE MOOD.

PRESENT TENSE.

Sing. 1. mū'niō   Plur. 1. mū nī' mus
2. mū'nis   2. mū nī'tis
3. mū'nit   3. mū'ni unt

IMPERFECT TENSE.

Sing. 1. mū ni ē'bam   Plur. 1. mū ni ē bā'mus
2. mū ni ē'bās   2. mū ni ē bā'tis
3. mū ni ē'bat   3. mū ni ē'bant

FUTURE TENSE.

Sing. 1. mū'ni am   Plur. 1. mū ni ē'mus
2. mū'ni ēs   2. mū ni ē'tis
3. mū'ni et   3. mū'ni ent

PERFECT TENSE (1st form).

Sing. 1. mū nī'vī   Plur. 1. mū ni'vi mus
2. mū nī vi'stī   2. mū nī vi'stis
3. mū nī'vit   3. mū nī vē'runt (-re)

PERFECT TENSE (2d form).

Sing. 1. mū'ni ī   Plur. 1. mū ni'i mus
2. mū ni i'stī   2. mū ni i'stis
3. mū'ni it   3. mū ni ē'runt (-re)

PLUPERFECT TENSE.

Sing. 1. mū nī′ve ram   Plur. 1. mū nī ve rā′mus
     2. mū nī′ve rās   2. mū nī ve rā′tis
     3. mū nī′ve rat   3. mū nī′ve rant

FUTURE PERFECT TENSE.

Sing. 1. mū nī′ve rŏ   Plur. 1. mū nī ve′ri mus
     2. mū nī′ve ris   2. mū nī ve′ri tis
     3. mū nī′ve rit   3. mū nī′ve rint

PASSIVE VOICE, INDICATIVE MOOD.

PRESENT TENSE.

Sing. 1. mū′ni or   Plur. 1. mū nī′mur
     2. mū nī′ris (-re)   2. mū nī′mi nī
     3. mū nī′tur   3. mū ni un′tur

IMPERFECT TENSE.

Sing. 1. mū ni ē′bar   Plur. 1. mū ni ē bā′mur
     2. mū ni ē bā′ris (-re)   2. mū ni ē bā′mi nī
     3. mū ni ē bā′tur   3. mū ni ē ban′tur

FUTURE TENSE.

Sing. 1. mū′ni ar   Plur. 1. mū ni ē′mur
     2. mū ni ē′ris (-re)   2. mū ni ē′mi nī
     3. mū ni ē′tur   3. mū ni en′tur

PERFECT TENSE.

Sing. 1. mū nī′tus sum   Plur. 1. mū nī′tī su′mus
     2. mū nī′tus es   2. mū nī′tī e′stis
     3. mū nī′tus est   3. mū nī′tī sunt

PLUPERFECT TENSE.

Sing. 1. mū nī′tus e′ram   Plur. 1. mū nī′tī e rā′mus
     2. mū nī′tus e′rās   2. mū nī′tī e rā′tis
     3. mū nī′tus e′rat   3. mū nī′tī e′rant

FUTURE PERFECT TENSE.

Sing. 1. mū nī'tus e'rō   Plur. 1. mū nī'tī e'rimus
      2. mū nī'tus e'ris   2. mū nī'tī e'ritis
      3. mū nī'tus e'rit   3. mū nī'tī e'runt

204.

1. The enemy are surrounding us treacherously. 2. We were reaching the vicinity of (ad) Vesontio. 3. You (sing.) will hear concerning (dē) this thing. 4. I have fortified my house by a rampart. 5. You (plur.) will have surrounded our forces on (ex) the march. 6. The day which Caesar had determined with the ambassadors came. 7. When Caesar arrives, I shall have obtained possession of the town. 8. You (sing.) had tried the same fortune of war. 9. No voice was heard unworthy of the majesty of the Roman people. 10. We shall always measure great men by valor, not by [good] fortune. 11. You (plur.) who have remained in camp are surrounded by the enemy. 12. The consuls have distributed the provinces among themselves.

FOURTH CONJUGATION, REMAINING MOODS AND FORMS.

205.

1. Sī veniam, bellī fortūnam experiar. 2. Caesar hōc audiēns nōn exspectat dum[1] in Santonēs Helvētiī perveniant. 3. Hōc faciam dum modō[2] (dummodō) vōs ab hostibus nē circumveniāminī. 4. Līterās ad Caesarem mīsimus antequam[3] in Italiam venīrēmus. 5. Līterās ad Caesarem ante[4] mīsī quam[4] in Italiam vēnissem. 6. Illī nōn dēstitērunt priusquam tōtīus Galliae[5] potīrentur. 7. Vōs nōn prius dēstitistis quam rērum potītī essētis. 8. Tametsī[6] ab duce nostrō dēserēbāmur, tamen bellī fortūnam experiēbāmur. 9. Etsī rēs sit multae labōris, tamen frūmentum mīlitibus mētiāmur. 10. Nisi pervēneris,[7] castra mūniam. 11. Caesar dīcit sēsē castra mūnītūrum, nisi pervēneris.[8] 12. Caesar dīxit sē potiundī (potiendī) oppidī causā vēnisse. 13. Hōc est nefās etiam audītū.

DIRECTION. — Learn A. & G.: ¹328. ²314 and *a*; Rule 73. ⁸327.
⁴262. ⁵223, *a*. ⁶313, *c*. ⁷307,*c*.
⁸336 and 2; Rule 80; 286, Remark (*b*), last part.

H.: ¹519, II. 2; Rule L. II. 2. ²513, I.;
Rule XLV. I. ⁸520 and II.; Rule
LI. II. ⁴520, foot-note 1. ⁵410,
V. and 3. ⁶515, II.; Rule XLVI.
⁷508, 2. ⁸524; Rule LIV.; 525, 2.

ACTIVE VOICE, SUBJUNCTIVE MOOD.

PRESENT TENSE.

Sing. 1. mū'ni am   Plur. 1. mū ni ā'mus
2. mū'ni ās   2. mū ni ā'tis
3. mū'ni at   3. mū'ni ant

IMPERFECT TENSE.

Sing. 1. mū nī'rem   Plur. 1. mū nī rē'mus
2. mū nī'rēs   2. mū nī rē'tis
3. mū nī'ret   3. mū nī'rent

PERFECT TENSE.

Sing. 1. mū ni've rim   Plur. 1. mū nī ve'ri mus
2. mū nī've ris   2. mū nī ve'ri tis
3. mū nī've rit   3. mū nī've rint

PLUPERFECT TENSE.

Sing. 1. mū nī vis'sem   Plur. 1. mū nī vis sē'mus
2. mū nī vis'sēs   2. mū nī vis sē'tis
3. mū nī vis'set   3. mū nī vis'sent

PASSIVE VOICE, SUBJUNCTIVE MOOD.

PRESENT TENSE.

Sing. 1. mū'ni ar   Plur. 1. mū ni ā'mur
2. mū ni ā'ris (-re)   2. mū ni ā'mi nī
3. mū ni ā'tur   3. mū ni an'tur

IMPERFECT TENSE.

Sing. 1. mū nī'rer   Plur. 1. mū nī rē'mur
     2. mū nī rē'ris (-re)   2. mū nī rē'mi nī
     3. mū nī rē'tur   3. mū nī ren'tur

PERFECT TENSE.

Sing. 1. mū nī'tus sim   Plur. 1. mū nī'tī sī'mus
     2. mū nī'tus sīs   2. mū nī'tī sī'tis
     3. mū nī'tus sit   3. mū nī'tī sint

PLUPERFECT TENSE.

Sing. 1. mū nī'tus es'sem   Plur. 1. mū nī'tī es sē'mus
     2. mū nī'tus es'sēs   2. mū nī'tī es sē'tis
     3. mū nī'tus es'set   3. mū nī'ti es'sent

IMPERATIVE MOOD.

ACTIVE VOICE.	*Present Tense.*	PASSIVE VOICE.
Sing. 2. mū'nī		Sing. 2. mū nī're
Plur. 2. mū nī'te		Plur. 2. mū nī'mi nī

Future Tense.

Sing. 2 and 3. mū nī'tō		Sing. 2 and 3. mū nī'tor
Plur. 2. mū nī tō'te		Plur. 2. ——
Plur. 3. mū ni un'tō		Plur. 3. mū ni un'tor

INFINITIVE MOOD.

ACTIVE VOICE.	*Present Tense.*	PASSIVE VOICE.
mū nī're		mū nī'rī

Perfect Tense.

mū ni vis'se		mū nī'tus es'se

Future Tense.

mū nī tū'rus es'se		mū nī'tum ī'rī
		mū nī'tus fo're

PARTICIPLES.

ACTIVE VOICE, *Pres.* mū'ni ēns ; *Fut.* mū nī tū'rus
PASSIVE VOICE, *Perf.* mū nī'tus ; *Fut.* mū ni en'dus (Gerundive).

THE GERUND AND SUPINES.

N., Gen. mū ni en'dī, Dat. mū ni en'dō, Acc. mū ni en'dum, Abl.
mū ni en'dō.
Former Supine, mū nī'tum. Latter Supine, mū nī'tū.

206.

1. The enemy will not wait until I have reached [the country of] the Santones. 2. We shall do this provided the camp is fortified. 3. I sent a scout to Vesontio before I came into Gaul. 4. We sent scouts to Avaricum before we had come into the province. 5. You (sing.) [did] not stop before (earlier than) you had become masters of all Gaul. 6. Our consuls [did] not stop before they had become masters of affairs. 7. Although our forces were being abandoned by their leaders, still they tried the fortune of war. 8. Even if the task had been great (if the thing had been of great labor) we should have distributed rations to the army. 9. Unless new legions arrive, we shall fortify the camp. 10. The commanders say that, unless new legions arrive, they will fortify the camp. 11. Our leaders say that they will try the fortune of war, unless they secure the authority. 12. Caesar says that he will come for the sake of obtaining possession of the town.

POSSUM, VOLŌ, NŌLŌ, MĀLŌ.

SUGGESTIONS. — 1. In translating the forms of **possum**, *can* and *could* should be commonly used; *e.g.* **prohibēre possunt,** 1, *can keep from.* But translate **plūrimum poterat,** 2, *was the most powerful man* (*was able the most*).

2. Find the inflection of these verbs at the end of Exercise 207.

207.

1. Perpaucī exercitum itinere facile prohibēre possunt. 2. Dumnorix apud Sēquanōs plūrimum poterat. 3. Nōn est dubium quīn tōtīus Galliae plūrimum Helvētiī possint. 4. Nostrī sequī[1] nōn potuērunt. 5. Lēgātī dīcunt nostrōs sequī nōn potuisse. 6. Sī quid voltis ad Īd.[2] Apr. (Īdūs Aprīlīs) revertere. 7. Sī interficī nōn voltis, arma pōnite. 8. Pūgnāre[3] quam servīre mālumus. 9. Sī veteris contumēliae[4] oblīviscī volō, recentium iniūriārum memoriam dēpōnere nōn possum. 10. Ego nūllī iter per prōvinciam dare possum,[5] sī volam. 11. Caesar negat sē posse[6] ūllī iter per prōvinciam dare sī velit.[7]

DIRECTIONS. — Learn A. & G. : [1] 271; Rule 59. [2] 376, a, b, c, d. [3] 331, b and 1. [4] 219; Rule 19. [5] 307, d. [6] 304, c. [7] 337, 1; Rule 80.

H.: [1] 533 and I. 1, 2; Rule LVI. [2] 642, I. 1, 2, 3, II. [3] 498, I. and Note. [4] 406, II.; Rule XIX. II. [5] 511 and 1. [6] 527 and I. [7] 524; Rule LIV.

Possum, *I am able* (*I can*).

INDICATIVE MOOD.

PRESENT TENSE.

Sing. 1. pos'sum   Plur. 1. pos'su mus
      2. po'tes   2. po te'stis
      3. po'test   3. pos'sunt

IMPERFECT TENSE.

Sing. 1. po'te ram   Plur. 1. po te rā'mus
      2. po'te rās   2. po te rā'tis
      3. po'te rat   3. po'te rant

FUTURE TENSE.

Sing. 1. po'te rō   Plur. 1. po te'ri mus
      2. po'te ris   2. po te'ri tis
      3. po'te rit   3. po'te runt

PERFECT TENSE.

Sing. 1. po'tu ī
     2. po tu i'stī
     3. po'tu it

Plur. 1. po tu'i mus
     2. po tu i'stis
     3. po tu ĕ'runt (-re)

PLUPERFECT TENSE.

Sing. 1. po tu'e ram
     2. po tu'e rās
     3. po tu'e rat

Plur. 1. po tu e rā'mus
     2. po tu e rā'tis
     3. po tu'e rant

FUTURE PERFECT TENSE.

Sing. 1. po tu'e rō
     2. po tu'e ris
     3. po tu'e rit

Plur. 1. po tu e'ri mus
     2. po tu e'ri tis
     3. po tu'e rint

SUBJUNCTIVE MOOD.

PRESENT TENSE.

Sing. 1. pos'sim
     2. pos'sīs
     3. pos'sit

Plur. 1. pos sī'mus
     2. pos sī'tis
     3. pos'sint

IMPERFECT TENSE.

Sing. 1. pos'sem
     2. pos'sēs
     3. pos'set

Plur. 1. pos sē'mus
     2. pos sē'tis
     3. pos'sent

PERFECT TENSE.

Sing. 1. po tu'e rim
     2. po tu'e ris
     3. po tu'e rit

Plur. 1. po tu e'ri mus
     2. po tu e'ri tis
     3. po tu'e rint

PLUPERFECT TENSE.

Sing. 1. po tu is'sem
     2. po tu is'sēs
     3. po tu is'set

Plur. 1. po tu is sē'mus
     2. po tu is sē'tis
     3. po tu is'sent

(No Imperative.)

INFINITIVES.

Pres. pos'se   *Perf.* po tu is'se

PARTICIPLE (as adjective).

Pres. po'tēns

Volō, *I am willing (I wish).*

INDICATIVE MOOD.

PRESENT TENSE.

Sing. 1. vo'lŏ	Plur. 1. vo'lu mus
2. vĭs	2. vol'tis (vul tis)
3. volt (vult)	3. vo'lunt

IMPERFECT TENSE.

Sing. 1. vo lě'bam	Plur. 1. vo lě bā'mus
2. vo lě'bās	2. vo lě bā'tis
3. vo lě'bat	3. vo lě'bant

FUTURE TENSE.

Sing. 1. vo'lam	Plur. 1. vo lě'mus
2. vo'lěs	2. vo lě'tis
3. vo'let	3. vo'lent

PERFECT TENSE.

Sing. 1. vo'lu ī	Plur. 1. vo lu'ï mus
2. vo lu ĭ'stī	2. vo lu ĭ'stis
3. vo'lu it	3. vo lu ē'runt (-re)

PLUPERFECT TENSE.

Sing. 1. vo lu'e ram	Plur. 1. vo lu e rā'mus
2. vo lu'e rās	2. vo lu e rā'tis
3. vo lu'e rat	3. vo lu'e rant

FUTURE PERFECT TENSE.

Sing. 1. vo lu'e rŏ   Plur. 1. vo lu e'ri mus
     2. vo lu'e ris   2. vo lu e'ri tis
     3. vo lu'e rit   3. vo lu'e rint

SUBJUNCTIVE MOOD.

PRESENT TENSE.

Sing. 1. ve'lim   Plur. 1. ve lī'mus
     2. ve'līs   2. ve lī'tis
     3. ve'lit   3. ve'lint

IMPERFECT TENSE.

Sing. 1. vel'lem   Plur. 1. vel lē'mus
     2. vel'lēs   2. vel lē'tis
     3. vel'let   3. vel'lent

PERFECT TENSE.

Sing. 1. vo lu'e rim   Plur. 1. vo lu e'ri mus
     2. vo lu'e ris   2. vo lu e'ri tis
     3. vo lu'e rit   3. vo lu'e rint

PLUPERFECT TENSE.

Sing. 1. vo lu is'sem   Plur. 1. vo lu is sē'mus
     2. vo lu is'sēs   2. vo lu is sē'tis
     3. vo lu is'set   3. vo lu is'sent

(NO IMPERATIVE.)

INFINITIVES.

Pres. vel'le   *Perf.* vo lu is'se

PARTICIPLE.

Pres. vo'lēns

Nōlō, *I am unwilling.*

INDICATIVE MOOD.

PRESENT TENSE.

Sing. 1. nō′lō
2. nōn vīs
3. nōn volt (vult)

Plur. 1. nō′lu mus
2. nōn vol′tis (vul′tis)
3. nō′lunt

IMPERFECT TENSE.

Sing. 1. nō lē′bam
2. nō lē′bās
3. nō lē′bat

Plur. 1. nō lē bā′mus
2. nō lē bā′tis
3. nō lē′bant

FUTURE TENSE.

Sing. 1. nō′lam
2. nō′lēs
3. nō′let

Plur. 1. nō lē′mus
2. nō lē′tis
3. nō′lent

PERFECT TENSE.

Sing. 1. nō′lu ī
2. nō lu i′stī
3. nō′lu it

Plur. 1. nō lu′i mus
2. nō lu i′stis
3. nō lu ē′runt (-re)

PLUPERFECT TENSE.

Sing. 1. nō lu′e ram
2. nō lu′e rās
3. nō lu′e rat

Plur. 1. nō lu e rā′mus
2. nō lu e rā′tis
3. nō lu′e rant

FUTURE PERFECT TENSE.

Sing. 1. nō lu′e rō
2. nō lu′e ris
3. nō lu′e rit

Plur. 1. nō lu e′ri mus
2. nō lu e′ri tis
3. nō lu′e rint

SUBJUNCTIVE MOOD.

PRESENT TENSE.

Sing. 1. nō′lim
2. nō′līs
3. nō′lit

Plur. 1. nō lī′mus
2. nō lī′tis
3. nō′lint

IMPERFECT TENSE.

Sing. 1. nōl'lem   Plur. 1. nōl lē'mus
     2. nōl'lēs   2. nōl lē'tis
     3. nōl'let   3. nōl'lent

PERFECT TENSE.

Sing. 1. nō lu'e rim   Plur. 1. nō lu e'ri mus
     2. nō lu'e ris   2. nō lu e'ri tis
     3. nō lu'e rit   3. nō lu'e rint

PLUPERFECT TENSE.

Sing. 1. nō lu is'sem   Plur. 1. nō lu is sē'mus
     2. nō lu is'sēs   2. nō lu is sē'tis
     3. nō lu is'set   3. nō lu is'sent

IMPERATIVE MOOD.

Pres. Sing. 2. nō'lī   Plur. 2. nō lī'te
Fut. Sing. 2 and 3. nō lī'tō   Plur. 2. nō lī tō'te

INFINITIVES.

Pres. nōl'le   *Perf.* nō lu is'se

PARTICIPLE.

Pres. nō'lēns

Mālō, *I wish rather (I prefer).*

INDICATIVE MOOD.

PRESENT TENSE.

Sing. 1. mā'lō   Plur. 1. mā'lu mus
     2. mā'vīs   2. mā vol'tis (-vul'tis)
     3. mā'volt (-vult)   3. mā'lunt

IMPERFECT TENSE.

Sing. 1. mā lē'bam   Plur. 1. mā lē bā'mus
     2. mā lē'bās   2. mā lē bā'tis
     3. mā lē'bat   3. mā lē'bant

FUTURE TENSE.

Sing. 1. mā′lam   Plur. 1. mā lē′mus
2. mā′lēs   2. mā lē′tis
3. mā′let   3. mā′lent

PERFECT TENSE.

Sing. 1. mā′lu ī   Plur. 1. mā lu′ī mus
2. mā lu i′stī   2. mā lu i′stis
3. mā′lu ĭt   3. mā lu ē′runt (-re)

PLUPERFECT TENSE.

Sing. 1. mā lu′e ram   Plur. 1. mā lu e rā′mus
2. mā lu′e rās   2. mā lu e rā′tis
3. mā lu′e rat   3. mā lu′e rant

FUTURE PERFECT TENSE.

Sing. 1. mā lu′e rŏ   Plur. 1. mā lu e′ri mus
2. mā lu′e ris   2. mā lu e′ri tis
3. mā lu′e rit   3. mā lu′e rint

SUBJUNCTIVE MOOD.

PRESENT TENSE.

Sing. 1. mā′lim   Plur. 1. mā lī′mus
2. mā′līs   2. mā lī′tis
3. mā′lit   3. mā′lint

IMPERFECT TENSE.

Sing. 1. māl′lem   Plur. 1. māl lē′mus
2. māl′lēs   2. māl lē′tis
3. māl′let   3. māl′lent

PERFECT TENSE.

Sing. 1. mā lu′e rim   Plur. 1. mā lu e′ri mus
2. mā lu′e ris   2. mā lu e′ri tis
3. mā lu′e rit   3. mā lu′e rint

PLUPERFECT TENSE.

Sing. 1. mā lu is'sem   Plur. 1. mā lu is sē'mus
    2. mā lu is'sēs   2. mā lu is sē'tis
    3. mā lu is'set   3. mā lu is'sent

(NO IMPERATIVE.)

INFINITIVES.

Pres. māl'le   *Perf.* mā lu is'se

(NO PARTICIPLES.)

208.

1. A very few could (were able to) keep our legions from the journey. 2. Dumnorix has been the most powerful man (has been able the most) among the Sequani. 3. There was no doubt that the Helvetii had been the most powerful people of all Gaul. 4. The auxiliaries cannot (are not able to) follow the enemy. 5. The leader says that the auxiliaries cannot follow the enemy. 6. If you (sing.) wish anything, return on the thirteenth day of April. 7. If you (sing.) [do] not wish to be put to death, lay down your arms. 8. I prefer to fight [rather] than to turn and flee. 9. If we shall be willing to forget the former insult, we cannot (are not able to) lay aside the memory of recent injuries. 10. We can give (are able to give) no one a way through the province, if we [shall] wish. 11. The commanders say that they cannot give to any one a way through the province, if they wish.

IMPERSONAL VERBS.   HISTORICAL INFINITIVES.

SUGGESTION. — In connection with Impersonal Verbs, A. & G. 145, 146, *a, b, c,* and *d*; H. 298, 300, 301 and 1 should be carefully studied.

209.

1. Caesaris[1] māximē interest, manūs hostium distinērī.[a]   2. Nihil[2] meā[3] intererat, manūs hostium distinērī.[4]   3. Sī volt mēcum conloquī, licet.   4. Sī velim in Ubiōrum fīnibus cōnsīdere, liceat.   5. Poenam, ut[5] īgnī cremārētur, eum damnātum[6] sequī[a] oportēbat.   6. Cōpiāsne[7] adversum hostem dūcere, an[7] castra dēfendere, an[7] fugā salūtem petere praestat?   7. Diū cum esset pūgnātum,[8] impedīmentīs castrīsque nostrī potītī sunt.   8. Nostrī sōsē in castra, ut erat imperātum,[9] recēpērunt.   9. Hanc Galliae partem Gallōs obtinēre dictum est.   10. Id[b] aliquot dē causīs accidēbat, ut[10] subitō Gallī bellī renovandī cōnsilium caperent.   11. Ea rēs[b] meritō populī Rōmānī nōn accidit.   12. Omnibus cōnstat hiemārī[11] in Galliā oportēre.[12]   13. Diem ex diē dūcere[13] Haeduī.   14. Haeduī dīcere frūmentum adesse.

> DIRECTION. — Read A. & G.: [a]29, c;   270 (1) and b.   [b]145 and
> foot-note.
>
>   H.: [a]42, Note;   538 and 1.   [b]298, foot-note 5.
>
> Learn A. & G.: [1]222.   [2]238 and b; Rule 31.   [3]222, a.
>   [4]270; Rule 58.   [5]329.   [6]292.   [7]211.
>   [8]145;   146, d.   [9]230.   [10]332, f.
>   [11]Rule 35.   [12]Rule 13.   [13]275.
>
>   II.: [1]406, III.; Rule XIX. III.   [2]378; Rule
>   VIII. [3]408, I. 2.   [4]538.   [5]501 and
>   III. [6]549, 1.   [7]353, 1, 2 and Note 5.
>   [8]298;   301 and 1.   [9]384, 5.   [10]501
>   and III.   [11]538 and 2.   [12]Rule III.
>   [13]536, 1.

210.

1. It especially concerned the republic that (inf.) we come as soon as possible.   2. It concerns you not at all that I have come. 3. If he wishes to try the fortune of war, [it] will be permitted. 4. If you (sing.) had wished to settle in the territory of the Ubii, [it] would have been permitted.   5. [It] is fitting that (inf.) the punishment of being burned to death (that he be burned by

fire) be inflicted upon him when condemned (to follow him condemned). 6. Was [it] better that I had led (to have led) the
forces against the enemy, or had sought safety in flight? 7. You
(plu.) will obtain possession of the town when the engagement
shall have continued a long time (when [it] shall have been
fought a long time). 8. We are betaking ourselves to camp
according to command (as [it] has been commanded). 9. [It]
was evident to all that we ought to pass the winter in Gaul (the-
winter-to-be passed (inf.) in Gaul to behoove, was evident).
10. Caesar demands (inf.) corn of the Haedui.

FERŌ. EŌ. FĪŌ.

211.

1. Equitātus, tripartītō dīvīsus, contrā hostem it. 2. Nostrī
subsidiō sociīs iērunt. 3. Sēquanī hāc viā[1] propter angustiās īre
nōn possunt. 4. Caesar Britanniae quoque[2] nātiōnēs[3] adīre volt.
5. Nostrī frūmentandī causā trāns Mosam ierant. 6. Hostēs nē
ūnum quidem[4] nostrōrum impetum ferunt. 7. Factum est, ut
hostēs nē ūnum[4] quidem nostrōrum impetum ferrent. 8. Nōs
propter ea, quae ferēbāmus, onera impediēbāmur. 9. Nōnnūllī[5]
nē voltum quidem hostium atque aciem oculōrum ferre potuerant.
10. Helvetiī nōn facile fīnitimīs bellum īnferre poterant. 11. Hīs
rēbus fit, ut[6] Helvetiī minus facile fīnitimīs bellum īnferre possint. 12. Hīs rēbus fiēbat, ut Haeduī sēsē ab Helvētiīs dēfendere
nōn possent. 13. Id sī fīat, māgnō cum perīculō prōvinciae sit,
ut (prōvincia) hominēs bellicōsōs locīs patentibus māximēque
frūmentāriīs fīnitimōs habeat.

DIRECTION. — Learn A. & G.: [1]258, g. [2]151, a. [3]228, a; 237, d.
[4]151, e, second part. [5]150 and a.
[6]332 and a, 2.
H.: [1]420, 1, 3); Rule XXV. [2]554, I. 4.
[3]372. [4]569, III. 2. [5]553 and 1.
[6]501, I. 1.

Ferō, *I bear* (*I endure*).

ACTIVE VOICE, INDICATIVE MOOD.

PRESENT TENSE.

Sing. 1. fe'rō   Plur. 1. fe'ri mus
     2. fers   2. fer'tis
     3. fert   3. fe'runt

IMPERFECT TENSE.

Sing. 1. fe rē'bam   Plur. 1. fe rē bā'mus
     2. fe rē'bās   2. fe rē bā'tis
     3. fe rē'bat   3. fe rē'bant

FUTURE TENSE.

Sing. 1. fe'ram   Plur. 1. fe rē'mus
     2. fe'rēs   2. fe rē'tis
     3. fe'ret   3. fe'rent

PERFECT TENSE.

Sing. 1. tu'lī   Plur. 1. tu'li mus
     2. tu li'stī   2. tu li'stis
     3. tu'lit   3. tu lē'runt (-re)

PLUPERFECT TENSE.

Sing. 1. tu'le ram   Plur. 1. tu le rā'mus
     2. tu'le rās   2. tu le rā'tis
     3. tu'le rat   3. tu'le rant

FUTURE PERFECT TENSE.

Sing. 1. tu'le rō   Plur. 1. tu le'ri mus
     2. tu'le ris   2. tu le'ri tis
     3. tu'le rit   3. tu'le rint

PASSIVE VOICE, INDICATIVE MOOD.

PRESENT TENSE.

Sing. 1. fe'ror   Plur. 1. fe'ri mur
     2. fer'ris (-re)   2. fe ri'mi nī
     3. fer'tur   3. fe run'tur

IMPERFECT TENSE.

Sing. 1. fe rē'bar   Plur. 1. fe rē bā'mur
2. fe rē bā'ris (-re)   2. fe rē bā'mi nī
3. fe rē bā'tur   3. fe rē ban'tur

FUTURE TENSE.

Sing. 1. fe'rar   Plur. 1. fe rē'mur
2. fe rē'ris (-re)   2. fe rē'mi nī
3. fe rē'tur   3. fe ren'tur

PERFECT TENSE.

Sing. 1. lā'tus sum   Plur. 1. lā'tī su'mus
2. lā'tus es   2. lā'tī e'stis
3. lā'tus est   3. lā'tī sunt

PLUPERFECT TENSE.

Sing. 1. lā'tus e'ram   Plur. 1. lā'tī e rā'mus
2. lā'tus e'rās   2. lā'tī e rā'tis
3. lā'tus e'rat   3. lā'tī e'rant

FUTURE PERFECT TENSE.

Sing. 1. lā'tus e'rō   Plur. 1. lā'tī e'ri mus
2. lā'tus e'ris   2. lā'tī e'ri tis
3. lā'tus e'rit   3. lā'tī e'runt

ACTIVE VOICE, SUBJUNCTIVE MOOD.

PRESENT TENSE.

Sing. 1. fe'ram   Plur. 1. fe rā'mus
2. fe'rās   2. fe rā'tis
3. fe'rat   3. fe'rant

IMPERFECT TENSE.

Sing. 1. fer'rem   Plur. 1. fer rē'mus
2. fer'rēs   2. fer rē'tis
3. fer'ret   3. fer'rent

PERFECT TENSE.

Sing. 1. tu'le rim	Plur. 1. tu le'ri mus
2. tu'le ris	2. tu le'ri tis
3. tu'le rit	3. tu'le rint

PLUPERFECT TENSE.

Sing. 1. tu lis'sem	Plur. 1. tu lis sē'mus
2. tu lis'sēs	2. tu lis sē'tis
3. tu lis'set	3. tu lis'sent

PASSIVE VOICE, SUBJUNCTIVE MOOD.

PRESENT TENSE.

Sing. 1. fe'rar	Plur. 1. fe rā'mur
2. fe rā'ris (-re)	2. fe rā'mi nī
3. fe rā'tur	3. fe ran'tur

IMPERFECT TENSE.

Sing. 1. fer'rer	Plur. 1. fer rē'mur
2. fer rē'ris (-re)	2. fer rē'mi nī
3. fer rē'tur	3. fer ren'tur

PERFECT TENSE.

Sing. 1. lā'tus sim	Plur. 1. lā'tī sī'mus
2. lā'tus sīs	2. lā'tī sī'tis
3. lā'tus sit	3. lā'tī sint

PLUPERFECT TENSE.

Sing. 1. lā'tus es'sem	Plur. 1. lā'tī es sē'mus
2. lā'tus es'sēs	2. lā'tī es sē'tis
3. lā'tus es'set	3. lā'tī es'sent

IMPERATIVE MOOD.

ACTIVE VOICE.	*Present Tense.*	PASSIVE VOICE.
Sing. 2. fer		Sing. 2. fer'rī
Plur. 2. fer'te		Plur. 2. fe ri'mi nī

Future Tense.

Sing. 2 and 3. fer'tō	Sing. 2 and 3. fer'tor
Plur. 2. fer tō'te	Plur. 2. ——
Plur. 3. fe run'tō	Plur. 3. fe run'tor

INFINITIVE MOOD.

ACTIVE VOICE.	*Present Tense.*	PASSIVE VOICE.
fer're		fer'rī

Perfect Tense.

tu lis'se		lā'tus es'se

Future Tense.

lā tū'rus es'se		lā'tum ī'rī
		lā'tus fo're

PARTICIPLES.

ACTIVE VOICE, *Pres.* fe'rēns, *Fut.* lā tū'rus.
PASSIVE VOICE, *Perf.* lā'tus, *Fut.* fe ren'dus (Gerundive).

THE GERUND AND SUPINES.

N. Gen. fe ren'dī, Dat. fe ren'dō, Acc. fe ren'dum, Abl. fe ren'dō.
Former Supine, lā'tum. Latter Supine, lā'tū.

Eō, *I go.*

INDICATIVE MOOD.

PRESENT TENSE.

Sing. 1. e'ō	Plur. 1. ī'mus
2. īs	2. ī'tis
3. it	3. e'unt

IMPERFECT TENSE.

Sing. 1. ī'bam   Plur. 1. ī bā'mus
      2. ī'bās   2. ī bā'tis
      3. ī'bat   3. ī'bant

FUTURE TENSE.

Sing. 1. ī'bō   Plur. 1. ī'bi mus
      2. ī'bis   2. ī'bi tis
      3. ī'bit   3. ī'bunt

PERFECT TENSE.

Sing. 1. ī'vī   (i'ī, etc.)   Plur. 1. ī'vi mus
      2. ī vi'stī   2. ī vi'stis
      3. ī'vit   3. ī vē'runt (-re)

PLUPERFECT TENSE.

Sing. 1. ī've ram (i'e ram, etc.) Plur. 1. ī ve rā'mus
      2. ī've rās   2. ī ve rā'tis
      3. ī've rat   3. ī've rant

FUTURE PERFECT TENSE.

Sing. 1. ī've rō   (i'e rō, etc.)   Plur. 1. ī ve'ri mus
      2. ī've ris   2. ī ve'ri tis
      3. ī've rit   3. ī've rint   .

SUBJUNCTIVE MOOD.

PRESENT TENSE.

Sing. 1. e'am   Plur. 1. e ā'mus
      2. e'ās   2. e ā'tis
      3. e'at   3. e'ant

IMPERFECT TENSE.

Sing. 1. ī'rem   Plur. 1. ī rē'mus
      2. ī'rēs   2. ī rē'tis
      3. ī'ret   3. ī'rent

PERFECT TENSE.

Sing. 1. ī've rim (i'e rim, etc.)   Plur. 1. ī ve'ri mus
     2. ī've ris   2. ī ve'ri tis
     3. ī've rit   3. ī've rint

PLUPERFECT TENSE.

Sing. 1. ī vis'sem (īs'sem, etc.)   Plur. 1. ī vis sē'mus
     2. ī vis'sēs   2. ī vis sē'tis
     3. ī vis'set   3. ī vis'sent

IMPERATIVE MOOD.

Pres. Sing. 2. ī   Plur. 2. ī'te
Fut. Sing. 2 and 3. ī'tō   Plur. 2. ī tō'te ; 3. e un'tō

INFINITIVES.

Pres. ī're   *Perf.* ī vis'se (īs'se)   *Fut.* i tū'rus es'se

PARTICIPLES.

Pres. i'ēns (gen. e un'tis).   *Fut.* i tū'rus

Gerund. Gen. e un'dī, Dat. e un'dō, Acc. e un'dum, Abl. e un'dō.
Former Supine, i'tum.   Latter Supine, i'tū.

Fīō, *I am made, I become.*

INDICATIVE MOOD.

PRESENT TENSE.

Sing. 1. fī'ō   Plur. 1. fī'mus
     2. fīs   2. fī'tis
     3. fit   3. fī'unt

IMPERFECT TENSE.

Sing. 1. fī ē'bam   Plur. 1. fī ē bā'mus
     2. fī ē'bās   2. fī ē bā'tis
     3. fī ē'bat   3. fī ē'bant

FUTURE TENSE.

Sing. 1. fī'am   Plur. 1. fī ē'mus
    2. fī'ēs   2. fī ē'tis
    3. fī'et   3. fī'ent

PERFECT TENSE.

Sing. 1. fac'tus sum   Plur. 1. fac'tī su'mus
    2. fac'tus es   2. fac'tī e'stis
    3. fac'tus est   3. fac'tī sunt

PLUPERFECT TENSE.

Sing. 1. fac'tus e'ram   Plur. 1. fac'tī e rā'mus
    2. fac'tus e'rās   2. fac'tī e rā'tis
    3. fac'tus e'rat   3. fac'tī e'rant

FUTURE PERFECT TENSE.

Sing. 1. fac'tus e'rō   Plur. 1. fac'tī e'ri mus
    2. fac'tus e'ris   2. fac'tī e'ri tis
    3. fac'tus e'rit   3. fac'tī e'runt

SUBJUNCTIVE MOOD.

PRESENT TENSE.

Sing. 1. fī'am   Plur. 1. fī ā'mus
    2. fī'ās   2. fī ā'tis
    3. fī'at   3. fī'ant

IMPERFECT TENSE.

Sing. 1. fi'e rem   Plur. 1. fi e rē'mus
    2. fi'e rēs   2. fi e rē'tis
    3. fi'e ret   3. fi'e rent

PERFECT TENSE.

Sing. 1. fac'tus sim   Plur. 1. fac'tī sī'mus
    2. fac'tus sīs   2. fac'tī sī'tis
    3. fac'tus sit   3. fac'tī sint

PLUPERFECT TENSE.

Sing. 1. fac'tus es'sem   Plur. 1. fac'tī es sē'mus
    2. fac'tus es'sēs   2. fac'tī es sē'tis
    3. fac'tus es'set   3. fac'tī es'sent

IMPERATIVE MOOD.

Pres. Sing. 2. fī   Plur. 2. fī'te
Fut. Sing. 2 and 3. fī'tō   Plur. 3. fī tō'te ; fī un'tō

INFINITIVES.

Pres. fi'e rī   *Perf.* fac'tus es'se   *Fut.* fac'tum ī'rī

PARTICIPLES.

Perf. fac'tus   *Fut.* fa ci en'dus (Gerundive)

212.

1. The infantry, separated into three divisions, attack (go against) the enemy. 2. We were going to reinforce the cavalry (for a reinforcement to the cavalry). 3. I could not have gone (was not able to have gone) by sea. 4. Why [do] you (sing.) wish to visit the nations of Britain ? 5. I am going for the sake of waging war. 6. You (plur.) will not endure even one attack of the enemy. 7. It did not happen without reason that we did not endure even one attack of the enemy. 8. I am hindered by this load which I am carrying. 9. Some cannot (are not able to) endure the enemies' expression-of-countenance and the glare of their eyes. 10. We could have made (were able to have made) war upon the enemy. 11. From these circumstances it happens that we can easily make war upon our neighbors. 12. It happened all along (imperfect tense) that we could not defend ourselves from the enemy. 13. If this happens (shall happen), it will be with great danger to the province that it has warlike men as neighbors in an open and especially fertile country.

QUESTIONS AND IMPERATIVE FORMS IN INDIRECT DISCOURSE. FUTURE PASSIVE INFINITIVES.

SUGGESTIONS. — 1. **Cum,** 1 and 2, is to be translated *since;* **cum,** 3, *although;* **fēcērunt ut profectiō vidērētur,** 2, *they caused that the departure seemed,* or concisely, *the departure seemed.*

2. The second sentences in 9 and 10 show two ways of expressing the *future passive infinitive.* The form in 10 is the common one. It is often used to express the *future active infinitive* with the verb of the *ut-clause* in the subjunctive active, and *must* be used when the verb has no future active participle. Since deponent verbs have the participles of both voices, the form given in 10, third sentence, may also be used with deponents.

213.

1. Perfacile[1] est, cum[2] virtūte omnibus praestēmus, tōtīus Galliae imperiō potīrī. 2. Cum quisque domum[3] pervenīre properāret, fēcērunt ut[4] cōnsimilis fugae profectiō vidērētur. 3. Cum[2] ea ita sint, pācem Helvētiīs faciam. 4. Quid tibi[5] vīs? Ariovistus rogāvit quid sibi[5] vellet.[6] 5. Num[7] recentium iniūriārum memoriam dēpōnere possum? Hīs Caesar respondit num[8] recentium iniūriārum memoriam dēpōnere posse?[6] 6. Sī[9] flūmen nostrī trānsīrent, hostēs exspectābant. 7. Fīnem ōrandī fac.[10] Caesar dīcit, fīnem ōrandī faciat.[11] 8. Vercingetorix prōditiōnis accūsātus est, quod castra propius Rōmānōs mōvisset,[12] quod sine imperiō cōpiās relīquisset, quod ēius discessū Rōmānī celeriter vēnissent. 9. Ea rēs longius[13] dūcētur. Lēgātus longius eam rem ductum īrī exīstimābat. 10. Sī opus erit, mīrābor. Caesar dīcit fore[14] (futūrum esse) ut[14] mīrētur, sī opus sit. Caesar dīcit sē mīrātūrum (esse), sī opus sit. 11. Sī opus esset, mīrārer. Caesar dīxit futūrum fuisse[15] ut[15] mīrārētur, sī opus esset.

DIRECTION. — Learn A. & G.: [1] Rule 2.   [2] **326**; Rule 79.   [3] **258,** *b.*
[4] **332,** *e.*   [5] **235** and Note; **236**;
Rule 29.   [6] **338.**   [7] **210,** 1, 2 and *c.*
[8] **210,** 2 and *f*, Remark.   [9] **334**
and *f.*   [10] **128,** *c.*   [11] **339**; Rule 82.
[12] **321**; **341** and *d*; Rule 83.
[13] **93,** *a.*   [14] **288,** *f.*   [15] **337,** *b* and 3.

Learn H.: [1]Rule XXXIV. [2]517; Rule XLVIII. [3]380, II. 2, 1); Rule X. [4]501, II. 1. [5]389. [6]523, II. 1, 2; Rule LIII. II. 1, 2. [7]351, 1, Note 3. [8]529, I., II. 1 and Note 3; Rule LV., I. [9]529, II. 1 and Note 1. [10]238. [11]523, III.; Rule LIII. III. [12]516, II.; Rule XLVII. II. [13]444 and 1. [14]537, 3 and Note 1. [15]527, III. and Note 1.

214.

1. It was very easy, since we excelled all in valor, to obtain control of the entire province. 2. Since we are all hastening to reach home, we make the departure seem (that the departure seems) very much like a flight. 3. Although these things were so, I made peace with them. 4. What do you want (for yourselves)? I asked what they wanted (for themselves). 5. Can we blot out the memory of our wrongs? The consuls asked whether they could blot out the memory of their wrongs. 6. We are waiting [to see] if you will cross the river. 7. Don't wait (make an end of waiting). Caesar asked [him] not to wait. 8. I am accused of treason because (as they say) I have moved camp nearer the enemy, and have left the forces without control. 9. Ariovistus will be condemned. They say that Ariovistus will be condemned. 10. If there should be need, I should wonder. The lieutenants said that if there should be need, they would wonder (express in two ways). 11. If there had been need, we should have wondered. The commanders said that if there had been need, they would have wondered.

PERIPHRASTIC CONJUGATIONS.

SUGGESTIONS. — 1. The inflections of the *periphrastic* conjugations are to be learned from A. & G. 129; H. 233, 234, and translated as suggested by the following illustrations: **laudātūrus sum**, *I am (about) to praise, I intend (propose) to praise;* **laudandus sum**, *I am to be praised, I must (ought to, need to) be praised.*

2. The subjunctive of the first periphrastic conjugation is used in *Indirect Questions* referring to future time. Learn A. & G. 333, 5, Note; 334 and *a*; H. 529, II. 4; e.g. *Sciō quid* **factūrus sim**, etc., *I know what I shall do,* etc. *Scīvī quid* **factūrus essem**, etc., *I knew what I should do,* etc. *Scīvī quid* **factūrus fuerim**, etc., *I knew what I should have done,* etc.

3. Such sentences as *hōc tibī* **faciendum est**, *this is to be* (*must be*) *done by you*, are best translated actively, *you must do this*.

215.

1. Repraesentābō quod in longiōrem diem conlātūrus fuī. Caesar dīcit sē, quod in longiōrem diem conlātūrus fuerit, repraesentātūrum[1] (esse). 2. Sciō quō itūrus sim.[2] Scīvī quō itūrus essem. Scīvī quō itūrus fuerim. 3. Caesarī[3] omnia ūnō tempore agenda erant; mīlitēs cohortandī, vexillum prōpōnendum, sīgnum tubā dandum, aciēs īnstruenda. 4. Mīlitibus[3] dē nāvibus erat dēsiliendum,[4] in fluctibus cōnsistendum[4] et cum hostibus pūgnandum.[4] 5. Caesar cōncēdendum[4] (esse) nōn putābat. 6. Caesar nōn expectandum[4] (esse) sibī[3] statuit. 7. Caesar partiendum (esse) sibī[3] exercitum putāvit, priusquam plūrēs cīvitātēs cōnspīrārent.

DIRECTION.— Learn A. & G.: [1]336, 2; Rule 80. [2]338; Rule 81. [3]232 and Note, first sentence; Rule 26. [4]Impersonal.

H.: [1]523, I.; Rule LIII. I.; 524; Rule LIV. [2]523, II. 1.; Rule LIII. II. 1. [3]388. [4]Impersonal.

216.

1. I am about-to-go. This you (sing.) were to-do-at-once. We have purposed-to-do this. They had intended-to-divide the army. 2. Caesar said that he would do-at-once what he had intended-to-postpone to a more distant day. 3. We often wish to know what will happen (will be). We have often wished to know what would happen. We have often wished to know what would have happened. 4. I must-be-protected. We ought-to-have-been (perfect) selected. 5. We need to encourage the legions, hang out the flag, give the signal with a trumpet, and arrange the battle-line (the legions need-to-be-encouraged by us, etc.). 6. You (plur.) will need to jump down from the ships, take position in the waves, and fight with the enemy (it will need-to-be-jumped-down by you, etc.). 7. Caesar [does] does not think that a concession ought to be made (it ought-to-be-conceded). 8. I think that I must divide the auxiliaries (that the auxiliaries ought-to-be-divided by me).

VOCABULARIES.

ABBREVIATIONS.

a.,	active (transitive).		N.,	neuter gender.
abl.,	ablative.		n.,	neuter (intransitive).
acc.,	accusative.		num.,	numeral.
adj.,	adjective.		ord.,	ordinal.
adv.,	adverb.		p.,	passive.
aux.,	auxiliary.		p.p.,	perfect participle.
c.,	common gender.		part.,	particle.
card.,	cardinal.		pass.,	passive.
comp.,	comparative.		perf.,	perfect.
conj.,	conjunction.		pers.,	personal.
coör.,	coördinate.		pl.,	plural.
dat.,	dative.		pluperf.,	pluperfect.
dem.,	demonstrative.		poss.,	possessive.
dep.,	deponent.		prep.,	preposition.
dist.,	distributive.		pres.,	present.
F.,	feminine gender.		pres. p.,	present participle.
fut.,	future.		pron.,	pronoun.
gen.,	genitive.		reflex.,	reflexive.
imperf.,	imperfect.		rel.,	relative.
impers.,	impersonal.		semi-dep.,	semi-deponent.
ind.,	indicative.		sing.,	singular.
indecl.,	indeclinable.		sub.,	subordinate.
indef.,	indefinite.		subj.,	subjunctive.
interrog.,	interrogative.		sup.	superlative.
irr.,	irregular.		v.,	verb.
M.,	masculine gender.			

LATIN–ENGLISH.

A.

ab (ū, abs), prep., *by, from.*
abdūcuntur, 3. v. p., *are led away.*
abest, irr. v. n., *is away.*
absum, -fuī, -futūrus, -esse, irr. v. n., *be absent.*
absunt, irr. v. n., *are away.*
āc, conj., *and.*
acceptus, -a, -um, adj., *acceptable.*
accidō, -cidī, —, -cidere, 3. v. n., *happen.*
accipiō, -cēpī, -ceptum, -cipere, 3. v. a., *receive, take.*
accipiunt, 3. v. a., *take.*
accommodō, -āvī, -ātum, -āre, 1. v. a., *put on.*
accūsō, 1. v. a., *accuse.*
ācer, -cris, -cre, adj., *active, violent.*
ācerrimē, adv., sup., *most (very) violently.*
ācerrimus, -a, -um, adj., sup., *most (very) active, violent.*
aciēs, -ēī, F., *(battle) line, glare.*
ācrior, -us, adj., comp., *more (rather) active, violent.*
ācriter, adv., *violently, with spirit.*
ācrius, adv., comp., *more violently.*
ad, prep., *to, towards, near.*
addūcō, -dūxī, -dūctum, -dūcere, 3. v. a., *lead to.*
adeō, -iī (-īvī), -itum, -īre, irr. v. a. and n., *visit.*
adfīnitās, -tātis, F., *relationship.*
aditus, -ūs, M., *approach.*
administrō, -āvī, -ātum, -āre, 1. v. a., *execute.*

adsum, -fuī, -futūrus, -esse, irr. v. n., *be here.*
adventus, -ūs, M., *an arrival.*
adversus, prep., *against.*
aedificium, -ī, N., *a building.*
aequus, -a, -um, adj., *fair.*
aestās, -tātis, F., *heat.*
aetās, -tātis, F., *age.*
ager, agrī, M., *a field.*
agit, 3. v. a., *treats.*
agmen, -minis, N., *an army* (on the march), *a column.*
agō, ēgī, āctum, agere, 3. v. a., *do, treat.*
agricultūra, -ae, F., *agriculture.*
alacritās, -tātis, F., *activity.*
aliēnus, -a, -um, adj., *unfavorable.*
aliquis, -qua, -quid (-quod), pron., *some, any.*
aliquot, pron. indecl., *several.*
alius, -a, -ud, adj. pron., *other, another.*
alius . . . alius, *one . . . another;* aliī . . . aliī, *some . . . others.*
Allobrogēs, -um, M. pl., *the Allobroges.*
Alpēs, -ium, M. pl., *the Alps.*
alter, -era, -erum, *the other.* In pl. *the other party.* Alter . . . alter, *the one . . . the other;* alterī . . . alterī, *one party . . . the other.*
altitūdō, -inis, F., *height, depth.*
altus, -a, -um, adj., *high, deep.*
Ambarrī, -ōrum, pl. of adj., *the Ambarri.*

3

amīcior, -us, adj., comp., *more (rather) friendly.*
amīcissimus, -a, -um, adj., sup., *most (very) friendly.*
amīcitia, -ae, F., *friendship.*
amīcus, -ī, M., *a friend.*
amīcus, -a, -um, adj., *friendly.*
āmīttō, -mīsī, -missum, -mittere, 3. v. a., *lose.*
amor, -ōris, M., *love.*
amplius, adv., comp., *more* (with abl., *more than*).
an, interrog. particle, *or* (used with second part of double question).
angustiae, -ārum, F., *narrowness of passage.*
animus, -ī, M., *disposition, mind, feelings.*
annus, -ī, M., *a year.*
annuus, -a, -um, adj., *annual.*
ante, prep., *before.*
antequam, adv., *before.*
appellantur, 1. v. p., *are called.*
appellat, 1. v. a., *calls.*
appellātur, 1. v. p., *is called.*
appellō, -āvī, -ātum, -āre, 1. v. a., *call.*
Apr., see *Aprilis.*
Aprīlis, -e, adj., *April.*
apud, prep., *among.*
Arar, -aris, M., *the Saône.*
arbor, -oris, F., *a tree.*
arduus, -a, -um, adj., *rugged.*
Ariovistus, -ī, M., *Ariovistus.*
arma, -ōrum, N. pl., *arms.*
armant, 1. v. a., *arm.*
armantur, 1. v. p., *are armed.*
armat, 1. v. a., *arms.*
armātur, 1. v. p., *is armed.*
armō, -āvī, -ātum, -āre, 1. v. a., *arm, equip.*
Arvernī, -ōrum, pl. of adj., *the Arverni.*
ascendit, 3. v. a., *ascends.*
ascendō, -scendī, -scēnsum, -scendere, 3. v. a. and n., *ascends.*

at, conj., *but.*
atque, conj., *and.*
auctor, -ōris, M., *an adviser.*
auctōritās, -tātis, F., *authority, influence.*
audācia, -ae, F., *boldness.*
audācior, -us, adj., comp., *more (rather) daring.*
audācissimē, adv., sup., *most (very) boldly.*
audācissimus, -a, -um, adj., sup., *most (very) daring.*
audācius, adv., comp., *more (rather, too) boldly.*
audācter, adv., *boldly.*
audāx, -ācis, adj., *daring.*
audeō, ausus, audēre, 2. v., semidep., *dare.*
audiō, -īvī, -ītum, -īre, 4. v. a., *hear.*
Aulus, -ī, M., *Aulus.*
auxilium, -ī, N., *assistance;* pl., *auxiliary forces, auxiliaries.*
Avaricum, -ī, N., *Avaricum.*

B.

barbarī, -ōrum, noun from adj., M., *barbarians.*
Belgae, -ārum, M. pl., *the Belgians.*
bellicōsus, -a, -um, adj., *warlike.*
bellō, -āvī, -ātum, -āre, 1. v. n., *make war.*
Bellovacī, -ōrum, M., *Bellovaci.*
bellum, -ī, N., *war.*
bene, adv., *well.*
Boiī, -ōrum, M., *Boii.*
bonus, -a, -um, adj., *good.*
Britannia, -ae, F., *Britain.*
Brūtus, -ī, M., *Brutus.*

C.

cadō, cecidī, cāsūrus, cadere, 3. v. n., *fall.*
cadunt, 3. v. n., *fall.*

caedēs, -is, F., *slaughter.*
Caesar, -aris, M., *Caesar.*
calamitās, -tātis, F., *misfortune.*
cālō, -ōnis, M., *a servant (of a soldier).*
capiō, cēpī, captum, capere, 3. v. a., *take, capture, adopt.*
captīvus, -ī, M., noun from adj., *a captive, prisoner.*
carrum, -ī, N., *cart, wagon.*
carrus, -ī, M., *cart, wagon.*
Cassiānus, -a, -um, adj., *of Cassius.*
castellum, -ī, N., *fortress.*
Casticus, -ī, M., *Casticus.*
castra, -ōrum, N. pl., *a camp.*
catēna, -ae, F., *chain.*
causa, -ae, F., *cause, sake.*
causā, *for the sake of.*
cautus, -a, -um, adj., *careful.*
celer, -eris, -ere, adj., *swift, fleet.*
celerior, -us, adj., comp., *swifter.*
celeriter, adv., *swiftly, quickly.*
celerius, adv., comp., *more (rather) swiftly.*
celerrimē, adv., sup., *most (very) swiftly.*
celerrimus, -a, -um, adj., sup., *swiftest.*
Celtae, -ārum, M., *Celts.*
centuriō, -ōnis, M., *a centurion.*
certus, -a, -um, adj., *definite.*
Cicerō, -ōnis, M., *Cicero.*
circiter, adv., *about.*
circum, prep., *around, about.*
circumveniō, -vēnī, -ventum, -venīre, 4. v. a., *surround.*
citerior, -us, adj., comp., *hither.*
citrā, prep., *this side.*
cīvis, -is, C., *a citizen.*
cīvitās, -tātis, F., *the state.*
clārior, -us, adj., comp., *more illustrious.*
clārissimus, -a, -um, adj., sup., *most (very) illustrious.*
clārus, -a, -um, adj., *illustrious.*

clāssis, -is, F., *a fleet.*
Claudius, -ī, M., *Claudius.*
clēmentia, -ae, F., *kindness.*
cohors, -ortis, F., *a cohort.*
cohortor, -ātus, -ārī, 1. v. dep., *exhort, encourage.*
collis, -is, M., *a hill.*
collocant (conlocant), 1. v. a., *locate.*
collocantur (conlocantur), 1. v. p., *are located.*
collocō (conlocō), -āvī, -ātum, -āre, 1. v. a., *locate.*
colloquium, see *conloquium.*
comes, -itis, C., *a companion.*
commeātus, -ūs, M., *supplies.*
commīttit, 3. v. a., *joins.*
commīttō, -mīsī, -missum, -mīttere, 3. v. a., *join.*
commoveō, -mōvī, -mōtum, -movēre, 2. v. a., *influence.*
commūnis, -e, adj., *common.*
complūrēs, -plūra (-plūria), adj., *very many.*
comportō, -āvī, -ātum, -āre, 1. v. a., *bring together.*
concēdō, -cēssi, -cēssum, -cēdere, 3. v. a. and n., *concede, grant.*
concidit, 3. v. a., *cuts to pieces.*
concīdō, -cīdī, -cīsum, -cīdere, 3. v. a., *cut to pieces.*
concilium, -ī, N., *a council.*
conclāmō, -āvī, -ātum, -āre, 1. v. n., *shout together.*
condōnō, -āvī, -ātum, -āre, 1. v. a., *pardon.*
cōnferō, -tulī, -lātum, -ferre, irr. v. a., *postpone.*
cōnfirmant, 1. v. a., *encourage.*
cōnfirmantur, 1. v. p., *are encouraged.*
cōnfirmat, 1. v. a., *encourages.*
cōnfirmātur, 1. v. p., *is encouraged.*
cōnfirmō, -āvī, -ātum, -āre, 1. v. a., *encourage, strengthen.*

6   VOCABULARIES.

cōniciō, -iēcī, -iectum, -icere, 3. v. a.,
  throw.
coniūrātiō, -ōnis, F., a conspiracy.
conlocō, etc., see collocō, etc.   .
conloquium, -ī, N., a conference.
conloquor, -locūtus, -loquī, 3. v.
  dep., confer.
cōnor, -ātus, -ārī, 1. v. dep., endeavor.
cōnscius, -a, -um, adj., conscious.
cōnscrībit, 3. v. a., enrolls.
cōnscrībō, -scrīpsī, -scrīptum, -scrī-
  bere, 3. v. a., enroll.
cōnsector, -ātus, -ārī, 1. v. dep., pursue, overtake.
cōnsēnsus, -ūs, M., consent.
cōnservō, -āvī, -ātum, -āre, 1. v. a.,
  spare.
Cōnsidius, -ī, M., Considius.
cōnsīdō, -sēdī, -sessūrus, -sīdere,
  3. v. n., settle.
cōnsilium, -ī, N., a plan.
cōnsimilis, -e, adj., very much like.
cōnsistō, -stitī, —, -sistere, 3. v. n.,
  take position.
cōnspectus, -ūs, M., sight.
cōnspīrō, -āvī, -ātum, -āre, 1. v. n.,
  conspire.
cōnstituō, -stituī, -stitūtum, -stitu-
  ere, 3. v. a. and n., determine.
cōnstō, -stitī, -stātūrus, -stāre, 1. v.
  n., impers., is evident.
cōnsuētūdō, -inis, F., custom.
cōnsul, -ulis, M., a consul.
cōnsulātus, -ūs, M., consulship.
contemptiō, -ōnis, F., contempt.
contendit, 3. v. n., hastens.
contendō, -tendī, -tentum, -tendere,
  3. v. n., hasten, contend.
continenter, adv. continually.
contineō, -tinuī, -tentum, -tinēre,
  2. v. a., keep, restrain, hem in;
  with reflexive, keep within.
continet, 2. v. a., keeps.
continuus, -a, -um, adj., successive.
contrā, prep., against.

contumēlia, -ae, F., insult.
convocō, -āvī, -ātum, -āre, 1. v. a.,
  call together, call.
cōpia, -ae, F., plenty, supply; pl.,
  troops, forces.
cornū, -ūs, (-ū), N., a wing (of an
  army).
corpus, -oris, N., body.
cotīdiē, adv., daily.
Cotta, -ae, M., Cotta.
creant, 1. v. a., elect.
creantur, 1. v. p., are elected.
creat, 1. v. a., elects.
creātur, 1. v. p., is elected.
cremō, -āvī, -ātum, -āre, 1. v. a.,
  burn.
creō, -āvī, -ātum, -āre, 1. v. a., elect.
cultus, -ūs, M., civilization.
cum, prep., (in company) with (abl.
  case).
cum, conj., although, since, when.
cupidē, adv., eagerly.
cupidissimē, adv., sup., most (very)
  eagerly.
cupiditās, -tātis, F., desire.
cupidius, adv., comp., more (too,
  rather) eagerly.
cupidus, -a, -um, adj., desirous of.
cūr, adv., why.
cūra, -ae, F., care.
currus, -ūs, M., chariot.
custōs, -ōdis, C., a guard.

D.

damnō, -āvī, -ātum, -āre, 1. v. a.,
  condemn.
dant, 1. v. a., give.
dantur, 1. v. p., are given.
dat, 1. v. a., gives.
datur, 1. v. p., is given.
dē, prep., concerning, for, from.
decem, card. num. adj., indecl., ten.
decimus, -a, -um, ord. num. adj.,
  tenth.

dēcrētum, -ī, N., a decree.

dēfendō, -fendī, -fēnsum, -fendere, 3. v. a., defend.

dēfendunt, 3. v. a., defend.

dēfessus, -a, -um, adj., wearied.

dēlectant, 1. v. a., delight.

dēlectantur, 1. v. p., are delighted.

dūlectat, 1. v. a., delights.

dēlectātur, 1. v. p., is delighted.

dēlectō, -āvī, -ātum, -āre, 1. v. a., delight.

dēligit, 3. v. a., selects.

dēligitur, 3. v. p., is selected.

dēligō, -lēgī, -lēctum, -ligere, 3. v. a., select.

dēligunt, 3. v. a., select.

dēliguntur, 3. v. p., are selected.

dēmōnstrant, 1. v. a., show.

dēmōnstrantur, 1. v. p., are shown.

dēmōnstrat, 1. v. a., shows.

dēmōnstrātur, 1. v. p., is shown.

dēmōnstrō, -āvī, -ātum, -āre, 1. v. a., show, point out.

dēpōnō, -posuī, -positum, -pōnere, 3. v. a., lay aside, blot out.

dēpopulor, -ātus, -ārī, 1. v. dep., devastate.

dēserō, -seruī, -sertum, -serere, 3. v. a., abandon.

dēsiliō, -siluī, -sultum, -silīre, 4. v. n., leap down.

dēsistō, -stitī, -stitūrus, -sistere, 3. v. n., stop.

dēsum, -fuī, -futūrus, -esse, irr. v. n., lack.

dēterreō, -terruī, -territum, -terrēre, 2. v. a., hinder.

dētineō, -tinuī, -tentum, -tinēre, 2. v. n., detain.

dēvastō, -āvī, -ātum, -āre, 1. v. a., devastate.

dexter, -era, -erum, and -tra, -trum, adj., right.

dīcō, dīxī, dictum, dīcere, 3. v. a. and n., say.

dīcor, dictus, dīcī, pass. of dīcō, 3. v. p. impers., it is said.

diēs, -ēī, M. (sometimes F.), a day.

difficilis, -e, adj., difficult.

difficultās, -tātis, F., a difficulty.

dīgnior, -us, adj., comp., more worthy.

dīgnissimus, -a, -um, adj., sup., most (very) worthy.

dignus, -a, -um, adj., worthy.

dīligēns, -entis, adj., diligent.

dīligenter, adv., diligently.

dīligentior, -us, adj., comp., more diligent, more careful.

dīligentissimē, adv., sup., most (very) diligently.

dīligentissimus, -a, -um, adj., most (very) diligent.

dīligentius, adv., comp., more diligently.

dīmicō, -āvī, -ātūrus, -āre, 1. v. n., fight (to the end).

discēssus, -ūs, M., departure.

dispōnō, -posuī, -positum, -pōnere, 3. v. a., station.

distineō, -tinuī, -tentum, -tinēre, 2. v. a., keep apart.

diū, adv., a long time.

Divicō, -ōnis, M., Divico.

dīvidit, 3. v. a., separates.

dīvidō, -vīsī, -vīsum, -videre, 3. v. a., separate.

dīvidunt, 3. v. a., separate.

dīvīsus, -a, -um, p.p. as adj., divided, separated.

Divitiacus, -ī, M., Divitiacus.

dō, dedī, datum, dare, 1. v. a., give.

domicilium, -ī, N., an abode.

dominus, -ī, M., a master, owner.

domus, -ī (-ūs), F., a house, home.

dubitātiō, -ōnis, F., doubt.

dubius, -a, -um, adj., doubtful.

dūcit, 3. v. a., leads.

dūcitur, 3. v. p., is led.

dūcō, dūxi, dūctum, dūcere, 3. v. a., *lead, draw.*

dūcunt, 3. v. a., *lead.*

dūcuntur, 3. v. p., *are led.*

dum, conj., *while, until.*

dummodō, conj., *provided.*

Dumnorix, -igis, M., *Dumnorix.*

duo, -ae, -o, card. num. adj., *two.*

duodecim, card. num. adj., indecl., *twelve.*

dux, ducis, C., *a leader.*

E.

ea, see *is.*

ēdūcit, 3. v. a., *leads out.*

ēdūcō, -dūxi, -dūctum, -dūcere, 3. v. a., *lead out, lead away.*

effēminō, -āvi, -ātum, -āre, 1. v. a., *enfeeble.*

egeō, eguī, —, egēre, 2. v. n., *need.*

ēnūntiō, -āvi, -ātum, -āre, 1. v. a., *reveal, disclose.*

eō, īvī (iī), itum, īre, irr. v. n., *go.*

eques, -itis, M., *a horseman;* pl., *cavalry.*

equitātus, -ūs, M., *cavalry.*

equus, -ī, M., *a horse.*

errō, -āvī, -ātūrus, -āre, 1. v. n., *be mistaken, go wrong.*

ērumpō, -rūpi, -ruptum, -rumpere, 3. v. a. and n., *break forth.*

es, see *sum.*

est, (*he, she, it, there*) *is.*

et, conj., *and.*

et ... et, *both ... and.*

etiam, conj., *even.*

etsī, conj., *even if.*

ex (ē), adv. and prep., *from, on.*

exeō, -īvī (-iī), -itum, -īre, irr. v. n., *go forth.*

exercitus, -ūs, M., *an army (in training).*

exeunt, irr. v. n., *go forth.*

exīstimō, -āvī, -ātum, -āre, 1. v. a., *think, believe.*

exit, irr. v. n., *goes forth.*

expellit, 3. v. a., *drives out.*

expellitur, 3. v. p., *is driven out.*

expellō, -pulī, -pulsum, -pellere, 3. v. a., *drive out.*

expellunt, 3. v. a., *drive out.*

expelluntur, 3. v. p., *are driven out.*

experior, -pertus, -perīrī, 4. v. dep., *try.*

explōrātor, -ōris, M., *a scout.*

expūgnantur, 1. v. p., *are captured.*

expūgnō, -āvī, -ātum, -āre, 1. v. a., *capture.*

exspectō, -āvī, -ātum, -āre, 1. v. a. and n., *wait.*

exsul, -ulis, C., *an exile.*

F.

faber, -brī, M., *an engineer* (in an army).

Fabius, -ī, M., *Fabius.*

facile, adv., *easily.*

facilis, -e, adj., *easy.*

facilius, adv., comp., *more easily.*

facillimē, adv., sup., *most (very) easily.*

facinus, -oris, N., *a crime.*

faciō, fēcī, factum, facere, irr. v. a. and n., *make.*

facit, irr. v. a. and n., *makes;* iter facit, *he makes a journey, marches.*

faciunt, irr. v. a. and n., *make.*

factiō, -ōnis, F., *a faction.*

factum, -ī, N. of p.p., *act;* opus factō, *need of action.*

facultās, -tātis, F., *opportunity.*

famēs, -is, F., *starvation, famine, hunger.*

favent, 2. v. n., *favor.*

faveō, fāvī, fautūrus, favēre, 2. v. n., *favor* (with dat.).

favet, 2. v. n., *favors.*

fēmina, -ae, F., *a woman.*

ferō, tulī, lātum, ferre, irr. v. a. and n., *bring.*

ferrum, -ī, N., *iron, sword.*

fert, irr. v. a. and n., *brings.*

ferunt, irr. v. a. and n., *bring, bear, carry, endure.*

fidēlior, -us, adj., comp., *more faithful.*

fidēlis, -e, adj., *faithful.*

fidēlissimus, -a, -um, adj., sup., *most (very) faithful.*

fīlia, -ae, F., *a daughter.*

fīlius, -ī, M., *a son.*

fīnis, -is, M., sing., *a boundary, limit;* pl., *territory.*

fīnitimus, -a, -um, adj., *adjacent.*

fīō, factus, fierī, pass. of faciō, *happen.*

fit, irr. v. p., *is made, becomes.*

fiunt, irr. v. p., *are made, become.*

flāgitant, 1. v. a., *(earnestly) demand.*

flāgitat, 1. v. a., *(earnestly) demands.*

flāgitō, -āvī, -ātum, -āre, 1. v. a., *(earnestly) demand.*

fluctus, -ūs, M., *wave.*

fluit, 3. v. n., *flows.*

flūmen, -inis, N., *a river.*

fluō, flūxī, flūxum, fluere, 3. v. n., *flow.*

foedus, -eris., N., *a treaty.*

fortior, -us, adj., comp., *more brave.*

fortis, -e, adj., *brave.*

fortissimē, adv., sup., *most (very) bravely.*

fortissimus, -a, -um, adj., sup., *most (very) brave.*

fortiter, adv., *bravely.*

fortitūdō, -inis, F., *bravery.*

fortius, adv., comp., *more bravely.*

fortūna, -ae, F., *fortune.*

fossa, -ae, F., *a trench, ditch.*

frāter, -tris, M., *a brother.*

frāternus, -a, -um, adj., *fraternal.*

frīgus, -oris, N., *cold;* pl., *cold weather, frosts.*

frūmentarius, -a, -um, adj., *fertile.*

frūmentor, -tātus, -tārī, 1. v. dep., *gather grain.*

frūmentum, -ī, N., *grain, rations.*

fuga, -ae, F., *flight.*

fugiō, fūgī, fugitūrus, fugere, 3. v. a. and n., *fly.*

fuī, see *sum.*

furor, -ōris, M., *frenzy.*

G.

G., see *Gāius.*

Gāius, -ī, M., *Gaius.*

Galba, -ae, M., *Galba.*

galea, -ae, F., *a helmet.*

Gallia, -ae, F., *Gaul.*

Gallī, -ōrum, M. pl., *Gauls.*

Gallicus, -a, -um, adj., *Gallic.*

gaudeō, gāvīsus, gaudēre, 2. v. n., *rejoice.*

Genāva, -ae, F., *Geneva.*

genus, generis, N., *a class.*

Germānī, -ōrum, adj. as noun, *the Germans.*

Germānia, -ae, F., *Germany.*

gerō, gessī, gestum, gerere, 3. v. a., *carry on.*

gerunt, 3. v. a., *carry on.*

glōria, -ae, F., *glory, fame.*

grātia, -ae, F., *popularity, favor.*

grātum, -ī, N. of adj., *favor.*

gravior, -us, adj., 3., comp. of *gravis; greater, more advanced.*

graviter, adv., *severely.*

H.

habent, 2. v. a. and n., *have, treat, regard.*

habentur, 2. v. p., *are treated (as), are regarded (as).*

habeo, habuī, habitum, habēre, 2. v. a. and n., *have, treat, regard.*

habet, 2. v. a. and n., *has, treats, regards.*

habētur, 2. v. p., *is treated (as), is regarded (as).*

Haeduī, -ōrum, M., noun from adj., *the Haedui.*

Haeduus, -a, -um, adj., *of the Haedui.*

Helvētiī, -ōrum, M., noun from adj., *the Helvetii.*

hībernus, -a, -um, adj., N. pl. as noun, *winter quarters.*

hīc, haec, hōc, dem. pron., *this, he, she, it.*

hiemō, -āvī, -ātūrus, -āre, 1. v. n., *pass the winter.*

homō, -inis, M., *a man.*

honor (-ōs), -ōris, M., *honor.*

horreō, horruī, —, horrēre, 2. v. n. and a., *shudder at.*

hospes, -itis, M., *a guest.*

hostis, -is, C., *an enemy.*

I.

ī, see *is.*

iam, adv., *already.*

ibī, adv., *there.*

Īd., see *Īdūs.*

īdem, eadem, idem, dem. pron., *the same.*

idōneus, -a, -um, adj., *suitable.*

Īdūs, Īduum, F. pl., *Ides.*

ignis, -is, M., *fire.*

ignōtus, -a, -um, adj., *unknown.*

ille, illa, illud, dem. pron., *that, he, she, it.*

impedīmentum, -ī, N., *baggage.*

impedio, -īvī, -ītum, -īre, 4. v. a., *obstruct, hinder.*

imperātor, -ōris, M., *commander (in chief).*

imperium, -ī, N., *(military) power, control, order.*

imperō, -āvī, -ātum, -āre, 1. v. a. and n., *command, order.*

imperor, -ātus, -ārī, pass. of *imperō,* 1. v. p., impers., *it is commanded.*

impetus, -ūs, M., *an attack.*

importō, -āvī, -ātum, -āre, 1. v. a., *import.*

improbus, -a, -um, adj., *wicked.*

īmus, see *infimus.*

in, prep., *in, into, upon, towards.*

incendō, -cendī, -cēnsum, -cendere, 3. v. a., *burn, set on fire.*

incolō, -coluī, —, -colere, 3. v. a. and n., *inhabit.*

incolunt, 3. v. a. and n., *inhabit.*

incommodum, -ī, N., noun from adj., *disaster.*

incrēdibilis, -e, adj., *extraordinary.*

incūsō, -āvī, -ātum, -āre, 1. v. a., *upbraid.*

indignus, -a, -um, adj., *unworthy.*

inferior, adj., comp., *inferior.*

inferō, intulī, illātum, īnferre, irr. v. a., *bring upon.*

īnfert, irr. v. a., *brings upon.*

īnfertur, irr. v. p., *is brought upon.*

inferunt, irr. v. a., *bring upon.*

inferuntur, irr. v. p., *are brought upon.*

infimus (īmus), adj., sup., *lowest part of, foot of.*

influō, -flūxī, -flūxum, -fluere, 3. v. n., *flow into.*

ingēns, -entis, adj., *enormous.*

inimīcus, -a, -um, adj., *unfriendly;* M. as noun, *an enemy (personal), rival.*

iniūria, -ae, F., *injury, violence;* pl., *wrongs.*

innāscor, -nātus, -nāscī, 3. v. dep., *spring up.*

inopia, -ae, F., *scarcity.*

insidiae, -ārum, F. pl., *treachery.*

īnsīgnis, -e, adj., N. as noun, *decorations.*

īnstruō, -ūxī, -ūctum, -uere, 3. v. a., *arrange.*

īnsuētus, -a, -um, adj., *ùnaccustomed.*

inter, prep., *between, among.*

interclūdō, -clūsi, -clūsum, -clūdere, 3. v. a., *cut off.*

interest, irr. v. n., *intervenes.*

interficiō, -fēcī, -fectum, -ficere, 3. v. a., *slay, put to death.*

interim, adv., *meanwhile.*

intersum, -fuī, -futūrus, -esse, irr. v. n., *intervene;* also impers., *it concerns.*

intrā, prep., *within.*

inūtilis, -e, adj., *unserviceable.*

invītissimus, -a, -um, adj., sup., *most (very) unwilling.*

invītus, -a, -um, adj., *unwilling.*

ipse, -a, -um, dem. pron., *himself, herself, itself.*

is, ea, id, dem. pron., *this, that, he, she, it.*

iste, ista, istud, dem. pron., *this, that.*

ita, adv., *so.*

Ītalia, -ae, F., *Italy.*

iter, itineris, N., *journey, road, way, march;* pl., *routes, roads, marches.*

iterum, adv., *again.*

iugum, -ī, N., *ridge.*

iūnior, -us, adj., comp., *younger.*

iūre, adv., ablative of iūs, *rightly.*

iūs, iūris, N., *right.*

iūstus, -a, -um, adj., *just.*

iuvant, 1. v. a., *assist, aid.*

iuvantur, 1. v. p., *are assisted, are aided.*

iuvat, 1. v. a., *assists, aids.*

iuvātur, 1. v. p., *is assisted, is aided.*

iuvenis, -is, M., noun from adj., *a young man, youth.*

iuvenis, -e, adj., *young.*

iuvō, iūvī, iūtum, iuvāre, 1. v. a., *assist, aid.*

L.

labor, -ōris, M., *labor, task.*

labōrō, -āvī, -ātum, -āre, 1. v. n., *struggle.*

lacus, -ūs, M., *a lake.*

laetior, -us, adj., comp., *more glad.*

laetissimus, -a, -um, adj., sup., *most (very) glad.*

laetus, -a, -um, adj., *glad.*

latrō, -ōnis, M., *a robber.*

laudant, 1. v. a., *praise.*

laudantur, 1. v. p., *are praised.*

laudat, 1. v. a., *praises.*

laudātur, 1. v. p., *is praised.*

laudō, -āvī, -ātum, -āre, 1. v. a., *praise.*

laus, laudis, F., *praise.*

lēgātiō, -ōnis, F., *an embassy.*

lēgātus, -ī, M., *a lieutenant, an ambassador.*

legiō, -ōnis, F., *a legion.*

Lemannus, -ī, M., *Lemannus.*

lēnitās, -tātis, F., *gentleness.*

lēx, lēgis, F., *a law.*

līberī, -ōrum, M. pl., *children.*

līberō, -āvī, -ātum, -āre, 1. v. a., *set free.*

lībertās, -tātis, F., *liberty.*

licet, licuit (licitum est), licēre, 2. v. impers., *is permitted.*

Liger, -eris, M., *the Loire.*

lingua, -ae, F., *language.*

Liscus, -ī, M., *Liscus.*

littera (lītera), -ae, F., *letter* (of the alphabet); pl., *letter, epistle.*

lītus, -oris, N., *a shore.*

locus, -ī, M. (pl. locī and neut. loca), N. pl., *places, country.*

longē, adv., *far.*

longissimē, adv., sup., *farthest, very far.*

longius, adv., comp., *farther.*

longus, -a, -um, adj., *distant.*

Lucius, -ī, M., *Lucius.*
lūx, lūcis, F., *light.*

M.

M., see *Mārcus.*
magis, adv., *more.*
magistrātus, -ūs, M., *a magistracy, a magistrate.*
māgnitūdō, -inis, F., *magnitude.*
māgnopere (māgnō opere), adv., *greatly, very much.*
māgnus, -a, -um, adj., *great, large.*
māiestās, -tātis, F., *majesty.*
māior, -us, adj., comp., *greater.*
mālō, māluī, —, mālle, irr. v. a. and n., *prefer.*
malus, -a, -um, adj., *bad.*
maneō, mānsī, mānsum, manēre, 2. v. n., *remain.*
manus, -ūs, F., *a hand, a band.*
Mārcus, -ī, M., *Marcus.*
mare, -is, N., *the sea.*
māter, -tris, F., *mother.*
mātrimōnium, -ī, N., *marriage.*
mātūrus, -a, -um, adj., *ripe.*
māximē, adv., sup., *very, in the highest degree, especially.*
māximus, -a,-um, adj., sup.,*greatest.*
melior, -us, adj., comp., *better.*
melius, adv., comp., *better.*
memoria, -ae, F., *memory.*
mercēs, -ēdis, F., *a reward.*
meritum, -ī, N., *desert.*
Messāla, -ae, M., *Messala.*
mētior, mēnsus, mētīrī, 4. v. dep., *distribute, measure.*
metus, -ūs, M., *fear.*
meus, -a, -um, poss. adj. pron., *my, mine.*
mīles, -itis, M., *a soldier.*
mīlia (millia), -ium, N., *thousand.*
mīlitāris, -e, adj., *military.*
mille, card. adj. indecl. ; and neut. noun, indecl. in sing., *a thousand.*

Minerva, -ae, F., *Minerva.*
minimus, -a, -um, adj., sup., *least.*
minor, -us, adj., comp., *less ;* N. as noun.
minus, adv., *less.*
mīror, -ātus, -ārī, 1. v. dep., a. and n., *wonder (at).*
miser, -era, -erum, adj., *unfortunate.*
mittit, 3. v. a., *sends.*
mittitur, 3. v. p., *is sent.*
mittō, mīsī, mīssum, mittere, 3. v. a., *send.*
mittunt, 3. v. a., *send.*
mittuntur, 3. v. p., *are sent.*
monent, 2. v. a., *warn.*
monentur, 2. v. p., *are warned.*
moneō, -uī, -itum, -ēre, 2. v. a., *warn.*
monet, 2. v. a., *warns, admonishes.*
monētur, 2. v. p., *is warned.*
mōns, montis, M., *a mountain.*
moror, -ātus, -ārī, 1. v. dep., *delay.*
mors, mortis, F., *death.*
mōs, mōris, M., *a custom.*
Mosa, -ae, M., *Meuse.*
moveō, mōvī, mōtum, movēre, 2. v. a., *disturb, move.*
multitūdō, -inis, F., *a multitude.*
multus, -a, -um, adj., *much, many.*
mūniō, -īvī (-iī), -ītum, -īre, 4. v. a. and n., *fortify.*
mūnitiō, -ōnis, F., *a fortification, fortifying.*
mūrus, -ī, M., *a wall.*

N.

Nantuātēs, -um, M. pl., *Nantuates.*
nātiō, -ōnis, F., *a nation.*
nātūra, -ae, F., *nature.*
nauta, -ae, M., *a sailor.*
nāvigō, -āvī, -ātum, -āre, 1. v. n., *navigate.*
nāvis, -is, F., *a ship.*
nē, conj., *lest, that . . . not, not.*

-ne ... an ... an, *or* ... *or*.

-ne, enclitic, asks a question, *did, etc., do, etc.*

nē ... quidem, adv., *not ... even*.

nefās, indecl., N., *crime*.

neglegō, -lēxī, -lēctum, -legere, 3. v. a., *neglect*.

negō, -āvī, -ātum, -āre, 1. v. a. and n., *say ... not*.

nēmō, nēminis, C., *no one*.

neque, adv., *neither*.

neque ... neque, adv., *neither ... nor*.

nex, necis, F., *death*.

nihil, indecl., N., as adv., *not at all*.

nisi, conj., *unless*.

nix, nivis, F., *snow*.

nōbilis, -e, adj., 3. pl. as M., noun, *nobles*.

nōbilitās, -tātis, F., *the nobility*.

nōlō, nōluī, —, nōlle, irr. v. a. and n., *be unwilling*.

nōmen, -minis, N., *a name*.

nōn, adv., *not*.

nōn ... modō, adv., *not only*.

nōn modō ... sed etiam, *not only ... but also*.

nōn ... sōlum, sed ... etiam, adv., *not only ... but also*.

nōnne, interrog. part., asks a question, *did not, etc., do not, etc.*

nōnnūllus (nōn nūllus), -a, -um, adj., *some*.

noster, -tra, -trum, poss. adj. pron., *our*.

nōtus, -a, -um, adj., *well-known*.

novem, card. num. adj. indecl., *nine*.

novissimus, -a, -um, adj., sup., *newest, rear*.

novus, -a, -um, adj., *new*.

nūllus, -a, -um, gen. nūllīus, dat. nūllī, adj. as M. noun, *no one*.

num, interrog. part., *does? is? it is not, is it?*

numerus, -ī, M., *a number*.

numquam (nunquam), adv., *never*.

nunc, adv., *now*.

nūntius, -ī, M., *a messenger*.

O.

Ō, exclamation, *o*.

ob, prep., *on account of*.

oblītus, -a, -um, adj., *forgetful*.

oblīviscor, -lītus, -līviscī, 3. v. dep., *forget*.

obses, -idis, C., *a hostage*.

obtineō, -tinuī, -tentum, -tinēre, 2. v. a., *obtain, hold, possess*.

occupō, -āvī, -ātum, -āre, 1. v. a., *occupy, take possession of, seize*.

octō, card. num. adj. indecl., *eight*.

oculus, -ī, M., *eye*.

offendō, -fendī, -fēnsum, -fendere, 3. v. a. and n., *hurt*.

officium, -ī, N., *duty*.

omnis, -e, adj., *all, every*.

onus, -eris, N., *load*.

opera, -ae, F., *care*.

oportet, -uit, —, -ēre, 2. v. impers., *it behooves, is fitting*.

oppidum, -ī, N., *town (walled), stronghold*.

oppūgnat, 1. v. a., *storms*.

oppūgnō, -āvī, -ātum, -āre, 1. v. a., *storm*.

optimē, adv., sup., *best*.

optimus, -a, -um, adj., sup., *best*.

opus, operis, N., *need*.

ōrātiō, -ōnis, F., *oration*.

ōrātor, -ōris, M., *an orator*.

orbis, -is, M., *a circle*.

ordō, -inis, M., *a rank, company*.

Orgetorix, -igis, M., *Orgetorix*.

ornāmentum, -ī, N., *an adornment*.

ōrō, -āvī, -ātum, -āre, 1. v. a. and n., *entreat*.

P.

pābulātiō, -ōnis, F., *a foraging*.

pābulum, -ī, N., *fodder*.

pācō, -āvī, -ātum, -āre, 1. v. a., *sub-due.*

paene, adv., *almost.*

parant, 1. v. a., *prepare.*

parantur, 1. v. p., *are prepared.*

parat, 1. v. a., *prepares.*

parātior, -us, adj., comp., *better prepared.*

parātur, 1. v. p., *is prepared.*

parātus, -a, -um, p.p. as adj., *prepared, ready.*

pāreō, pāruī, pāritūrus, pārēre, 2. v. n., *obey.*

parō, -āvī, -ātum, -āre, 1. v. a., *prepare.*

pars, partis, F., *a part, some.*

partior, -ītus, -īrī, 4. v. dep., *divide.*

parvus, -a, -um, adj., *small, little.*

passus, -ūs, M., *a pace.*

patēns, -entis, pres. p. as adj., *open.*

pater, -tris, M., *father;* pl., *ancestors.*

patrius, -a, -um, adj., *ancestral.*

paucus, -a, -um, adj., *few.*

pāx, pācis, F., *peace.*

pecūnia, -ae, F., *money.*

pedes, -itis, M., *foot-soldier;* pl., *infantry.*

pēior, -us, adj., comp., *worse.*

per, prep., *through.*

perdūcit, 3. v. a., *constructs.*

perdūcō, -dūxī, -dūctum, -dūcere, 3. v. a., *construct.*

pereō, -iī (-īvī), -itūrus, -īre, irr. v. n., *perish.*

pereunt, irr. v. n., *perish.*

perfacilis, -e, adj., *very easy.*

perfidia, -ae, F., *treachery.*

perfuga, -ae, M., *a deserter.*

perīculum, -ī, N., *danger, peril.*

perit, irr. v. n., *perishes.*

perītissimus, -a, -um, adj., sup., *very skilful.*

perītus, -a, -um, adj., *skilful.*

perpaucus, -a, -um, adj., pl., *very few.*

persuādent, 2. v. a. and n., *persuade.*

persuādeō, -suāsī, -suāsum, -suādēre, 2. v. a. and n., *persuade.*

persuādet, 2. v. a. and n., *persuades.*

pertineō, -tinuī, —, -tinēre, 2. v. n., *tend.*

perveniō, -vēnī, -ventum, -venīre, 4. v. n., *reach, arrive.*

perveniunt, 4. v. n., *arrive, reach.*

pēs, pedis, M., *a foot.*

pessimus, -a, -um, adj., sup., *worst.*

petō, petīvī, petītum, petere, 3. v. a. and n., *request, seek.*

phalanx, -angis, F., *a phalanx.*

Pīsō, -ōnis, M., *Piso.*

plēbs, -is, F., *the populace.*

plēnus, -a, -um, adj., *full.*

plerumque, adv., *generally.*

plūrimum, adv., sup., *the most.*

plūrimus, -a, -um, adj., sup., *most.*

plūs, plūris, adj., comp., *more.*

poena, -ae, F., *punishment.*

pōnit, 3. v. a., *places, pitches, lays down.*

pōnō, posuī, positum, pōnere, 3. v. a., *place, pitch, lay down.*

pōns, pontis, M., *a bridge.*

populor, -ātus, -ārī, 1. v. dep., *devastate.*

populus, -ī, M., *a people.*

porta, -ae, F., *gate.*

possessiō, -ōnis, F., *possession.*

possum, potuī, posse, irr. v. n., *be able, can.*

post, prep., *after.*

posterus, -a, -um, adj., *the next.*

postrīdē, adv., *the next day.*

postulant, 1. v. a., *demand.*

postulat, 1. v. a., *demands.*

postulō, -āvī, -ātum, -āre, 1. v. a., *demand.*

potēns, -entis, adj., *powerful, influential.*

potentātus, -ūs, M., *chief command.*

potentior, -us, adj., comp., *more powerful.*

potentissimus, -a, -um, adj., sup., *most (very) powerful.*

potestās, -tātis, F., *civil power.*

potior, potītus, potīrī, 4. v. dep., *obtain control of, become master of.*

praecō, -ōnis, M., *a herald.*

praedor, -ātus, -ārī, 1. v. dep., *plunder.*

praeest, irr. v. n., *in charge of.*

praefectus, -ī, M., *a commander.*

praeficiō, -fēcī, -fectum, -ficere, 3. v. a., *put (place) in charge of.*

praeficit, 3. v. a., *puts (places) in charge of.*

praemittit, 3. v. a., *sends forward.*

praesēns, -entis, adj., *present.*

praesidium, -ī, N., *a garrison.*

praestō, -stitī, -stātum, -stāre, 1. v. a. and n., *excel;* impers., *is better.*

praesum, -fuī, -esse, irr. v. n., *be in charge of.*

praeter, prep., *beyond.*

praeterita, -ōrum, adj., N. pl. as noun, *the past.*

prīma lūx, *daybreak.*

prīmus, -a, -um, adj., sup., *first, front.*

prīnceps, -cipis, M. adj. as noun, *leading man, chief.*

prīncipātus, -ūs, M., *leadership.*

prior, -us, adj., comp., *the former.*

priusquam, adv., *before.*

prīvātus, -a, -um, adj., *private.*

prō, prep., *in place of, as.*

probō, -āvī, -ātum, -āre, 1. v. a., *approve.*

prōcōnsul, -ulis, M., *a proconsul.*

prōditiō, -ōnis, F., *treason.*

proelium, -ī, N., *a battle.*

profectiō, -ōnis, F., *departure.*

prohibent, 2. v. a., *keep from.*

prohibentur, 2. v. p., *are kept from.*

prohibeō, -hibuī, -hibitum, -hibēre, 2. v. a., *keep from.*

prohibet, 2. v. a., *keeps from.*

prope, adv. and prep., *near.*

properō, -āvī, -ātum, -āre, 1. v. a. and n., *hasten.*

propinquitās, -tātis, F., *vicinity.*

propior, -us, adj., comp., *nearer.*

prōpōnō, -posuī, -positum, -pōnere, 3. v. a., *represent.*

propter, prep., *on account of.*

prōvincia, -ae, F., *the province.*

proximus, -a, -um, adj., sup., *nearest, (very) near.*

publicus, -a, -um, adj., *public.*

puer, -ī, M., *a boy.*

pūgna, -ae, F., *a fight.*

pūgnō, -āvī, -ātum, -āre, 1. v. n., *fight.*

pūgnor, -ātus, -ārī, pass. of pūgnō, 1. v. p. impers., *it is fought.*

putō, -āvī, -ātum, -āre, 1. v. a., *think.*

Q.

quam, adv. and conj., *than, as much as possible, how.*

quāre, conj., *why.*

quartus, -a, -um, ord. num. adj., *fourth.*

quattuor, card. num. adj. indecl., *four.*

-que, conj., enclitic, *and.*

quī, quae, quod, cūius, etc., rel. pron., *who, which, that.*

quibuscum, prep. phrase, *with whom.*

quīn, conj., *but that.*

quīndecim, card. num. adj. indecl., *fifteen.*

quīngentī, -ae, -a, card. num. adj., *five hundred.*

quīnī, -ae, -a, dist. num. adj., *five (at a time).*

quīnque, card. num. adj. indecl., *five.*

quis (quī), quae, quid (quod),
cūius, etc., interrog. pron., *who,
which, what.*
quis (quī), quae, quod (quid),
cūius, etc., indef. pron., *anyone.*
quisquam, quae-, quid-, cūius-, etc.,
indef. pron., *anyone, anything.*
quisque, quae-, quid- (quod-), indef. pron., *each one.*
quō, rel. adv., *whither;* conj., *that, in
order that.*
quod, conj., *because.*
quōminus, conj., (*the less by which*),
from (with subj.).
quoque, conj., *also.*

R.

recēns, -entis, adj., *recent.*
recipiō, -cēpī, -ceptum, -cipere, 3. v.
a., with reflexive, *betake himself
(themselves), recover, retreat.*
recipiunt, 3. v. a., sē recipiunt, *betake themselves, retreat.*
regiō, -ōnis, F., *a region.*
rēgnum, -ī, N., *the throne.*
regō, rēxī, rēctum, regere, 3. v. a.,
rule.
relinquō, -līquī, -lictum, -linquere,
3. v. a., *leave.*
reliquus, -a, -um, adj., *remaining.*
remaneō, -mānsī, -mānsūrus, -ma-
nēre, 2. v. n., *remain.*
Rēmī, -ōrum, M. pl., *Remi.*
removeō, -mōvī, -mōtum, -movēre,
2. v. a., *remove.*
renovō, -āvī, -ātum, -āre, 1. v. a.,
renew.
repraesentō, -āvī, -ātum, -āre, 1. v.
a., *do at once.*
rēs, reī, F., *thing, affair, circumstance, undertaking, property.*
rescindit, 3. v. a., *destroys.*
respondeō, -spondī, -spōnsum, -spon-
dēre, 2. v. n., *to respond, reply.*

respondet, 2. v. n., *responds, replies.*
rēs publica, reī publicae, F., *commonwealth, republic.*
revertō, -vertī, -versum, -vertere,
3. v. n., *return.*
revocō, -āvī, -ātum, -āre, 1. v. a.,
call away.
rēx, rēgis, M., *a king.*
Rhēnus, -ī, M., *the Rhine.*
Rhodanus, -ī, M., *the Rhone.*
rogō, -āvī, -ātum, -āre, 1. v. a., *ask.*
Rōma, -ae, F., *Rome.*
Rōmānus, -a, -um, adj., *Roman.*
rūmor, -ōris, M., *a rumor.*

S.

saepe, adv., *often.*
saepissimē, adv., sup., *most often.*
saepius, adv., comp., *more (rather)
often.*
salūs, -ūtis, F., *safety.*
Santonēs, -um (-ī, -ōrum), M. pl.,
Santones.
satis, adv., *sufficiently;* with gen.,
sufficient.
satisfaciō, -fēcī, -factūrus, -facere,
irr. v. n., *satisfy, make amends.*
satisfactiō, -ōnis, F., *amends.*
saucius, -a, -um, adj., *wounded.*
scapha, -ae, F., *a boat.*
sciō, scīvī, scītum, scīre, 4. v. a.,
know.
sē (sēsē), see *sui.*
sēcum, prep. phrase, *with him,
etc.*
sed, conj., *but.*
sēdecim, card. num. adj. indecl.,
sixteen.
sēdēs, -is, F., *a dwelling-place.*
sēmentis, -is, F., *a sowing;* sēmentīs
facere, *sow grain.*
semper, adv., *always.*
senātor, -ōris, M., *a senator.*
senātus, -ūs, M., *the senate.*

senex, senis, M. adj. as noun, *an old man.*
sēnī, -ae, -a, dist. num. adj., *six each.*
senior, -us, adj., *older.*
septem, card. num. indecl., *seven.*
Sēquanī, -ōrum, M. pl. from adj., *the Sequani.*
sequor, secūtus, sequī, 3. v. dep., *follow, be inflicted upon.*
sermō, -ōnis, M., *conversation.*
servant, 1. v. a., *protect.*
servantur, 1. v. p., *are protected.*
servat, 1. v. a., *protects.*
servātur, 1. v. p., *is protected.*
serviō, -iī (-īvī), -itūrus, -īre, 4. v. n., *to be a slave.*
servitūs, -ūtis, F., *servitude.*
servō, -āvī, -ūtum, -āre, 1. v. a., *protect.*
servus, -ī, M., *a slave.*
sevēritās, -tātis, F., *strictness.*
sex, card. num. adj. indecl., *six.*
sexcentī, -ae, -a, card. num. adj., *six hundred.*
sī, conj., *if.*
sīc, adv., *so.*
signum, -ī, N., *signal.*
silentium, -ī, N., *silence.*
silva, -ae, F., *a forest.*
similior, -us, adj., comp., *more like.*
similis, -e, adj., *like.*
simillimus, -a, -um, adj., sup., *most like.*
sine, prep., *without.*
singulī, -ae, -a, dist. num. adj. pl., *single, one by one.*
sinister, -tra, -trum, adj., *left.*
socius, -ī, M., *an ally.*
sōlus, -a, -um, adj., *alone.*
soror, -ōris, F., *a sister.*
spatium, -ī, N., *space.*
spērō, -āvī, -ātum, -āre, 1. v. a. and n., *hope, expect.*
spēs, -eī, F., *hope.*

statuō, -uī, -ūtum, -uere, 3. v. a., *decide.*
student, 2. v. n., *desire.*
studeō, studuī, —, studēre, 2. v. n., *desire.*
studet, 2. v. n., *desires.*
studium, -ī, N., *zeal.*
sub, prep. with acc. and abl., *under, at the foot of.*
subitō, adv., *suddenly.*
subsidium, -ī, N., *re-enforcement.*
Suessiōnēs, -um, M. pl., *Suessiones.*
suī, sibī, sē, reflex. pron., *himself, herself, itself, etc.*
Sulla, -ae, M., *Sulla.*
sum, fuī, futūrus, esse, irr. v. n., *be.*
sunt, *are.*
superior, -us, adj., comp., *higher, superior.*
superō, -āvī, -ātum, -āre, 1. v. a. and n., *conquer, overcome, overpower.*
supersum, -fuī, -futūrus, -esse, irr. v. n., *survive, remain.*
supplex, -icis, C., *a suppliant.*
suprēmus, -a, -um, adj., sup., *highest, supreme.*
suspīciō, -ōnis, F., *suspicion.*
sustineō, -tinuī, -tentum, -tinēre, 1. v. a. and n., *sustain.*
suus, -a, -um, reflex. adj. pron., *his, hers, its, their; his own, etc.*

T.

taceō, tacuī, tacitum, tacēre, 2. v. a. and n., *be silent.*
tam, adv., *so.*
tamen, adv., *still, yet.*
tametsī, adv., *although.*
tandem, adv., *at length.*
tantus, -a, -um, adj., *so great.*
tēcum, prep. phrase, *with you.*
tegō, tēxī, tēctum, tegere, 3. v. a., *cover, conceal.*

tempĕrō, -āvī, -ātum, -āre, 1. v. a.,
refrain.
tempestās, -ātis, F., storm.
temptant, 1. v. a., attempt, try.
temptō, -āvī, -ātum, -āre, 1. v. a.,
attempt, try.
tempus, -oris, N., time.
teneō, tenuī, tentum, tenēre, 2. v, a.,
hold, keep, bind.
tergum, -ī, N., back.
terra, -ae, F., land.
terreō, terruī, territum, terrēre, 2. v.
a., terrify.
territō, -āvī, -ātum, -āre, 1. v. a.,
frighten.
tertius, -a, -um, ord. num. adj., third.
testis, -is, C., a witness.
timeō, -uī, —, -ēre, 2. v. a. and n.,
be afraid (of).
timidus, -a, -um, adj., cowardly.
timor, -ōris, M., fear.
tōtus, -a, -um, adj., the whole (of),
entire.
trāns, prep., beyond, across.
trānsdūcitur, 3. v. p., is led over.
trānsdūcō (trādūcō), -dūxī, -ductum,
-dūcere, 3. v. a., lead over.
trānsdūcunt, 3. v. a., lead over.
trānsdūcuntur, 3. v. p., are led over.
trānseō, -iī, -itum, -īre, irr. v. a. and
n., cross.
trānseunt, irr. v. a. and n., cross.
trānsit, irr. v. a. and n., crosses.
trānsitur, irr. v. p., is crossed.
trānsportō, -āvī, -ātum, -āre, 1. v. a.,
transport.
Trebonius, -ī, M., Trebonius.
trēs, tria, gen. trium, card. num.
adj., three.
Trēverī, -ōrum, M. pl., the Treveri.
tribūnus, -ī, M., a tribune.
trīduum, -ī, N., space of three days.
tripartītō, abl. as adv., in three divisions.
tuba, -ae, F., trumpet.

tum, adv., then.
turris, -is, F., a tower.
tūtus, -a, -um, adj., safe.
tuus, -a, -um, poss. adj. pron., your,
yours.

U.

ubī, adv., when, where.
Ubiī, -ōrum, M., the Ubii.
ūllus, -a, -um, gen. ūllīus, dat. ūllī,
adj., any; as noun, anybody, anyone.
undique, adv., from every side.
ūnus, -a, -um, card. num. adj., one,
alone, only.
urbs, urbis, F., a city.
ūsus, -ūs, M., use.
ut (utī), conj. (with subj.), that, in
order that, so as to; (with ind.)
as.
ut . . . ita, as . . . so.
ūtilior, -us, adj., comp., more useful.
ūtilis, -e, adj., useful.
ūtilissimus, -a, -um, adj., sup.,
most (very) useful.
ūtor, ūsus, ūtī, 3. v. dep., employ,
exercise, use.
uxor, -ōris, F., a wife.

V.

vadum, -ī, N., a ford.
vallum, -ī, N., a rampart, palisade.
vastant, 1. v. a., lay waste.
vastantur, 1. v. p., are laid waste.
vastat, 1. v. a., lays waste.
vastātur, 1. v. p., is laid waste.
vastō, -āvī, -ātum, -āre, 1. v. a., lay
waste.
vectīgal, -ālis, N., tribute; pl., revenues.
vehementer, adv., severely.
velutsī, adv., (just) as if.
veniō, vēnī, ventūrus, venīre, 4. v.
n., come.

venit, 4. v. n., *comes.*
veniunt, 4. v. n., *come.*
vereor, -itus, -ērī, 2. v. dep., *fear.*
Vergobretus, -ī, M., *Vergobretus.*
versō, -āvī, -ātum, -āre, 1. v. a., *turn* (this way and that).
vertō, vertī, versum, vertere, 3. v. a., *turn;* terga vertere, *turn and flee.*
Vesontiō, -ōnis, F., *Vesontio.*
vester, -tra, -trum, poss. adj. pron., *your, yours.*
veterānus, -a, -um, adj., *veteran.*
vetus, -eris, adj., *former.*
vexant, 1. v. a., *harass.*
vexillum, -ī, N., *flag.*
vexō, -āvī, -ātum, -āre, 1. v. a., *harass.*
via, -ae, F., *way.*
victor, -ōris, M., *a victor.*
victōria, -ae, F., *victory.*
vīcus, -ī, M., *village.*
videō, vīdī, vīsum, vidēre, 2. v. a., *see;* pass., videor, *seem.*

vincō, vīcī, victum, vincere, 3. v. a. and n., *conquer.*
vir, virī, M., *a man.*
virtūs, -ūtis, F., *valor;* pl., *virtues.*
vīs, vīs, F., *force.*
vita, -ae, F., *life.*
vītō, -āvī, -ātum, -āre, 1. v. a., *avoid.*
vīvō, vīxī, vīctum, vīvere, 3. v. n., *live.*
vix, adv., *with difficulty.*
vocant, 1. v. a., *summon.*
vocantur, 1. v. p., *are summoned.*
vocat, 1. v. a., *summons.*
vocātur, 1. v. p., *is summoned.*
vocō, -āvī, -ātum, -āre, 1. v. a., *summon.*
volnus (vulnus), -eris, N., *wound.*
volō, voluī, —, velle, irr. v. a. and n., *be willing, wish, want.*
vōx, vōcis, F., *a voice.*
vulgus, -ī, N., *common people.*
vultus, -ūs, M., *expression of countenance.*

A.

A., see *Aulus*.

a, untranslated.

abandon, *dēserō, -seruī, -sertum, -serere*, 3. v. a.

able, *possum, potuī, posse*, irr. v. n.

abode, *domicilium, -ī*, 2. N.

about, *circiter*, adv.

about, *circum*, prep. with acc.

absent, *absum, -fuī, -futūrus, -esse*, irr. v. n.

acceptable, *acceptus, -a, -um*, 1. and 2. adj.

accomplish, *faciō, fēcī, factum, facere*, 3. v. a.

accordance (in . . . with), abl. case.

account (on . . . of), *ob*, prep.

account (on . . . of), *causā* with gen.

accuse, *accūsō, -āvī, -ātum, -āre*, 1. v. a.

across, *trāns*, prep. with acc.

act, *factum, -ī*, 2. N.

action, see *act*.

active, *ācer, ācris, ācre*, 3. adj.

actively, *ācriter*, adv.

activity, *alacritās, -tātis*, 3. F.

adjacent, *fīnitimus, -a, -um*, 1. and 2. adj.

admiral, *praefectus clāssis*.

adopt, *capiō, cēpī, captum, capere*, 3. v. a.

adornment, *ornāmentum, -ī*, 2. N.

advanced, *gravis, -e*, 3. adj.

affair, see *thing*.

afraid of, *timeō, -uī, —, -ēre*, 2. v. a. and n.

again, *iterum*, adv.

against, *contra, adversus*, preps. with acc.

against . . . will, see *unwillingly*.

age, *aetās, -tātis*, 3. F.

agriculture, *agricultūra, -ae*, 1. F.

aid, see *assist*.

aid, *praesidium, -ī*, 2. N.

alarmed, *commōtus, -a, -um*, p.p. 1. and 2. as adj.

all, *omnis, -e*, 3. adj.

all along, imperfect tense.

Allobroges, *Allobrogēs, -um*, pl., 3. M.

ally, *socius, -ī*, 2. M.

almost, *paene*, adv.

alone, see *one*.

alone, *sōlus, -a, -um*, 1. and 2. adj.

Alps, *Alpēs, -ium*, pl., 3. F.

already, *iam*, adv.

also, *quoque*, adv.

although, *cum, etsī, tametsī*, conjs.

always, *semper*, adv.

am, *sum, fuī, futūrus, esse*, irr. v. n.

Ambarri, *Ambarrī, -ōrum*, pl., 2. M.

ambassador, *lēgātus, -ī*, 2. M.

amends, *satisfactiō, -ōnis*, 3. F.

among, *in*, prep. with abl.

among, *apud*, prep. with acc.

among themselves, *inter sē*.

ancestors, *patrēs, -trum*, pl., 3. M., see *father*.

ancestral, *patrius, -a, -um,* 1. and 2. adj.

and, *et, -que, atque, āc,* coör. conj.

and (both . . . and), *et . . . et, -que . . . -que.*

announce, see *reveal.*

annually, *annuus, -a, -um,* 1. and 2. adj.

another, *alius, alia, aliud,* adj. pron.

another (one . . . another), see *one.*

any, *aliquis, -qua, -quid,* adj. pron.

any, *ūllus, -a, -um,* 1. and 2. adj.

anybody, see *anyone (ūllus).*

anyone (indefinite), *quisquam, quaequam, quidquam,* pron.

anyone (very indefinite), *quis (quī), quae, quid(quod),* pron.

anyone, *ūllus, -a, -um,* gen. *ūllius,* dat. *ūllī,* adj. as mas. noun, 1. and 2.

anything, see *anyone.*

anxiety, *metus, -ūs,* 4. M.

approach, *aditus, -ūs,* 4. M.

approve, *probō, -āvī, -ātum, -āre,* 1. v. a.

are, see *am.*

April, *Aprīlis, -e,* M. adj. as noun, 3.

Ariovistus, *Ariovistus, -ī,* 2. M.

arm, *armō, -āvī, -ātum, -āre,* 1. v. a.

arm, *armant,* 1. v. a.

armed (are), *armantur,* 1. v. p.

armed (is), *armātur,* 1. v. p.

arms, *armat,* 1. v. a.

arms, *arma, -ōrum,* pl., 2. N.

army (in training), *exercitus, -ūs,* 4. M.

army (on the march), *agmen, agminis,* 3. N.

arrange, *īnstruō, -strūxī, -structum, -struere,* 3. v. a.

arrival, *adventus, -ūs,* 4. M.

arrive, *perveniō, -vēnī, -ventum, -venīre,* 4. v. n.

Arverni, *Arvernī, -ōrum,* pl., 2. M.

as, mark of apposition, untranslated.

as, see *for.*

as . . . as possible, *quam* with sup.

as if, *velut sī,* conj.

as . . . so, *ut . . . ita,* conj.

ascend, *ascendō, -cendī, -cēnsum, -cendere,* 3. v. a. and n.

ask, *rogō, -āvī, -ātum, -āre,* 1. v. a. and n.

ask (as a right), *flāgitō, -āvī, -ātum, -āre,* 1. v. a.

assist, *iuvō, iūvī, iūtum, iuvāre,* 1. v. a.

assist, *iuvant,* 1. v. a.

assisted (are), *iuvantur,* 1. v. p.

assisted (is), *iuvātur,* 1. v. p.

assists, *iuvat,* 1. v. a.

assistance, *auxilium, -ī,* 2. N.

at length, *tandem,* adv.

attack, *impetus, -ūs,* 4. M.

attempt, *temptō, -āvī, -ātum, -āre,* 1. v. a.

Aulus, *Aulus, -ī,* 2. M.

authority, *auctōritās, -tātis,* 3. F.

auxiliary forces, *auxilia, -ōrum,* pl., 2. N.

auxiliaries, see *auxiliary forces.*

Avaricum, *Avaricum, -ī,* 2. N.

avoid, *vītō, -āvī, -ātum, -āre,* 1. v. a.

away (to be), *absum, -fuī, -futūrus, -esse,* irr. v. n.

B.

back, *tergum, -ī,* 2. N.

bad, *malus, -a, -um,* 1. and 2. adj.; comp., *pēior ;* superl., *pessimus.*

baggage, *impedīmenta, -ōrum,* pl., 2. N.

band, *manus, -ūs,* 4. F.

barbarians, *barbarī, -ōrum,* pl., 2. M.

battle, *proelium, -ī,* 2. N.

be, see *am.*

be able, *possum, potuī, posse,* irr. v. n.

because, *quod,* conj.

because of, abl. with or without a prep.
become, *fīō, fierī, factus*, pass. of *faciō*.
become masters of, *potior, potītus, potīrī*, 4. v. dep.
before, *antequam, priusquam*, conjs.
before, *ante*, prep. with acc.
behoove, *oportet, -uit*, —, *-ēre*, 2. v. impers.
Belgae, *Belgae, -ārum*, pl., 1. M.
believe, *exīstimō, -āvī, -ātum, -āre*, 1. v. a. and n.
Bellovaci, *Bellovacī, -ōrum*, pl., 2. M.
best, *optimus, -a, -um*, 1. and 2., sup. of *bonus*.
best, *optimē*, adv., sup. of *bene*.
betake themselves, *recipiō, -cēpī, -ceptum, -cipere*, with reflex. pron., 3. v. a.
better, *melior, -us*, 3. adj., comp. of *bonus*.
better, *melius*, adv., comp. of *bene*.
better (is), *praestō, -stitī, -stātum, -stāre*, 1. v. a. and n. impers.
between, *inter*, prep. with acc.
beyond, *praeter*, prep. with acc.
bind, *teneō, tenuī, tentum, tenēre*, 2. v. a.
bitter, see *active*.
blot out, *dēpōnō, -posuī, -positum, -pōnere*, 3. v. a.
boat, *scapha, -ae*, 1. F.
body, *corpus, -oris*, 3. N.
Boii, *Boiī, -ōrum*, pl., 2. M.
boldly, *audācter*, adv.
boldness, *audācia, -ae*, 1. F.
both, see *and*.
bound, *teneō, tenuī, tentum, tenēre*, 2. v. a.
boundary, *fīnis, -is*, 3. M.
boy, *puer, -erī*, 2. M.
brave, *fortis, -e*, 3. adj.
bravely, *fortiter*, adv.
bravery, *fortitūdō, -inis*, 3. F.

break forth, *ērumpō, -rūpī, -ruptum, -rumpere*, 3. v. a. and n.
bridge, *pōns, pontis*, 3. M.
bring, *ferō, tulī, lātum, ferre*, irr. v. a.
bring together, *comportō, -āvī, -ātum, -āre*, 1. v. a.
bring upon, *īnferō, -tulī, -lātum, -ferre*, irr. v. a.
Britain, *Britannia, -ae*, 1. F.
brother, *frāter, -tris*, 3. M.
Brutus, *Brūtus, -ī*, 2. M.
building, *aedificium, -ī*, 2. N.
burn, *incendō, -cendī, -cēnsum, -cendere*, 3. v. a.
burn, *cremō, -āvī, -ātum, -āre*, 1. v. a.
burst out, *ērumpō, -rūpī, -ruptum, -rumpere*, 3. v. n.
but, *at, sed*, coör. conj.
but that, *quīn*, rel. conj.
by, *ab (ā, abs)*, prep. with abl.

C.

Caesar, *Caesar, -aris*, 3. M.
call, *appellō, -āvī, -ātum, -āre*, 1. v. a.
call away, *revocō, -āvī, -ātum, -āre*, 1. v. a.
call together, *convocō, -āvī, -ātum, -āre*, 1. v. a.
camp, *castra, -ōrum*, pl., 2. N.
can, *possum, potuī, posse*, irr. v. n.
captive, *captīvus, -ī*, 2. M.
capture, see *take*.
capture (by storming), *expūgnō, -āvī, -ātum, -āre*, 1. v. a.
care, *cūra, -ae*, 1. F.
care, *opera, -ae*, 1. F.
careful, *cautus, -a, -um*, 1. and 2. adj.
carefully, *dīligenter*, adv.
carry, *ferō, tulī, lātum, ferre*, irr. v. a. and n.
carry on, *gerō, gessī, gestum, gerere*, 3. v. a.

cart, *carrus, -ī*, 2. M., also *carrum, -ī*, 2. N.

Cassius (of), *Cassiānus, -a, -um*, 1. and 2. adj.

Cassius, *Cassius, -ī*, 2. M.

Casticus, *Casticus, -ī*, 2. M.

cause, *causa, -ae*, 1. F.

cavalry, *equitātus, -ūs*, 4. M.

cavalry, *equites, -um*, pl., 3. M.; see *horseman*.

cease, *fīnem facere;* see *faciō.*

Celts, *Celtae, -ārum*, pl., 1. M.

censure, see *accuse.*

centurion, *centuriō, -ōnis*, 3. M.

certain, *certus, -a, -um*, 1. and 2. adj.

chain, *catēna, -ae*, 1. F.

charge of (to be in), *praesum, -fuī, —, -esse*, irr. v. n. (with dat.).

chariot, *currus, -ūs*, 4. M.

chief, *prīnceps, -ipis*, 3. M.

chief command, *potentātus, -ūs*, 4. M.

children, *līberī, -ōrum*, pl., 2. M.

choose, *dēligō, -lēgī, -lēctum, -ligere*, 3. v. a.

choose, *capiō, cēpī, captum, capere*, 3. v. a.

Cicero, *Cicerō, -ōnis*, 3. M.

circle, *orbis, -is*, 3. M.

circumstance, *rēs, reī*, 5. F.

citizen, *cīvis, -is*, 3. C.

city, *urbs, urbis*, 3. F.

civilization, *cultus, -ūs*, 4. M.

class, *genus, generis*, 3. N.

Claudius, *Claudius, -ī*, 2. M.

cohort, *cohors, -hortis*, 3. F.

cold, *frīgus, frīgoris*, 3. N.

collect, see *locate.*

column, *agmen, -minis*, 3. N.

come, *veniō, vēnī, ventūrus, venīre*, 4. v. n.

coming, see *approach.*

command, *imperō, -āvī, -ātum, -āre*, 1. v. a. and n.

commanded (it is), *imperor, -ātum*,

-*ārī*, pass. of *imperō*, used impers., 1. v. p.

commander, *praefectus, -ī*, 2. M.

commander (in chief), *imperātor, -ōris*, 3. M.

common, *commūnis, -e*, 3. adj.

common people, *vulgus, -ī*, 2. N.

commonwealth, *rēs publica, reī publicae*, F.

companion, *comes, -itis*, 3. C.

company (of soldiers), *ordō, -inis*, 3. M.

company with (in), see *with.*

conceal, *tegō, tēxī, tēctum, tegere*, 3. v. a.

concede, *concēdō, -cēssī, -cēssum, -cēdere*, 3. v. a. and n.

concern (it concerns), *intersum, -fuī, -futūrus, -esse*, irr. v. n., also impers.

concerning, *dē*, prep.

condemn, *damnō, -āvī, -ātum, -āre*, 1. v. a.

confer, *conloquor (colloquor), -locūtus, -loquī*, 3. v. dep.

conference, *colloquium (conloquium), -ī*, 2. N.

conquer, *superō, -āvī, -ātum, -āre*, 1. v. a.

conquer, *vincō, vīcī, victum, vincere*, 3. v. a. and n.

conscious, *cōnscius, -a, -um*, 1. and 2. adj.

consent, *cōnsēnsus, -ūs*, 4. M.

consider, *dūcō, dūxī, dūctum, dūcere*, 3. v. a.

Considius, *Cōnsidius, -ī*, 2. M.

conspiracy, *coniūrātiō, -ōnis*, 2. F.

conspire, *cōnspīrō, -āvī, -ātum, -āre*, 1. v. n.

construct, *perdūcō, -dūxī, -dūctus, -dūcere*, 3. v. a.

consul, *cōnsul, -ulis*, 3. M.

consulship, *cōnsulātus, -ūs*, 4. M.

contempt, *contemptiō, -ōnis*, 3. F.

contend, *contendō, -tendī, -tentum, -tendere*, 3. v. n.
continually, *continenter*, adv.
control, *imperium, -ī*, 2. N.
conversation, *sermō, -ōnis*, 3. M.
Cotta, *Cotta, -ae*, 1. M.
could, see *can*.
council, *concilium, -ī*, 2. N.
counsel, *cōnsilium, -ī*, 2. N.
countenance (expression of), *voltus* (*vultus*), *-ūs*, 4. M.
country, *loca, -ōrum*, pl., 2. N.
courage, *virtūs, -tūtis*, 3. F.
course, *modus, -ī*, 2. M.
cover, *tegō, tēxī, tēctum, tegere*, 3. v. a.
cowardly, *timidus, -a, -um*, 1. and 2. adj.
crime, *nefās*, indecl., N.
crime, *facinus, -oris*, 3. N.
crops, *frūmentum, -ī*, 2. N.
cross, *trānseō, -īvī (-iī), -itum, -īre*, irr. v. a. and n.
custom, *cōnsuētūdō, -inis*, 3. F.
custom, *mōs, mōris*, 3. M.
cut off, *interclūdō, -clūsī, -clūsum, -clūdere*, 3. v. a.
cut to pieces, *concīdō, -cīdī, -cīsum, -cīdere*, 3. v. a.

D.

daily, *cotīdiē*, adv.
danger, *perīculum, -ī*, 2. N.
dare, *audeō, ausus, audēre*, 2. v. semi-dep.
daring, *audāx, -ācis*, 3. adj.
daughter, *fīlia, -ae*, 1. F.
dawn, see *daybreak*.
day, *diēs, diēī (di-ē'-ī)*, 5. M. (sometimes F.).
daybreak, *prīma lūx*, gen. *prīmae lūcis*, F.
death, *mors, mortis*, 3. F.
death (violent), *nex, necis*, 3. F.
decide, *statuō, -uī, -ūtum, -uere*, 3. v. a.

decorations, *īnsīgnis, -e*, 3. adj., N. pl. as noun.
decree, *dēcrētum, -ī*, 2. N.
deep, *altus, -a, -um*, 1. and 2. adj.
defeat, *vincō, vīcī, victum, vincere*, 3. v. a. and n.
defend, *dēfendō, -fendī, -fēnsum, -fendere*, 3. v. a.
definite, *certus, -a, -um*, 1. and 2. adj.
delay, *moror, -ātus, -ārī*, 1. v. dep.
delight, *dēlectō, -āvī, -ātum, -āre*, 1. v. a.
delight, *dēlectant*, 1. v. a.
delighted (are), *dēlectantur*, 1. v. p.
delighted (is), *dēlectātur*, 1. v. p.
delights, *dēlectat*, 1. v. a.
demand (earnestly), *flāgitō, -āvī, -ātum, -āre*, 1. v. a.
departure, *discēssus, -ūs*, 4. M.; *profectiō, -ōnis*, 3. F.
depth, *altitūdō, -inis*, 3. F.
desert, *meritum, -ī*, 2. N.
deserter, *perfuga, -ae*, 1. M.
desire, *studeō, -uī, —, -ēre*, 2. v. n. (with dat.).
desire, *petō, petīvī, petītum, petere*, 3. v. a. and n.
desire, *cupiditās, -tātis*, 3. F.
desirous, *cupidus, -a, -um*, 1. and 2. adj.
detain, *dētineō, -tinuī, -tentum, -tinēre*, 2. v. a.
determine, *cōnstituō, -stituī, -stitūtum, -stituere*, 3. v. a. and n.
devastate, *populor, -ātus, -ārī*, 1. v dep.
devastate, see *lay waste*.
did, see *do*.
difficult, *difficilis, -e*, 3. adj.
difficulty, *difficultās, -tātis*, 3. F.
difficulty (with), *vix*, adv.
diligent, *dīligēns, -entis*, 3. adj.
disaster, *incommodum, -ī*, 2. N.
disclose, *ēnūntiō, -āvī, -ātum, -āre*, 1. v. a.

disposition, see *spirit.*
distant (to be), see *away (to be).*
distant, *longus, -a, -um,* 1. and 2. adj.
distribute, *mētior, mēnsus, mētīrī,* 4. v. dep.
disturb, *moveō, mōvī, mōtum, movēre,* 2. v. a.
ditch, *fossa, -ae,* 1. F.
Divico, *Divicō, -ōnis,* 3. M.
divide, *partior, -ītus, -īrī,* 4. v. dep.
divided, *dīvīsus, -a, -um,* p.p. as adj. 1. and 2.
Divitiacus, *Divitiacus, -ī,* 2. M.
do, untranslated, when used instead of the common form of the verb. See *-ne, -num,* and *nōnne.*
do, *agō, ēgī, āctum, agere,* 3. v. a.
do a favor, *grātum facere.*
do at once, *repraesentō, -āvī, -ātum, -āre,* 1. v. a.
doubt, *dubium, -ī,* 2. N.
doubt, *dubitātiō, -ōnis,* 3. F.
doubtful, *dubius, -a, -um,* 1. and 2. adj.
draw, *dūcō, dūxī, dūctum, dūcere,* 3. v. a.
drive out, *expellō, -pulī, -pulsum, -pellere,* 3. v. a.
Dumnorix, *Dumnorix, -igis,* 3. M.
duty, *officium, -ī,* 2. N.
dwelling-place, *sēdēs, -is,* 3. F.

E.

each one, *quisque, quae-, quid-* (*quod-*), indef. pron.
eagerly, *cupidē,* adv.
eagerness, *cupiditās, -tātis,* 3. F.
earnestly demands, see *demands.*
easily, *facile,* adv.
easy, *facilis, -e,* 3. adj.
eight, *octō,* card. num. adj. indecl.
elect, *creō, creāvī, creātum, creāre,* 1. v. a.
embassy, *lēgātiō, -ōnis,* 3. F.

employ, *ūtor, ūsus, ūtī,* 3. v. dep.
encourage, *cohortor, -ātus, -ārī,* 1. v. dep.
encourage, *cōnfirmō, -āvī, -ātum, -āre,* 1. v. a.
encourage, *cōnfirmant,* 1. v. a.
encouraged (are), *cōnfirmantur,* 1. v. p.
encouraged (is), *cōnfirmātur,* 1. v. p.
encourages, *cōnfirmat,* 1. v. a.
end, *fīnis, -is,* 3. M.
endeavor, *cōnor, -ātus, -ārī,* 1. v. dep.
endure, *ferō, tulī, lātum, ferre,* irr. v. a. and n.
enemy (in war), *hostis, -is,* 3. C.
enemy (personal), *inimīcus, -ī,* 2. M.
enfeeble, *effēminō, -āvī, -ātum, -āre,* 1. v. a.
engagement continues,(it is fought), pass. of *pūgnō, -āvī, -ātum, -āre,* 1. v. n.
engineer, *faber, fabrī,* 2. M.
enormous, *ingēns, -entis,* 3. adj.
enroll, *cōnscrībō, -scrīpsī, -scrīptum, -scrībere,* 3. v. a.
entire, *tōtus, -a, -um,* 1. and 2. adj.
entreat, *ōrō, -āvī, -ātum, -āre,* 1. v. a. and n.
equip, *armō, -āvī, -ātum, -āre,* 1. v. a.
especially, *māximē,* adv.
even, *etiam,* conj.
even if, *etsī,* conj.
every, see *all.*
evident (is), *cōnstō, -stitī, -stātūrus, -stāre,* 1. v. n. impers.
excel, *praestō, -stitī, -stitum, -stāre,* 1. v. a. and n.
execute, *administrō, -āvī, -ātum, -āre,* 1. v. a.
exercise, *ūtor, ūsus, ūtī,* 3. v. dep.
exhort, *cohortor, -ātus, -ārī,* 1. v. dep.
exile, *exsul, -ulis,* 3. C.
expect, *spērō, -āvī, -ātum, -āre,* 1. v. a. and n.

expression (of countenance), *voltus* (*vultus*), *-ūs*, 4. M.

extent, see *magnitude*.

extraordinary, *incrēdibilis, -e*, 3. adj.

eye, *oculus, -ī*, 2. M.

F.

Fabius, *Fabius, -ī*, 2. M.

fact, see *thing*.

faction, *factiō, -ōnis*, 3. F.

fair, *aequus, -a, -um*, 1. and 2. adj.

faithful, *fidēlis, -e*, 3. adj.

fall, *cadō, cecidī, cāsūrus, cadere*, 3. v. n.

fame, *glōria, -ae*, 1. F.

famine, *famēs, -is*, F.

far, *longē*, adv.

father, *pater, -tris*, 3. M.

favor, *grātia, -ae*, 1. F.

favor, *faveō, fāvī, fautūrus, favēre*, 2. v. n. (with dat.).

fear, *vereor, -itus, -ērī*, 2. v. dep.

fear, *timor, -ōris*, 3. M.

feeble, *īnfirmus, -a, -um*, 1. and 2. adj.

feelings, *animus, -ī*, 2. M.

fertile, *frūmentārius, -a, -um*, 1. and 2. adj.

few, *paucus, -a, -um*, 1. and 2. adj.

field, *ager, agrī*, 2. M.

fifteen, *quīndecim*, card. num. adj. indecl.

fifteen hundred, *mille et quīngentī*.

fight, *pūgna, -ae*, 1. F.

fight, *pūgnō, -āvī, -ātum, -āre*, 1. v. a.

fight (decisively), *dīmicō, -āvī, -ātū-rus, -āre*, 1. v. n.

fire, *īgnis, -is*, 3. M.

first, *prīmus, -a, -um*, 1. and 2. adj. sup.

fitting (is), *oportet, -uit*, ——, *-ēre*, 2. v. impers.

five, *quīnque*, card. num. adj. indecl.

five (at a time), *quīnī, -ae, -a*, pl., 1. and 2. dist. num. adj.

five hundred, *quīngentī, -ae, -a*, pl., 1. and 2. card. num. adj.

flag, *vexillum, -ī*, 2. N.

flee, see *fly*.

fleet, *clāssis, -is*, 3. F.

fleet, see *swift*.

flight, *fuga, -ae*, 1. F.

flow, *fluō, flūxī, fluxūrus, fluere*, 3. v. n.

flow into, *īnfluō, -flūxī, -fluxūrus, -fluere*, 3. v. a.

fly, *fugiō, fūgī, fugitūrus, fugere*, 3. v. a. and n.

fodder, *pābulum, -ī*, 2. N.

follow, *sequor, secūtus, sequī*, 3. v. dep.

following day, see *next day*.

foot, *pēs, pedis*, 3. M.

foot of, *īnfimus* (*īmus*), *-a, -um*, 1. and 2. adj. sup.

foot-soldier, *pedes, -itis*, 3. M.; pl., infantry.

for, untranslated, dat. case.

for (the purpose of), see *in order that*.

for (the sake of), *causā* with gen.

for, *ob*, prep.

foraging, *pābulātiō, -ōnis*, 3. F.

force, *vīs, vīs*, 3. F., irr.

forced (march), *māximus, -a, -um*, 1. and 2. adj. sup.

forces, *cōpiae, -ārum*, pl., 1. F.

ford, *vadum, -ī*, 2. N.

forest, *silva, -ae*, 1. F.

forget, *oblīviscor, -lītus, -līviscī*, 3. v. dep.

forgetful, *oblītus, -a, -um*, 1. and 2. adj.

form, see *make*.

former, *prior, prius*, 3. adj. comp.

former, *vetus, -eris*, 3. adj.

fortification, *mūnītiō, -ōnis*, 3. F.

fortify, *mūniō, -īvī (-iĭ), -ītum, -īre,*
4. v. a. and n.
fortifying, *mūnītiō, -ōnis,* 3. F.
fortress, *castellum, -ī,* 2. N.
fortune, *fortūna, -ae,* 1. F.
fought (it is), *pūgnor, -ātus, -ārī,*
pass. of *pūgnō,* impers. 1. v. p.
four, *quattuor,* card. num. adj.
indecl.
fourth, *quartus, -a, -um,* 1. and 2.
ord. num. adj.
fraternal, *frāternus, -a, -um,* 1. and
2. adj.
frenzy, *furor, -ōris,* 3. M.
friend, *amīcus, -ī,* 2. M.
friendly, *amīcus, -a, -um,* 1. and
2. adj.
friendship, *amīcitia, -ae,* 1. F.
frighten, *territō, -āvī, -ātum, -āre,*
1. v. a.
from, *quōminus,* (with subj.), conj.
from (away from), *ab (ā, abs),*
prep. with abl.
from (out of), *ex (ē),* prep.
from every side, *undique,* adv.
front (front rank), *prīmus, -a, -um,*
1. and 2. adj.
frosts, *frīgora, -um,* 3. N. pl. of
frīgus.
full, *plēnus, -a, -um,* 1. and 2. adj.

G.

Gabinius, *Gabinius, -ī,* 2. M.
gate, *porta, -ae,* 1. F.
gather grain, *frūmentor, -tātus, -tārī,*
1. v. dep.
Galba, *Galba, -ae,* 1. M.
Gallic, *Gallicus, -a, -um,* 1. and
2. adj.
garrison, *praesidium, -ī,* 2. N.
Gaul, *Gallia, -ae,* 1. F.
Gauls, *Gallī, -ōrum,* pl. 2. M.
generally, *plērumque,* adv.
Geneva, *Genāva, -ae,* 1. F.

gentleness, *lēnitās, -tātis,* 3. F.
Germans, *Germānī, -ōrum,* pl. 2. M.
Germany, *Germānia, -ae,* 1. F.
give, *dō, dedī, datum, dare,* 1. v. a.
give, *dant,* 1. v. a.
given (are), *dantur,* 1. v. p.
given (is), *datur,* 1. v. p.
gives, *dat,* 1. v. a.
give battle, see *join battle.*
glad, *laetus, -a, -um,* 1. and 2. adj.
gladly, *laetus, -a, -um,* 1. and 2. adj.,
as English adv.
glare, *aciēs, -ēī,* 5. F.
glory, *glōria, -ae,* 1. F.
go, *eō, īvī (iĭ), itum, īre,* irr. v. n.
go forth, *exeō, -īvī (-iĭ), -itum, -īre,*
irr. v. n.
go over, *trānseō, -īvī (-iĭ), -itum, -īre,*
irr. v. a. and n.
go wrong, *errō, -āvī, -ātum, -āre,*
1. v. n.
good, *bonus, -a, -um,* 1. and 2. adj.
government, *imperia, -ōrum,* pl. 2. N.
grain, *frūmentum, -ī,* 2. N.
grant, see *give.*
grant, *concēdō, -cēssī, -cēssum, -cēdere,*
3. v. a. and n.
great, *māgnus, -a, -um,* 1. and 2. adj.;
comp. *māior,* sup. *māximus.*
greater, *māior, -us,* 3. adj., comp. of
māgnus.
greater (age), *gravior, -us,* 3. adj.,
comp. of *gravis.*
greatest, *māximus, -a, -um,* 1. and 2.
adj. sup.
greatly, see *severely.*
greatly, *māgnopere,* adv.
guest, *hospes, -itis,* 3. M.

H.

had (aux.), pluperf. ind. or subj.
Haedui, *Haeduī, -ōrum,* pl. 2. M.
Haedui (of the), *Haeduus, -a, -um,*
1. and 2. adj.

habit of (in the), imperf. tense.

hand, *manus, -ūs,* 4. F.

hang out, *prōpōnō, -posuī, -positum, -pōnere,* 3. v. a.

happens (it happens), *accidit, -cidit,* —, *-cidere,* 3. v. n.; *fit, factum, fierī,* pass. of *faciō.*

harass, *vexō, -āvī, -ātum, -āre,* 1. v. a.

hard pressed, *labōrāns, -antis,* 3., pres. p. of *labōrō,* as adj.

has (aux.), perf. ind.

hasten, *contendō, -tendī, -tentum, -tendere,* 3. v. n.

hasten, *properō, -āvī, -ātum, -āre,* 1. v. n.

have, *habeō, habuī, habitum, habēre,* 2. v. a. and n.

have (aux.), see *has.*

he (she, it), *is (ea, id); hīc (haec, hōc); ille (illa, illud);* often untranslated.

hear, *audiō, -īvī, -ītum, -īre,* 4. v. a.

height, *altitūdō, -inis,* 3. F.

helmet, *galea, -ae,* 1. F.

Helvetii (Helvetians), *Helvētiī, -ōrum,* pl., 2. M.

hem in, *contineō, -tinuī, -tentum, -tinēre,* 2. v. a.

her, see *she.*

herald, *praecō, -ōnis,* 3. M.

here (be), *adsum, -fuī, -futūrus, -esse,* irr. v. n.

hers, see *his,* poss. pron.

herself (her-, it-), *suī, sibī, sē,* reflex. pron.

herself, see *himself,* intensive pron.

high, *altus, -a, -um,* 1. and 2. adj.

higher places, *superiōra, -um,* pl., 3. N.

highest, *summus, -a, -um,* 1. and 2. adj.

hill, *collis, -is,* 3. M.

him, see *he.*

himself (her-, it-), *ipse, ipsa, ipsum,* intensive pron.

hinder, *dēterreō, -terruī, -territum, -terrēre,* 2. v. a.; *impediō, -īvī, -ītum, -īre,* 4. v. a.

his, *suus, -a, -um,* 1. and 2. adj.

his own (her, its), see *his.*

hither, *citerior, -us,* 3. adj. comp. (no positive).

hold, *teneō, tenuī, tentum, tenēre,* 2. v. a.

hold (against some one), *obtineō, -tinuī, -tentum, -tinēre,* 2. v. a.

home, see *house.*

honor, *honor, -ōris,* 3. M.

hope, *spēs, speī (spe'-ī),* 5. F.

hope, *spērō, -āvī, -ātum, -āre,* 1. v. a. and n.

horse, *equus, -ī,* 2. M.

horseman, *eques, -itis,* 3. M.

hostage, *obses, -idis,* 3. C.

hostile, see *unfriendly.*

house, *domus, -ī (-ūs),* 2. and 4. F.

how, *quam,* adv.

hundred, *centum,* card. num. adj. indecl.

hunger, *famēs, -is,* 3. F.

hurt, *offendō, -fendī, -fēnsum, -fendere,* 3. v. a. and n.

I.

I, *ego,* pers. pron.

Ides, *Īdūs, -uum,* pl., 4. F.

if, *sī,* conj.

illustrious, *clārus, -a, -um,* 1. and 2. adj.

import, *importō, -āvī, -ātum, -āre,* 1. v. a.

in, *in,* prep. with abl.

in (with names of towns and small islands), locative case.

in charge of (to be), *praesum, -fuī, -futūrus, -esse,* irr. v. n.

in company with, *cum,* prep. with abl.

in front of, *prō,* prep. with abl.

in order that, *ut* (*utī*), conj.
in order to, see *in order that.*
in regard to, *dē*, prep. with abl.
in the highest degree, *māximē*, adv. sup.
in three divisions, *tripartītō*, adv.
infantry, see *pedes.*
inferior, *īnferior, -us*, 3. adj. comp.
inflicted upon (be), *sequor, secūtus, sequī*, 3. v. dep.
influence, *auctōritās, -tātis*, 3. F.
influence, *commoveō, -mōvī, -mōtum, -mōvēre*, 2. v. a.
influential, see *powerful.*
inform, *certiōrem facere.*
inhabit, *incolō, -coluī, —, -colere*, 3. v. a. and n.
injury, *iniūria, -ae*, 1. F.
insult, *contumēlia, -ae*, 1. F.
intervene, *intersum, -fuī, -futūrus, -esse*, irr. v. n.
into, *in*, prep. with acc.
iron, *ferrum, -ī*, 2. N.
is, see *am.*
it, see *he.*
Italy, *Ītalia, -ae*, 1. F.
its, see *his.*
itself, see *himself*, intens. or reflex.

J.

join (join battle), *committō, -mīsī, -missum, -mittere*, 3. v. a.
journey, *iter, itineris*, 3. N. irr.
joyful, *laetus, -a, -um*, 1. and 2. adj.
jump down, *dēsiliō, -siluī, -sultum, -silīre*, 4. v. n.
just, *iūstus, -a, -um*, 1. and 2. adj.
justly, see *rightly.*

K.

keep, see *hold.*
keep apart, *distineō, -tinuī, -tentum, -tinēre*, 2. v. a.

keep from, *prohibeō, -buī, -bitum, -bēre*, 2. v. a.
keep together, *contineō, -tinuī, -tentum, -tinēre*, 2. v. a.
kindness, *clēmentia, -ae*, 1. F.
king, *rēx, rēgis*, 3. M.
know, *sciō, scīvī, scītum, scīre*, 4. v. a.
known, *nōtus, -a, -um*, 1. and 2. adj.

L.

L., *Lucius, -ī*, 2. M.
labor, *labor, -ōris*, 3. M.
lacking (is), *dēsum, -fuī, -futūrus, -esse*, irr. v. n.
lake, *lacus, -ūs*, 4. M.
land, *terra, -ae*, 1. F.
language, *lingua, -ae*, 1. F.
large, see *great.*
law, *lēx, lēgis*, 3. F.
lay aside, *dēpōnō, -posuī, -positum, -pōnere*, 3. v. a.
lay down, *pōnō, posuī, positum, pōnere*, 3. v. a.
lay waste, *vastō, -āvī, -ātum, -āre*, 1. v. a.
lay waste, *vastant*, 1. v. a.
laid waste (are), *vastantur*, 1. v. p.
laid waste (is), *vastātur*, 1. v. p.
lays waste, *vastat*, 1. v. a.
lead, *dūcō, dūxī, dūctum, dūcere*, 3. v. a.
lead away, *abdūcō, -dūxī, -dūctum, -dūcere*, 3. v. a.
lead out, *ēdūcō, -dūxī, -dūctum, -dūcere*, 3. v. a.
lead over, *trānsdūcō (trādūcō), -dūxī, -dūctum, -dūcere*, 3. v. a.
lead to, *addūcō, -dūxī, -dūctum, -dūcere*, 3. v. a.
leader, *dux, ducis*, 3. M.
leadership, *prīncipātus, -ūs*, 4. M.
leading man, see *chief.*
least, *minimus, -a, -um*, 1. and 2. adj., sup. of *parvus.*

leave, *relinquō*, *-liquī*, *-lictum*, *-lin-quere*, 3. v. a.

led on, *indūctus*, *-a*, *-um*, 1. and 2. adj.

left, *sinister*, *-tra*, *-trum*, 1. and 2. adj.

legion, *legiō*, *-ōnis*, 3. F.

Lemannus, *Lemannus*, *-ī*, 2. M.

less, *minor*, *-us*, 3. adj., comp. of *parvus*.

less, *minus*, *-ōris*, N. of comp. as noun, 3.

lest, *nē*, conj.

letter (of the alphabet), *lītera*, *-ae ;* pl., a letter, an epistle, 1. F.

liberate, see *set free.*

liberty, *lībertās*, *-tātis*, 3. F.

lieutenant, see *ambassador.*

life, *vīta*, *-ae*, 1. F.

light, *lūx*, *lūcis*, 3. F.

like, *similis*, *-e*, 3. adj.

limit, *fīnis*, *-is*, 3. M.; pl., territory.

line (of battle), *aciēs*, *aciēī* (*aci-ē'-ī*), 5. F.

line (on the march), *agmen*, *-inis*, 3. N.

line, *fīnis*, *-is*, 3. M.

Liscus, *Liscus*, *-ī*, 3. M.

little, see *small.*

live, *vīvō*, *vīxī*, *vīctum*, *vīvere*, 3. v. n.

load, *onus*, *-eris*, 3. N.

locate, *collocō* (*conlocō*), *-āvī*, *-ātum*, *-āre*, 1. v. a.

Loire, *Liger*, *-eris*, 3. M.

long time, *diū*, adv.

lose, *āmīttō*, *-mīsī*, *-mīssum*, *-mīttere*, 3. v. a.

loud, see *great.*

love, *amor*, *-ōris*, 3. M.

lowest part of, see *foot of.*

Lucius, *Lucius*, *-ī*, 2. M.

M.

magistracy, *magistrātus*, *-ūs*, 4. M.

magistrate, *magistrātus*, *-ūs*, 4. M.

magnitude, *māgnitūdō*, *-inis*, 3. F.

majesty, *māiestās*, *-tātis*, 3. F.

make, *faciō*, *fēcī*, *factum*, *facere*, 3. v. a.

make amends, *satisfaciō*, *-fēcī*, *-factūrus*, *-facere*, irr. v. n. (with dat.).

make upon, see *bring upon.*

make war, *bellō*, *-āvī*, *-ātum*, *-āre*, 1. v. n.

man, *vir*, *virī*, 2. M.

man (human being), *homō*, *-inis*, 3. M.

many, *multus*, *-a*, *-um*, 1. and 2. adj.

many (very), *complūrēs*, *-plūra* (*-ia*), pl. 3. adj.

march, see *journey.*

marriage, *mātrimōnium*, *-ī*, 2. N.

master, *dominus*, *-ī*, 2. M.

may (aux.), pres. subj.

me, see *I.*

means (by . . . of), abl. case.

meanwhile, *interim*, adv.

measure, *mētior*, *mēnsum*, *mētīrī*, 4. v. dep.

Mediterranean Sea, *mare nostrum.*

memory, *memoria*, *-ae*, 1. F.

message, *nūntius*, *-ī*, 2. M.

messenger, *nūntius*, *-ī*, 2. M.

Meuse, *Mosa*, *-ae*, 1. M.

might (aux.), imp. subj.

mile, *mīlia passuum.*

military, *mīlitāris*, *-e*, 3. adj.

mind, see *spirit.*

mine, see *my.*

Minerva, *Minerva*, *-ae*, 1. F.

mistaken (to be), see *go wrong.*

money, *pecūnia*, *-ae*, 1. F.

more, comparative degree.

more, *plūs*, *plūris*, 3. N.; pl. as adj.

more, *magis*, adv.

more, *amplius*, N. indecl.

more than, *amplius* with abl.

morning (in the), *māne*, adv.

most, *plūrimus*, *-a*, *-um*, 1. and 2. adj.

most, *plūrimum*, adv.
mother, *māter, -tris*, 3. F.
mountain, *mōns, montis*, 3. M.
move, *moveō, mōvī, mōtum, movēre*,
2. v. a.
much, *multus, -a, -um*, 1. and 2.
adj.
multitude, *multitūdō, -inis*, 3. F.
my, *meus, mea, meum*, 1. and 2. poss.
pron.

N.

name, *nōmen, -inis*, 3. N.
name a day, *diem dīcere*.
Nantuates, *Nantuātēs, -um*, pl., 3. M.
narrowness of passage, *angustiae,
-ārum*, pl., 1. F.
nation, *nātiō, -ōnis*, 3. F.
native, *nātīvus, -a, -um*, 1. and 2.
adj.
nature, *nātūra, -ae*, 1. F.
navigate, *nāvigō, -āvī, -ātum, -āre*,
1. v. n.
near, *prope*, prep. with acc.; adv.
near (with names of places), *ad*,
prep. with acc.
nearer, *propior, -us*, 3. adj. comp.
nearest, *proximus, -a, -um*, 1. and 2.
adj., sup. of *propior*.
need, *egeō, eguī, —, egēre*, 2. v. n.
with gen. or abl.
need, *opus, operis*, 3. N.
need of action, *opus factū*.
neglect, *neglegō, -lēxī, -lēctum, -legere*,
3. v. a.
neither, *neque*, conj.
neither . . . nor, *neque . . . neque*,
conj.
never, *numquam (nunquam)*, adv.
new, *novus, -a, -um*, 1. and 2. adj.
next, *posterus, -a, -um*, 1. and 2. adj.
next day, *postrīdiē*, adv.
next day after that, *postrīdiē ēius
diēī*.
no, see *not any*.

no one, *nūllus, -a, -um*, gen. *nūllīus*,
dat. *nūllī*, adj. 1. and 2., M. as noun.
no one, *nēmō, -inis*, 3. C.
nobility, *nōbilitās, -tātis*, 3. F.
noble, *nōbilis, -is*, adj. 3., M. as
noun.
nobleman, *nōbilis, -is*, noun from
adj., 3. M.
nobles, *nōbilēs*, 3. adj., M. pl. as
noun.
not, *nōn*, adv.
not (with subj.), *nē*, adv.
not alone . . . but also, *nōn solum
. . . sed etiam*, conj.
not any, *nūllus, -a, -um*, 1. and 2.
adj.
not at all, *nihil*, N. indecl., acc. as
adv.
not even, *nē . . . quidem*, conj.
not only . . . but also, *nōn modō
. . . sed etiam*, conj.
now, *nunc*, adv.
number, *numerus, -ī*, 2. M.
number (great), see *multitude*.

O.

O, exclamation, *ō*.
obey, *pāreō, pāruī, pāritūrus, pārēre*,
2. v. n. (with dat.).
obstruct, *impediō, -dīvī, -dītum, -dīre*,
4. v. a.
obtain, *obtineō, -tinuī, -tentum, -tinēre*,
2. v. a.
obtain control (possession) of, *potior, potītus, potīrī*, 4. v. dep.
occupy, *occupō, -āvī, -ātum, -āre*,
1. v. a.
of, translated usually by gen.
of a father, *patrius, -a, -um*, 1. and
2. adj.
often, *saepe*, adv.
oh, *ō*, interj.
old, *senex, senis*, 3. M.
older, *senior, -us*, 3. adj. comp.

old man, see *old*.

on, *in*, prep. with abl.; abl. case.

on, *ex*, prep.

on account of, *ob, propter*, preps.

on this account, *ob*, prep. with acc.

one, *ūnus, ūna, ūnum*, 1. and 2. card. num. adj.

one another, *alius . . . alius*, 1. and 2. adj. pron.

one (the one . . . the other), *alter . . . alter*, 1. and 2. adj. pron.

one by one, *singulī, -ae, -a*, pl. dist. num. adj. 1. and 2.

only, *sōlus, -a, -um; ūnus, ūna, ūnum*, adjs. 1. and 2.

open, *patēns, -entis*, pres. p. as adj. 3.

opportunity, *facultās, -tātis*, 3. F.

oration, *ōrātiō, -ōnis*, 3. F.

orator, *ōrātor, -ōris*, 3. M.

order, *imperō, -āvī, -ātum, -āre*, 1. v. a.

order, see *line*.

order, *imperium, -ī*, 2. N.

Orgetorix, *Orgetorix, -igis*, 3. M.

other (another), *alius, alia, aliud*, 1. and 2. pron.

other (the other), *alter, -era, -erum*, 1. and 2. adj. pron.

others (some . . . others), *aliī . . . aliī*, 1. and 2. adj. pron.

our, *noster, -tra, -trum*, 1. and 2. poss. pron.

ours, see *our*.

over, *trāns*, prep. with acc.

overcome, see *conquer*.

over, dative case, see *Dumnorigī*, Ex. 195, sentence 7.

overpower, *superō, -āvī, -ātum, -āre*, 1. v. a.

overtake, *cōnsector, -ātus, -ārī*, 1. v. dep.

own, see *his own*.

owner, see *master*.

P.

pace, *passus, -ūs*, 4. M.

palisade, *vallum, -ī*, 2. N.

pardon, *condōnō, -āvī, -ātum, -āre*, 1. v. a.

part, *pars, partis*, 3. F.

party, see *faction*.

pass the winter, *hiemō, -āvī, -ātum, -āre*, 1. v. n.

passage, *iter, itineris*, 3. N.

past (the), *praeterita*, N. pl. of adj. as noun, 2.

peace, *pāx, pācis*, 3. F.

people, *populus, -ī*, 2. M.

peril, see *danger*.

perish, *pereō, -iī (-īvī), -itūrus, -īre*, irr. v. n.

permitted (it is), *licet, licuit (licitum est), licēre*, impers., 2. v. n.

persuade, *persuādeō, -suāsī, -suāsum, -suādēre*, 2. v. a. and n.

phalanx, *phalanx, -angis*, 3. F.

Piso, *Pīsō, -ōnis*, 3. M.

pitch, see *place*.

place, *pōnō, posuī, positum, pōnere*, 3. v. a.

place, *locus, -ī*, 2. M., pl. *loca*, N.

place in charge of, see *put in charge of*.

place of (in), *prō*, prep. with abl.

plan, see *counsel*.

pleasant, *facilis* with the latter supine of *video*.

plenty, *cōpia, -ae*, 1. F.

plunder, *praedor, -ātus, -ārī*, 1. v. dep.

point out, *dēmōnstrō, -āvī, -ātum, -āre*, 1. v. a.

populace, *plēbs, plēbis*, 3. F.

popularity, *grātia, -ae*, 1. F.

possess, *obtineō, -tinuī, -tentum, -tinēre*, 2. v. a.

possession, *possessiō, -ōnis*, 3. F.

possible, see *as . . . as possible*.

postpone, *cōnferō*, *-tulī*, *-lalum,-ferre*, irr. v. a.

power (civil), *potestās*, *-tātis*, 3. F.

power (military), *imperium*, *-ī,* 2. N.

powerful, *potēns*, *-entis*, 3. adj.

praise, *laudō*, *-āvī*, *-ātum*, *-āre*, 1. v. a.

praise, *laudant*, 1. v. a.

praise, *laus*, *laudis*, 3. F.

praised (are), *laudantur*, 1. v. p.

praised (is), *laudātur*, 1. v. p.

praises, *laudat*, 1. v. a.

pray, *tandem*, adv.

prefer, *mālō*, *mālul*, —, *mālle*, irr. v. a. and n.

prepare, *parō*, *-āvī*, *-ātum*, *-āre*, 1. v. a.

prepare, *parant*, 1. v. a.

prepared (are), *parantur*, 1. v. p.

prepared (is), *parātur*, 1. v. p.

prepared, *parātus*, *-a*, *-um*, 1. and 2. adj.

prepares, *parat*, 1. v. a.

present (to be), *adsum*, *-fuī*, *-futūrus*, *-esse*, irr. 1. v. n.

present, *praesēns*, *-entis*, 3. adj.

prisoner, see *captive*.

private, *privātus*, *-a*, *-um*, 1. and 2. adj.

proconsul, *prōcōnsul*, *-ulis*, 3. M.

property, *sua*, *suōrum*, pl., 2. N., see *his*; *rēs*, *reī*, 5. F.

protect, *servō*, *-āvī*, *-ātum*, *-āre*, 1. v. a.

protect, *servant*, 1. v. a.

protected (are), *servantur*, 1. v. p.

protected (is), *servātur*, 1. v. p.

protects, *servat*, 1. v. a.

protection, see *garrison*.

provided (that), *dummodō*, conj.

province, *prōvincia*, *-ae*, 1. F.

public, *publicus*, *-a*, *-um*, 1. and 2. adj.

punishment, *poena*, *-ae*, 1. F.

purchase, *redimō*, *-ēmī*, *-emptum*, *-imere*, 3. v. a.

pursue, *consector*, *-ātus*, *-ārī*, 1. v. dep.

put in charge of, *praeficiō*, *-fēcī*, *-fectum*, *-ficere*, 3. v. a. (with dat.).

put on, *accommodō*, *-āvī*, *-ātum*, *-āre*, 1. v. a.

put to death, *interficiō*, *-fēcī*, *-fectum*, *-ficere*, 3. v. a.

Q.

quickly, *celeriter*, adv.

quite, adv., superlative degree.

R.

rampart, *vallum*, *-ī*, 2. N.

rank (of soldiers), *ordō*, *-inis*, 3. M.; *agmen*, *-inis*, 3. N.

rapid, see *swift*.

rations, *frūmentum*, *-ī*, 2. N.

reach, *perveniō*, *-vēnī*, *-ventum*, *-venīre*, 4. v. n.

ready, see *prepared*.

rear rank, *novissimum agmen*, 3. N.

reason (for this), *causā* with gen.; *hōc*.

rebuke, *accūsō*, *-āvī*, *-ātum*, *-āre*, 1. v. a.

receive, *accipiō*, *-cēpī*, *-ceptum*, *-cipere*, 3. v. a.

recent, *recēns*, *-ntis*, 3. adj.

recover, *recipiō*, *-cēpī*, *-ceptum*, *-cipere*, with reflex., 3. v. a.

re-enforcements, *subsidium*, *-ī*, 2. N.

refrain, *temperō*, *-āvī*, *-ātum*, *-āre*, 1. v. a.

regard, see *have*.

region, *regiō*, *-ōnis*, 3. F.

rejoice, *gaudeō*, *gavīsus*, *gaudēre*, 2. semi-dep.

relationship, *adfīnitās*, *-tātis*, 3. F.

remain, *maneō*, *mānsī*, *mānsūrus*, *manēre*, 2. v. n.; *supersum*, *-fuī*, *-futūrus*, *-esse*, irr. v. n.

remain, *remaneō*, *-mānsī*, *-mānsūrus*, *-manēre*, 2. v. n.

remaining, *reliquus*, -a, -um, 1. and 2. adj.
remove, *removeō*, -mōvī, -mōtum, -mo-vēre, 2. v. a.
renew,*'renovō*, -āvī, -ātum, -āre, 1. v. a.
repent, *paenitet*, -nituit, -tēre, 2. v. a. impers. •
reply, *respondeō*, -spondī, -spōnsum, -spondēre, 2. v. n.
represent, *prōpōnō*, -posuī, -positum, -pōnere, 3. v. a.
republic, *rēspublica*, *reīpublicae*, 5. and 1. F.
repulse, *pellō*, *pepulī*, *pulsum*, *pellere*, 3. v. a.
request, *petō*, *petīvī*, *petītum*, *petere*, 3. v. a. and n.
request (at my, thy, etc.), *mē petente*, see *seek*.
respond, *respondeō*, -spondī, -spōnsum, -spondēre, 2. v. n.
rest of, see *remaining*.
restrain, see *keep together*.
retreat, *sē* (*mē*, *tē*, etc.), *recipere*, 3. v. a.
return, *revertō*, -vertī, -versum, -vertere, 3. v. n.
reveal, *ēnūntiō*, -āvī, -ātum, -āre, 1. v. a.
revenues, *vectīgalia*, -ium, pl., 3. N.
revolution, *rēs novae*, *rērum novārum*, F.
reward, *mercēs*, -ēdis, 3. F.
Rhine, *Rhēnus*, -ī, 2. M.
Rhone, *Rhodanus*, -ī, 2. M.
ridge, *iugum*, -ī, 2. N.
right, *dexter*, -era, -erum, and -tra, -trum, 1. and 2. adj.
right, *iūs*, *iūris*, 3. N.
rightly, *iūre*, adv.
ripe, *matūrus*, -a, -um, 1. and 2. adj.
rival, *inimīcus*, -ī, 2. M.
river, *flūmen*, -inis, 3. N.
road, *iter*, *itineris*, 3. N.
robber, *latrō*, -ōnis, 3. M.

Roman, *Rōmānus*, -a, -um, 1. and 2. adj.
Rome, *Rōma*, -ae, 1. F.
routes, *itinera*, -um, 3. N., pl. of *iter*.
rugged, *arduus*, -a, -um, 1. and 2. adj.
rule, *regō*, *rēxī*, *rēctum*, *regere*, 3. v. a.
rumor, *rūmor*, -ōris, 3. M.

S.

safe, *tūtus*, -a, -um, 1. and 2. adj.
safety, *salūs*, -ūtis, 3. F.
sailor, *nauta*, -ae, 1. M.
sake, *causa*, -ae, 1. F.
same, *idem*, *eadem*, *idem*, dem. adj. pron.
Santones, *Santonēs*, -um (-ī, -ōrum), pl., 3. M.
Saône, *Arar*, *Araris*, 3. M.
satisfy, *satisfaciō*, -fēcī, -factūrus, -facere, 3. v. n. (with dat.).
said (it is), *dīcor*, *dictus*, *dīcī*, pass. of *dīcō*, used impers., 3. v. p.
say, *dīcō*, *dīxī*, *dictum*, *dīcere*, 3. v. a. and n.
say . . . not, *negō*, -āvī, -ātum, -āre, 1. v. a. and n.
scarcity, *inopia*, -ae, 1. F.
scout, *explōrātor*, -ōris, 3. M.
sea, *mare*, *maris*, 3. N.
season, see *time*.
secure, *potior*, -ītus, -īrī, 4. v. dep.
see, *videō*, *vīdī*, *vīsum*, *vidēre*, 2. v. a.
seek, *petō*, *petīvī*, *petītum*, *petere*, 3. v. a. and n.
seeking to gain, *appetēns*, -entis, 3. adj.
seem, *videor*, *vīsus*, *vidērī*, pass. of *videō*.
seize, *occupō*, -āvī, -ātum, -āre, 1. v. a.
select, *dēligō*, -lēgī, -lectum, -ligere, 3. v. a.
senate, *senātus*, -ūs, 4. M.
senator, *senātor*, -ōris, 3. M.

send, *mittō, mīsī, missum, mittere*, 3. v. a.

send forward, *praemittō, -mīsī, -missum, -mittere*, 3. v. a.

separate, *dīvidō, -vīsī, -vīsum, -vīdere*, 3. v. a.

separated, *dīvīsus, -a, -um*, p.p. as adj. 1. and 2.

Sequani, *Sēquanī, -ōrum*, pl., 2. N.

servant (soldiers'), *cālō, -ōnis*, 3. M.

service, see *assistance*.

servitude, *servitūs, -tūtis*, 3. F.

set free, *līberō, -āvī, -ātum, -āre*, 1. v. a.

set on fire, *incendō, -cendī, -cēnsum, -cendere*, 1. v. a.

settle, *cōnsīdō, -sēdī, -sessūrus, -sīdere*, 3. v. n.

several, *aliquot*, pron. indecl.

severe, *dūrus, -a, -um*, 1. and 2. adj.

severely, *vehementer*, adv.

severely, *graviter*, adv.

severity, see *strictness*.

shall (aux.), fut. ind., and future imperative.

shall have (aux.), fut. perf. ind.

she, see *he*.

ship, *nāvis, -is*, 3. F.

shore, *lītus, -oris*, 3. N.

should (aux.), pres. subj.

shout together, *conclāmō, -āvī, -ātum, -āre*, 1. v. n.

show, *dēmōnstrō, -āvī, -ātum, -āre*, 1. v. a.

show, *dēmōnstrant*, 1. v. a.

shown (are), *dēmōnstrantur*, 1. v. p.

shown (is), *dēmōnstrātur*, 1. v. p.

shows, *dēmōnstrat*, 1. v. a.

shudder, *horreō, horruī, —, horrēre*, 2. v. a. and n.

sight, *cōnspectus, -ūs*, 4. M.

signal, *signum, -ī*, 2. N.

silence, *silentium, -ī*, 2. N.

silent, *taceō, tacuī, tacitum, tacēre*, 2. v. a. and n.

since, *cum*, conj. (with subj.).

single, *singulī, -ae, -a*, pl. 1. and 2. dist. num. adj.

sister, *soror, sorōris*, 3. F.

six, *sex*, card. num. adj. indecl.

six (each), *sēnī, -ae, -a*, pl. 1. and 2. dist. num. adj.

six hundred, *sexcentī, -ae, -a*, pl. 1. and 2. card. num. adj.

sixteen, *sēdecim*, card. num. adj. indecl.

skilful, *perītus, -a, -um*, 1. and 2. adj.

slaughter, *caedēs, -is*, 3. F.

slave, *servus, -ī*, 2. M.

slave (be a), *serviō, -iī (-īvī), -ītūrus, -īre*, 4. v. n.

slay, *interficiō, -fēcī, -fectum, -ficere*, 3. v. a.

small, *parvus, -a, -um*, 1. and 2. adj.; comp. *minor;* sup. *minimus.*

snow, *nix, nivis*, 3. F.

so, *ita, sic, tam*, advs.

so as to, *ut (utī)*, sub. conj.

so great, *tantus, -a, -um*, 1. and 2. adj.

soldier, *mīles, -itis*, 3. M.

some, *aliquis (-quī), -qua, -quid (-quod)*, indef. pron.

some (some . . . others), *aliī . . . aliī*, pl. 1. and 2. adj.

some, *nōnūllus, -a, -um*, M. adj. as noun, 1. and 2.

son, *fīlius, -ī*, 2. M.

sovereignty, see *throne*.

sow, *faciō*, with *sēmentis*.

sowing (a), *sēmentis, -is*, 3. F.

space, *spatium, -ī*, 2. N.

space of three days, *trīduum, -ī*, 2. N.

spare, *cōnservō, -āvī, -ātum, -āre*, 1. v. a.

spend the winter, *hiemō, -āvī, -ātum, -āre*, 1. v. n.

spirit, *animus, -ī*, 2. M.

spirit (with), see *severely*.

spring up, *innāscor, -nātus, -nāscī,*
3. v. dep.
stand, *cōnsistō, -stitī, —, -sistere,* 3.
v. n.
starvation, *famēs, -is,* 3. F.
state, *cīvitās, -tātis,* 3. F.
station, *dispōnō, -posuī, -positum,*
-ponere, 3. v. a.
stature, *māgnitūdō corporis.*
still, *tamen,* adv.
stop, *dēsistō, -stitī, -stitūrus, -sistere,*
3. v. n.
storm, *tempestās, -tātis,* 3. F.
storm, *oppūgnō, -āvī, -ātum, -āre,*
1. v. a.
strength, *vīrēs, -ium,* pl., 3. F.
strengthen, *cōnfirmō, -āvī, -ātum, -āre,*
1. v. a.
strictness, *sevēritās, -tātis,* 3. F.
stronghold, *oppidum, -ī,* 2. N.
struggle, *labōrō, -āvī, -ātum, -āre,*
1. v. n.
subdue, *pācō, -āvī, -ātum, -āre,* 1. v. a.
successive, *continuus, -a, -um,* 1. and
2. adj.
successive, *continēns, -entis,* 3. adj.
suddenly, *subitō,* abl. as adv.
Suessiones, *Suessiōnēs, -um,* pl., 3. M.
sufficient, *satis* with gen., adv.
sufficiently, *satis,* adv.
suitable, *idōneus, -a, -um,* 1. and 2.
adj.
Sulla, *Sulla, -ae,* 1. M.
summit of, see *top of.*
summon, *vocō, -āvī, -ātum, -āre,* 1. v. a.
summon, *vocant,* 1. v. a.
summoned (are), *vocantur,* 1. v. p.
summoned (is), *vocātur,* 1. v. p.
summons, *vocat,* 1. v. a.
superior, *superior, -us,* 3. adj. comp.
suppliant, *supplex, -icis,* 3. C.
supplies, *commeātus, -ūs,* 4. M.
supply, see *plenty.*
supreme, *suprēmus, -a, -um,* 1. and
2. adj. sup.

surround, *circumveniō, -vēnī, -ventum,*
-venīre, 4. v. a.
survive, *supersum, -fuī, -futūrus, -esse,*
irr. v. n.
suspicion, *suspīciō, -ōnis,* 3. F.
sustain, *sustineō, -tinuī, -tentum, -ti-*
nēre, 2. v. a. and n.
swift, *celer, -eris, -ere,* 3. adj.
swiftly, *celeriter,* adv.
sword, *ferrum, -ī,* 2. N.

T.

take, *capiō, cēpī, captum, capere,*
3. v. a.
take a stand, see *stand.*
take away, *tollō, sustulī, sublātum,*
tollere, 3. v. a.
take care, *dō* with *opera.*
take care to, *cūra ut.*
take position, *cōnsistō, -stitī, —, -sis-*
tere, 3. v. n.
take possession of, *occupō, -āvī,*
-ātum, -āre, 1. v. a.
task, *labor, -ōris,* 3. M.
tend, *pertineō, -tinuī, —, -tinēre,*
2. v. n.
tenth, *decimus, -a, -um,* 1. and 2.
ord. num. adj.
terrify, *terreō, terruī, territum, ter-*
rēre, 2. v. a.
territory, *fīnēs, -ium,* 3. M., pl. of
fīnis.
than, *quam,* adv.
that, *is, ea, id; ille, illa, illud,* dem.
prons.
that, see *who,* rel. pron.
that (in order that), *ut,* sub. conj.
that (in order that), *quō,* rel. adv.
that (of yours), *iste, ista, istud,* dem.
pron.
that not, *nē,* conj. (with subj.).
the, untranslated.
their, see *his,* etc.
them, see *they.*

themselves, see *himself*, etc.
then, *tum*, adv.
there, *ibī*, adv.
there (there is, etc.), untranslated.
these, pl. of *this*.
they, pl. of *he, she, it.*
thing, *rēs, reī*, 5. F.
thing which, *id quod* or *quae rēs.*
think, *exīstimō, -āvī, -ātum, -āre,*
1. v. a.
think, *putō, -āvī, -ātum, -āre,* 1. v. a.
third, *tertius, -a, -um,* 1. and 2. ord.
num. adj.
this, *hīc, haec, hōc ;* sometimes *is, ea,
id,* dem. pron.
this side of, *citrā,* prep. with acc.
those, pl. of *that.*
thousand, *mille,* indecl. card. num.
adj. and noun, N.
thousand, *mīlia, -ium,* pl., 3. N.
three, *trēs, tria,* 3. card. num. adj.
three days (space of), *trīduum, -ī,*
2. N.
throne, *regnum, -ī,* 2. N.
through, *per,* prep. with acc.
throw, *cōniciō, -iēcī, -iectum, -icere,*
3. v. a.
thus, see *so.*
time, *tempus, -oris,* 3. N.
to (place to which), *ad,* prep. with
acc.
to, dat. case.
top of, *summus, -a, -um,* 1. and 2.
adj.
towards, *in,* prep. with acc.
towards, *ad,* prep. with acc.
tower, *turris, -is,* 3. F.
town (walled), *oppidum, -ī,* 2. N.
transport, *trānsportō, -āvī, -ātum, -āre,*
1. v. a.
treacherously, *per īnsidiās.*
treachery, *īnsidiae, -ārum,* pl., 1. F.
treachery, *perfidia, -ae,* 1. F.
treason, *prōditiō, -ōnis,* 3. F.
treat, see *have.*

treaty, *foedus, -eris,* 3. N.
tree, *arbor, -oris,* 3. F.
trench, *fossa, -ae,* 1. F.
Treveri, *Trēverī, -ōrum,* pl., 2. M.
tribune, *tribūnus, -ī,* 2. M.
tribute, *vectīgal, -ālis,* 3. N.
troops, *cōpiae, -ārum,* F., pl. of *cōpia.*
trumpet, *tuba, -ae,* 1. F.
try, *experior, -pertus, -perīrī,* 4. v.
dep.
try, *temptō, -āvī, -ātum, -āre,* 1. v. a.
turn, *vertō, vertī, versum, vertere,*
3. v. a.
turn (this way and that), *versō,
-āvī, -ātum, -āre,* 1. v. a.
turn and flee, *vertō* with *tergum.*
twelve, *duodecim,* card. num. adj.
indecl.
two, *duo, duae, duo,* card. num. adj.

U.

Ubii, *Ubiī, -ōrum,* pl., 2. M.
unaccustomed, *īnsuētus, -a, -um,*
1. and 2. adj.
under arms, *in armīs.*
undertaking, *rēs, reī,* 5. F.
unfavorable, *aliēnus, -a, -um,* 1. and
2. adj.
unfortunate, *miser, -era, -erum,* 1.
and 2. adj.
unfriendly, *inimīcus, -a, -um,* 1. and
2. adj.
unjustly, *iniuste,* adv.
unknown, *īgnōtus, -a, -um,* 1. and 2.
adj.
unless, *nisi,* conj.
unserviceable, *inūtilis, -e,* 3. adj.
until, *dum,* conj.
unwilling (be), *nōlō, nōluī, —, nōlle,*
irr. v. a. and n.
unwilling, *invītus, -a, -um,* 1. and 2.
adj.
unworthy of, *indīgnus, -a, -um,* 1.
and 2. adj. (with abl.).

upbraid, *incūsō*, *-āvī*, *-ātum*, *-āre*, 1. v. a.

upon, *in*, prep. with abl.

use, *ūsus*, *ūsūs*, 4. M.

use, *ūtor*, *ūsus*, *ūtī*, 3. v. dep.

used to, imp. ind.

useful, *ūtilis*, *-e*, 3. adj.

V.

valor, *virtūs*, *-ūtis*, 3. F.

Vergobretus, *Vergobretus*, *-ī*, 2. M.

very, *māximē*, adv., or the sup. degree.

very easy, *perfacilis*, *-e*, 3. adj.

very few, *perpaucī*, *-ae*, *-a*, pl., 1. and 2. adj.

very many, *complūrēs*, *-plūra* (*-plūria*), 3. adj.

very much, *māgnopere* (*māgnō opere*), adv.

very much like, *cōnsimilis*, *-e*, 3. adj.

Vesontio, *Vesontiō*, *-ōnis*, 3. F.

veteran, *veterānus*, *-a*, *-um*, 1. and 2. adj.

vicinity, *propinquitās*, *-tātis*, 3. F.

vicinity of, *ad*.

victor, *victor*, *-ōris*, 3. M.

victorious, see *victor*.

victory, *victōria*, *-ae*, 1. F.

village, *vīcus*, *-ī*, 2. M.

violence, *iniūria*, *-ae*, 1. F.; see also *force*.

violent, see *active*.

virtues, *virtūtēs*, *-um*, 3. F., pl. of *virtūs*.

visit, *adeō*, *-iī* (*-īvī*), *-itūrus*, *-īre*, irr. v. a. and n.

voice, *vōx*, *vōcis*, 3. F.

W.

wage, see *carry on*.

wagon, *carrus*, *-ī*, 2. M.

wait, *exspectō* (*expectō*), *-āvī*, *-ātum*, *-āre*, 1. v. a. and n.

wall, *mūrus*, *-ī*, 2. M.

want, *volō*, *voluī*, *velle*, irr. v. a. and n.

war, *bellum*, *-ī*, 2. N.

warlike, *bellicōsus*, *-a*, *-um*, 1. and 2. adj.

warn, *moneō*, *monuī*, *monitum*, *monēre*, 2. v. a.

wave, *fluctus*, *-ūs*, 4. M.

way, *via*, *-ae*, 1. F.; *iter*, *itineris*, 3. N.

we, see *I*.

wearied, *dēfessus*, *-a*, *-um*, 1. and 2. adj.

well, *bene*, adv.

well-known, *nōtus*, *-a*, *-um*, 1. and 2. adj.

were, imp. ind. or subj.

were in the habit of, imp. ind.

were wont to, imp. ind.

what, see *who*, interrog. or rel.

when, *ubī*, *cum*, conjs.

where, *ubī*, conj.

whether, *sī*, conj.

which, see *who*, interrog. or rel. pron.

while, *dum*, conj.

whither, *quō*, conj.

who (what, which, that), *quī*, *quae*, *quod*, rel. pron.

who (what, which), *quis* (*quī*), *quae*, *quid* (*quod*), interrog. pron.

whole, *tōtus*, *-a*, *-um*, 1. and 2. adj.

whom, see *who*.

why, *cūr*, *quāre*, advs.

wicked, *improbus*, *-a*, *-um*, 1. and 2. adj.

wife, *uxor*, *-ōris*, 3. F.

will (aux.), fut. ind.

will have (aux.), fut. perf. ind.

willing (be), *volō*, *voluī*, *velle*, irr. v. a. and n.

wing, *cornū*, *-ūs* (*-ū*), 4. N.

winter, *hĭbernus*, -*a*, -*um*, 1. and 2. adj.

winter quarters, *hiberna*, -*ōrum*, pl., 2. N.

wish, *volō*, *voluī*, *velle*, irr. v. a. and n.

with, *cum*, prep. with abl.

within (of time), abl.

within, *intrā*, prep. with acc.

without, *sine*, prep. with abl.

with spirit, see *actively*.

witness, *testis*, -*is*, 3. C.

woman, *fēmina*, -*ae*, 1. F.

wonder at, *mīror*, -*ātus*, -*ārī*, 1. v. dep.

wont (to be), imperfect tense.

work, *opera*, -*ae*, 1. F.

world, *orbis terrae* (*terrārum*).

worse, *pēior*, -*us*, 3. adj., comp. of *malus*.

worst, *pessimus*, -*a*, -*um*, 1. and 2. adj., sup. of *malus*.

worthy of, *dignus*, -*a*, -*um*, 1. and 2. adj. (with abl.).

would, pres. subj.

would have, perf. subj.

wound, *volnus* (*vulnus*), -*eris*, 3. N.

wounded, *saucius*, -*a*, -*um*, 1. and 2. adj.

wretched, see *unfortunate*.

wrong, *iniūria*, -*ae*, 1. F.

Y.

year, *annus*, -*i*, 2. M.

yet, *tamen*, adv.

you, *tū*, gen. *tuī*, pers. pron.

young, *iuvenis*, -*e*, 3. adj.

young man, see *young*.

younger, *iunior*, -*ius*, 3. adj.

your (sing.), *tuus*, *tua*, *tuum*, poss. pron. 1. and 2.

your (pl.), *vester*, -*tra*, -*trum*, poss. pron. 1. and 2.

yours, see *your*.

youth, see *young man*.

Z.

zeal, *studium*, -*i*, 2. N.

www.ingramcontent.com/pod-product-compliance
Lightning Source LLC
Chambersburg PA
CBHW020110030726

47498CB00006B/2042